Nathaniel Hawthorne

Hawthorne's Short Stories

WITH ESSAYS IN CRITICSM

Annotated with
Critical Introduction
by
Lee, Young-Oak

Shinasa

Nathaniel Hawthorne

Nathaniel Hawthorne (July 4, 1804–May 19, 1864) was an American novelist and short story writer.

CONTENTS

INTRODUCTION

호손의 단편 세계

호손만큼 인생의 깊이를 사유하고 또 사유하는 작가도 없을 것이다. 바로 이 점이 나로 하여금 호손을 놓지 못하게 한다. 이 선집에 실은 단편들은 작가의 영혼의 깊이를 담아내는 것들로 구성하였다. 점점 더 빨라지는 생의 속도 하에서 사람들은 인생을 사유할 시간을 떼어내지 못한다. 시간이 가빠질수록 우리는 사유를 등한히 하고 건성 살아간다. 먹고 마시고 자고 하는 동물적인 본능 차원을 벗어나지 못한다. 그러다 보면, 우리는 우리도 모르는 사이에 동물적으로 생각하고 동물적으로 행동하다가, 동물적으로 죽음을 맞이하게 될 것이다. 이러한 우려가 나로 하여금 호손을 끄집어내어 일반 삶의 지평선에 노정하게 만들었다. 사람이 사람이려면, 적어도 사람의 영혼의 모습을 조금이라도 지키려면 호손이 제시하는 면면을 보고 생각해야 할 것이다.

호손의 일생을 살펴보면 특이한 점이 몇 가지 보인다. 그가 미국의 독립기념일인 7월 4일에 태어난 것은 마치 그가 미국의 문학을 탄생시킬 운명을 지니고 있었던 것처럼 보인다, 영국으로부터 1776년 정치적 독립을 쟁취한 미국이지만 호손이 태어날 무렵 즉 독립 후 삼 십여 년이 지난 시점에도 문학적으로는 이렇다 할 작가를 산출하고 있지 못했기 때문이다. 그가 태어난 가문도 특기할 점이 있다. 호손의 증조부 (William Hathorne)는 세일럼 (Salem) 초기 정착민으로 공을 세

우면서 소위 명문가로 집안을 일으켰다. 그러나 철저한 청교도였던 그는 많은 업적과 함께 씻지 못할 과오도 저질렀으니 퀘이커교도들에 대한 박해로 이름을 남기게 되었다. 윌리엄의 아들 존 호손(John Hathorne) 판사도 명망이 높았으나, 그 역시 1692년에 있었던 소위 마녀재판에서 영향력을 발휘한 것으로 알려져 있어 후손인 작가 호손에게는 조상의 과거에 대한 죄의식이 큰 부담이었다. 게다가 잘 나가던 집안은 작가 호손 당대에 이르러 가세가 기울게 되니 호손은 조상들의 업보가 현 세대를 벌하는 것으로 받아들이지 않을 수 없었던 것 같다. 불행하게도 호손이 4세가 되었을 때, 선장이었던 아버지가 남아메리카 북부의 수리남(Surinam)에서 황열병으로 죽음을 맞게 되었고, 달리 생활방편이 없던 어머니 엘리자베스 매닝 호손(Elizabeth Manning Hathorne) 부인은 아들 나사니엘과 두 딸을 데리고 친정의 도움을 받게 된다. 겹치는 불행에 젊은 호손은 조상들의 불미스런 과거와 단절하고 싶었을 것이고 이것이 그로 하여금 작가로 데뷔하면서 자신의 성 'Hathorne'에 조상과 구별되는 "w"를 추가하여 'Hawthorne'가로 새로 태어나게 하였는지도 모른다. 더불어 본래 사교적이지 못했던 어머니의 삶은 고립의 시대로 들어간다. 설상가상으로 호손이 아홉 살 되던 해에는 발을 다쳐 2년 여 바깥출입을 못하여 뛰놀지도 못하고 친구들도 없이 지내게 되었는데 이러한 환경은 호손을 작가로 키우는데 적잖은 영향을 주었던 것이다. 소년 호손은 뛰노는 대신 집에서 셰익스피어, 존 번년, 존 밀톤 등 거대한 작가들을 접하게 되었다.

호손은 청년기에 이르러 집과 가까운 보든 대학(Bowdoin College)으로 진학하기로 결정한다. 작은 학교이긴 하나, 그곳에서 호손은 일생동안 친교를 맺은 급우들을 만나게 된다. 당대 시인으로 이름을 떨친 롱펠로우(Henry W. Longfellow), 브리지(Horatio Bridge), 그리고 미국의 대통령이 된 피어스(Franklin Pierce) 등이다. 학교 시절에 관하여 특기할 것이 있다면, 호손은 학교 공부에 크게 재미를 느끼지 못했으나, 글쓰기에 관심을 가지고 습작을 냈으며, 작가로 불멸의 이름을 얻고 싶다는 야심을 품게 되었다는 것이다. 장래의 직업을 구상하면서 호손은, 나무처럼 한 곳에서 살며 웅덩이에 고인 물처럼 고요하게 평안한, 그런 "a dull way of life"를 살기를 원치 않으며, 그렇다고 변호사는 이미 너무 많아 절반은 굶어죽기 직전이니 그도 그의 길이 아니요, 의사라는 직업으로 병과 병균 사이에서 혹시라도 환자를 지옥으로 보내는 실수를 하게 되면 큰일이라는 식으로 어머니에게 생각을 토로한 바 있다. 일생 먹을 걱정이 없어, 직업이 없이 산다면 얼마나 좋을까 하면서 그는 글 쓰는 일이 자신에게는 가장 적합하고 멋있는 길이라고 말한다. 그런 가운데 나온 그의 첫 작품『팬쇼』(*Fanshawe*)는 익명으로 출간되었으나 작가로서의 첫 걸음을 증명할 뿐 아니라 후일 호손이 보이는 작품세계의 주제를 선보였다는 점에서 의의를 갖는다.

젊은 호손은 학교를 졸업한 후 십 여 년을 별 일없이 세일럼 집에서 뉴 잉글런드 역사 등을 읽으면서 소일하고 익명으로 작품을 발표하다가, 1837년 그간 발표한 글들을 추려, 이번에는 본명으로『다시 듣는 이야기』(*Twice-Told Tales*)를 출간함으로써 긴 동면을 벗어나 본격적인 작가로의 생애를 시작한다. 이때에 발표된 주요작품들은 다음과 같다.

"The Minister's Black Veil"
"The May-Pole of Merry Mount"
"The Great Carbuncle"
"Dr. Heidegger's Experiment"

"The Ambitious Guest"

『다시 듣는 이야기』의 출간은 호손에게 인생의 전환을 이루는 계기가 되었다. 사회개혁을 주창하던 엘리자베스 피바디(Elizabeth Peabody)가 이 스토리를 높이 평가한 나머지 저자를 찾아왔고, 사람들에게 그의 작품을 알리고 하더니, 드디어는 여동생 소피아(Sophia)를 호손에게 소개한 것이다. 이제 호손에게 결혼은 매우 현실적인 일이 되면서, 직업적인 작가를 소망하고 있던 그는 가정을 꾸려나갈 방편에 관심을 갖게 된다. 그리고 마침 이상주의자들이 시도하던 Brook Farm 농장(매서추세츠 주 소재)은 생활수단을 해결하는 하나의 가능성일 수 있겠다고 생각한다. 호손은 1841년 자기 몫의 자본을 대고 4월부터 7개월간 농장생활에 합류하여 외양간을 치우는 등 농부의 일을 하며 창작을 병행하고자 한다. 그러나 결국 노동과 집필은 양립할 수 없다는 결론을 내리고 이상향 실험에서 빠져 나오는데, 이 경험을 후일의 작품『블라이드데일 로맨스』(*The Blithedale Romance*) 속에 불멸의 기록으로 남긴다.

이상향 실험 프로젝트의 실패로 생활수단은 아직 불확실하게 되었다. 그러나 다행하게도 호손은 소피아를 설득하여 결혼하고 에머슨이 살던 콩코드(Concord)의 Old Manse로 들어가 살림을 차리게 된다. 이 결정은 작가인 호손에게 좋은 기회를 주었던 것이, 당시 초월주의 거장들 즉 에머슨(Ralph Waldo Emerson), 리플리(George Ripley), 소로(Henry David Thoreau) 등의 존재로 인하여 지적인 열기가 활발하던 콩코드에 살면서 호손은 자연스럽게 이 특이한 문화현상을 관찰하며 작품 활동을 할 수 있었다는 것이다.『올드맨스 이끼』(*Mosses from an Old Manse*, 1846)는 다음과 같은 단편들이 대표한다.

"The Birth-Mark"
"Young Goodman Brown"
"Rappaccini's Daughter"
"Egotism; or, The Bosom-Serpent"
"Roger Malvin's Burial"
"P.'s Correspondence"
"The Artist of the Beautiful"
"A Virtuoso's Collection"
"Feathertop"

『이끼』(*Mosses*)의 출간은 미국문학사상 행운이라 할 수 있는 또 하나의 사건의 계기가 된다. 당시 젊은 작가로서 발돋움하던 멜빌(Herman Melville)과의 교우가 그것이다. 멜빌은 1850년 "Hawthorne and His *Mosses*"라는 글에서 호손이 그려낸 악의 세계에 깊이 공감한다며 호손을 진리의 탐구자로서 셰익스피어와 비교하고 있다. 멜빌이 그의 역작『모비 딕』(*Moby-Dick or the Whale*)을 집필하는 동안 그와 호손과의 우정은 서로에게 영향을 준 매우 소중한 관계로 남았다. 멜빌은 그가 심혈을 기울여 탈고한 장편『모비 딕』을 호손에게 헌정하는 것으로서 대작가 호손에 대한 그의 깊은 존경심을 표현하였다.

* *

<우리 집안 멀리뉴 어르신 "My Kinsman, Major Molineux" 1832>은 왕성하게 발전해가는 영국의 식민지 미국사회를 배경으로, 입신양명의 꿈을 안고 그에게 힘이 되어 줄 집안의 어른 멀리뉴 소령을 찾아 상경하는 18세의 시골청년 로빈(Robin)의 이야기다. 다시 말하면, 이

단편은 한 청년의 성장소설로, 식민지의 번창과 성공의 꿈, 도시의 타락과 환멸을 주제로 하고 있다.

독립 이전의 식민지 미국은 영국과의 얽힌 관계 속에서 주민에 의해 선출된 주지사의 통치를 거쳐 영국 왕이 임명하는 식민지의 총독 체제 하에서 날로 인구가 증가하고 산업은 번창한다. 호손은 이 독특한 역사적 순간을 배경으로 청년의 이니시에이션(initiation)이라는 보편적인 이야기를 꾸려내었다. 그런데 여니 스토리와는 달리 호손의 이야기는 달 밝은 밤을 배경으로 한다. 사물이 달리 보이는 달빛의 영향 하에서 일어난 일련의 사건들은 로빈이 실제로 경험하는 것인지 그가 꿈의 세계에서 경험한 것인지가 불분명해지는 효과를 낳는다.

때는 달 밝은 어느 여름 밤 9시경, 보트 한 척이 단 한 사람의 손님을 싣고 도착한다. 열여덟 살이 될까 말까한 이 시골뜨기 청년은 도시라곤 처음 온 듯한데, 밝고 유쾌한 눈빛과 준수한 용모를 하고 있으나, 허름한 회색 복장에 아버지로부터 물려받은 삼각모자를 쓴 남루한 모습이다. 로빈의 등장은 여러모로 의미가 있다. 밝은 성격에 순진한 청년 로빈은 미국적 순수성을 인물화한 것으로 볼 수 있으며, 후일 헤밍웨이(Ernest Hemingway), 셔우드 앤더슨(Sherwood Anderson), 핏츠제럴드(F. Scott Fitzgerald) 등이 제시한 청년 주인공들이 그 계보를 잇는다고 볼 수 있다.

또 한편으로는 시골뜨기 소년의 상경 모습은 이 삼십 년 후, 호레이쇼 알저(Horatio Alger)의 주인공들의 등장 모습을 예견하고 있어 미국의 건설과 함께 미국의 꿈을 향한 미국청년의 등장을 알리는 셈이다. 알저는 백여 권의 베스트셀러를 통해, 풍부한 기회의 나라에서 근면과 정직과 절약 정신만 갖추면 아무리 가난한 젊은이라도 부자가 될 수 있음을 보여 주었으며, 당시의 젊은이들로 하여금 가난한 시골집을 떠나 도시로 가서 고생 끝에 물질적 부를 성취하는 인생을 동경하게 만들었다.

둘째로, <우리 집안 멀리뉴 어르신>은 인간성의 타락을 발견하는 이야기다. 일견, 20세기의 영국 소설가 콘라드(Joseph Conrad)가 <어둠의 속 "Heart of Darkness">에서 청년 말로우(Marlow)가 우상화하던 커츠(Kurtz)의 실상을 대면하고 성장하듯이 로빈은 집안의 성공 신화의 상징인 멀리뉴 어르신의 실체를 알게 됨으로써 아는 사람에 의존하여 세상적인 출세를 하려던 마음을 버리게 된다. 어려운 환경을 극복하고 자수성가 하는 알저의 주인공들과 비교해 볼 때, 호손의 소년 주인공은 미리감치 물질적 성공의 꿈은 헛된 것으로 알고 마음을 접고 있다.

셋째로, 이 작품에서 우리가 주목할 수 있는 것은 도시의 이미지다. <우리 집안 멀리뉴 어르신>에서 도시는 인간의 순수성을 타락시키고 인간을 파멸로 이끄는 환경으로 제시되어 있다. 도시의 발달이 본격적인 문제점을 드러내지 않은 19세기에 호손이 도시와 인간의 타락을 예상하고 연계하고 있는 점은 이 작품의 현대 소설적인 요소로 볼 수 있다.

<로저 맬빈의 장례 "Roger Malvin's Burial">는 역사적인 배경과 함께 시작하고 있다. 때는 18세기 초, 신대륙을 동해안에서 시작하여 서진(西進)하며 점거해 가고 있던 식민지인들은 생활터전을 빼앗기지 않으려는 본토 인디언들과 피치 못할 접전을 일삼을 때다. 호손은 인종과 인종 간에 벌어지는 전쟁 자체보다는 전쟁의 결과에 주목하고 있다. 즉 이 작품은 일반 전쟁소설과는 달리, 전투가 끝난 상황에서의 두 부상병을 통해, 인간의 궁극적인 선택 문제를 깊이 있게 다루고 있다.

호손의 이 스토리가 주목을 받는 것은 다음의 몇 가지로 요약할 수

있다. 첫째는 자신의 처절한 죽음의 공포를 충분히 인지하면서도 자기로 인하여 상대방의 삶의 기회에 차질을 가져오지 않는 고귀한 결단의 가치다. 스토리의 사실상의 첫 문단은 부상을 입고 지친 두 군인이 거대한 묘비 같은 화강석 발치에 누워있는 모습을 제시한다. 거대하고 힘 있는 자연 앞에 중년을 넘은 부상군인 로저 맬빈은 자신의 순례의 끝을 예지하고 묘비를 언급한다. 삶의 마지막을 예감하고 있는 것이다. 인디언과의 전투에서 다쳐 죽어가고 있는 군인은 개척지에서의 백인과 인디언 간의 전쟁의 종식을 상징한다고도 볼 수 있다. 그러면 양 종족 간의 전쟁이 정치 경제적 의미 외에 의미하는 바는 무엇일까? 이 문제를 탐색하는 것이 호손이 전쟁이야기를 쓴 목적이 될 것이다.

이 두 사람—연장자와 청년, 로저와 루번(Reuben)—이 직면한 문제는 생과 사의 문제다. 로저는 더 이상 힘이 없어 엄청난 황무지를 헤치고 고향마을을 찾아갈 형편이 못된다. 청년 루번 자신도 부상이 깊어서 오래 버티지 못할 것이므로 그가 어른을 부축하고 진행한다면 결국은 둘 다 죽고 말 것이다. 연장자는 어려운 결정을 내린다. 인간은 누구나 자기 자신을 먼저 돌보고 살아나기에 집착할 것이지만 작품의 주인공은 생명의 욕심을 젊은 미래를 위하여 양보하는 결단을 하는 것이다. 자연의 섭리에 순응하기 위하여 자신을 접는다. 그리고 망설이는 젊은이를 설득하기 위하여 자신의 딸 도카스(Dorcas)를 부탁한다고 말하고, 결정적으로는 자신이 지난날 부상당한 동지를 두고 떠났기 때문에 도움을 구하여 두 사람이 다 살아났던 경험을 말하여 청년의 마음을 움직인다.

둘째는, 합당한 이유에 근거한 행위였음에도 불구하고 첫 번 기회의 유실로 말미암아 약속을 이행하지 못하는 지극히 인간적인 운명적 상황이다. 로저를 빈사상태로 두고 떠난 청년은 예상과 달리 며칠을 악

조건에서 헤매다가 탈진해 쓰러지고 며칠 후 의식을 회복했을 때는 로저를 구하기가 불가능해진데다, 일부의 진실을 말하고 망설이던 순간에, 도카스가 결론을 내리게 되어 그것이 진실인양 되어버린 것이다.

셋째는, 가당치 않은 칭찬과 털어놓을 수 없는 진실에 갇혀 사는 도덕적 소심증과 그 결과의 문제다. 루번이 어려운 상황에서도 충실하게 장인어른의 시체를 거두었다고 믿고 그를 추켜세움을 받을 때, 루번의 가슴 속은 감추어진 진실에 대한 죄의식이 커져간다. 그 죄의식은 그의 일상생활에 영향을 미치고 급기야는 그의 가족에게도 파멸을 가져온다는 것이다. 때를 놓쳐 망설이는 소심증의 결과는 크나큰 파멸을 가져온다. 도의적 소심증이 가져온 침묵은 비밀의 방을 루번의 가슴 속에 만들어 놓으며, 비밀의 방이 있음으로 해서 루번은 자신을 고립시키고 가족이나 친지들과 소통이 불가한 상황에 놓인다. 그리고 소통의 불가는 곧 관계의 파탄을 불러온다. 작가의 치밀한 영혼의 탐구는 순간적인 실기(失機)가 용기의 부족으로 인하여 자신 뿐 아니라 가장 가까운 가족에게까지 엄청난 비극을 초래함을 보이고 있다.

<유령 챔피언 “The Gray Champion”>은 십 칠세기 후반, 미국이 영국의 식민지 상태를 벗어나지 못하고 신음하던 시절, 본국과 식민지간의 첨예한 갈등이 드러난 역사적 시기를 배경으로 하고 있다. 영국에는 오렌지 공(William of Orange)의 승리로 종교의 자유를 허락하는 관대한 분위기가 조성되고 있었으나, 제임스 2세로부터 식민지 통치권을 받은 안드로스 경(Sir Andros)은 식민지를 여전히 가혹하게 다스리면서, 식민지에 불어오는 자유의 바람을 차단하려한다. 제왕적 통치세력과 힘없는 식민지의 종교지도자, 위압적인 영국의 붉은 군대와 조직되지 못한 주민집단, 당당하고 화려한 무력의 시위와 우중충한 피지배자들의 복장 등은 두 세력이 대치할 경우 결과는 명백한 듯

하다.

그러나 작가는 이 예상을 뒤집는다. 두 진영이 대치하는 시간은 하루의 저녁, 즉 황혼 무렵이다. "황혼"이 낮과 밤의 경계선으로 정체가 불분명하고 애매한 시점이므로 호손은 이 시점을 작품에 도입하여 사실과 환상의 구분을 불분명하게 함으로써 애매모호성을 가미한다. 지극히 확실한 사실도 황혼의 배경에서는 약간의 twist가 일어난다. 호손은 사실적인 상황에 잠깐의 twist를 사용하여 유령 챔피언이 등장하도록 한다. 이 작품의 원제 "The Gray Champion"의 "gray" 역시 밝음과 어두움의 불분명한 경계색을 나타낸다. 주인공 The Gray Champion이 살아있는 존재인지, 이미 죽은 장수가 위기의 식민지인을 구하러 불려나온 것인지 그 정체가 아리송하다. 호손은 이와 같이 초자연적인 인물을 설정하면서 존재의 실재여부에 대한 논란을 처음부터 대처해 놓았다고 생각된다.

<야심 찬 손님 "The Ambitious Guest">은 실화에 기초하고 있다. 1826년 8월 28일 뉴 잉글란드 산사태에 희생된 윌리(Willey) 일가족 이야기를 기초로 쓰여 졌기 때문이다. 그러나 어찌 보면 청년시절의 호손의 정신세계의 갈등을 그려낸 것이라 볼 수도 있다. 대부분의 사람들은 이 작품에 등장하는 한 가족처럼 특별한 야심을 품고 살지는 않는다. 여기서 특별한 야심이란 이 작품의 주인공 청년이 목표하는 '불멸성'인데, 영국으로부터 독립을 성취한지 반세기도 안 된 미국에 태어난 호손은 불멸의 작가가 되는 것이 개인으로서의 그의 '야심'이었다.

'불멸'에 대한 '야심'을 가진 청년이 찾아오는 깊은 골짜기의 외딴 집은 아이로니컬하게도 산 자의 생명이 순간순간 위협받는 곳이다. 춥고 위험한 곳에, 험준한 산이 머리 위로 높게 깎아지르듯 솟아 있어

무시로 돌들이 산허리를 굴러 그들 머리 위로 떨어지는 곳이다. 말하자면 이 집에 도란도란 모여 사는 식구들—행복의 표상인 할머니, 아버지와 어머니, 한창 아리따운 행복의 표상인 딸, 그리고 어린아이들—은 밖에서 우르르 쾅 소리가 날 때마다 죽음의 문턱에 선다. 이들에게 청년이 말하는 불멸이란 매우 생소한 개념이다.

그러나 청년의 불멸에 대한 야심을 듣고 나서, 죽음과 이웃하고 살면서도 죽음을 초월하여 웃음을 잃지 않던 가족들의 생각에 변화가 일어난다. 예컨대, 할머니는 자신의 죽음을 대비하고, 아버지는 자신의 생을 달리 살 수도 있었다고 생각하며, 십 대의 딸은 외롭다고 느낀다. 즉 자신들에게 주어진 삶이 유한하다는 사실을 깨닫는 것이다. 평화롭고 화기애애 하던 가족들 마음에, 그들이 과거에 가능했을 수도 있던 길에 대한 미련과 후회를 일으키는 무명의 청년은 일면, 에덴의 동산에 들어와 만족한 삶을 영위하던 아담과 이브에게 그들에게 주어진 삶 이외의 삶의 가능성에 대한 유혹을 떨치지 못하게 한 사탄과 비슷한 면이 있다. 주어진 운명에 대한 불만과 인간적 도전이다.

그리고 그 도전은 그리스 작가 소포클레스의『오이디프스 왕』의 주인공 청년 오이디프스가 신탁에서 들려 준 운명, 즉 아버지를 살해하고 어머니와 살게 되는 재앙을 피하기 위하여 도망했듯이, 이 스토리의 작중 인물들도 '야심찬 손님'이 되어, "운명"을 피하여 산사태를 대비해 둔 대피소로 뛰어든다. 그러나 이는 자기들의 운명을 스스로 타개해 나가겠다는 오만의 죄로서 비극적 결과를 맺게 된다.

<목사의 검은 색 베일 "The Minister's Black Veil">은 "우화"라는 부제를 달고 있다. 호손은 주인공 후퍼(Hooper) 목사로 하여금 인간의 원죄를 상징하는 검은 색 베일을 얼굴에 착용케 함으로써 몇 가지 효과를 기대한다. 즉 베일은 가리는 물건으로서 보는 사람과 베일을 쓴

사람 사이에 끼어들어 둘 간의 소통을 가로막는다. 목사와 신도 간의 소통은 하나님과 신도들 간의 소통을 도와 신도들이 창조주와의 올바른 관계를 되찾고 유지하는데 필수적이다. 그런데 목사 얼굴 위의 베일이 신도들로 하여금 얼굴 없는 성직자와 대면하는듯한 괴이한 느낌을 주고 있는 것이다. 베일을 중간에 두고서는 신도들이 편안한 마음으로 속마음을 털어놓을 수도 없고 고민이나 어려움을 설명하기도 어렵다. 즉 목사의 베일은 목사와 신도들 간의 소통 장애를 암시하고 있다.

뿐만 아니라, 베일은 그것을 쓰고 있는 사람에게 모종의 권위 내지 권력을 부여한다. 베일을 쓴 사람은 인간성에 대한 지식을 소유하고 있으면서 그를 대하는 사람들로 하여금 자아의 죄성 정체성에 동의하는 것은 물론, 끊임없는 자아성찰을 할 것을 강력하게 요구하면서도 베일 뒤에 숨어 있어 그가 어떤 표정을 짓는지 어떤 생각을 하는지 짐작할 수가 없다. 따라서 사람들은 강한 압박과 위압을 느낀다.

호손의 <에고티즘 — 가슴 속의 뱀 "Egotism — the Bosom Serpent">은 주제나 은유사용 면에서 <목사의 검은 색 베일>과 유사하다. 즉 부제로 달린 '가슴 속의 뱀'은 목사가 얼굴에 드리운 검은 색 베일과 유사한 의미를 지닌다. 목사의 검은 색 베일이 그를 보는 사람들로 하여금 각자의 내면을 직시하게 하고 성찰하게 만드는 것처럼, 가슴 속의 뱀은 사람들로 하여금 각자의 안에 도사리고 있는 뱀, 곧 각자의 이기심이라는 악의 존재와 크기를 상기하고 성찰하도록 강요한다. 주인공 로데릭 엘리스톤(Roderick Elliston)은 얼마 전까지만 해도 자신은 보통 사람들과는 다르다고 보고 사람들을 우습게 여겼었다. 이 생각은 가슴 속에 뱀을 품은 것같이 되어 그의 이기심이 커지고, 악을 경배할수록 뱀은 괴물같이 커진다. 그는 이제 뱀처럼 눈을 번득이고 뱀처럼 걷게 되어, 완전치는 않으나 뱀 같은 모습으로 전락하였다. 호손은 인간의 마음 상태에 따라 외형이 변하는 현상을 작품에 많이 활용하였는데, 이 작품에서도 엘리스톤의 죄가 거대해짐에 따라 그의 외모가 악의 상징인 뱀과 닮아가는 모습으로 재현되었다.

엘리스톤의 변화된 외모와 그것이 전하는 메시지는 사람들이 외면하고 감추고 싶어 하는 추악한 자신의 실제의 모습으로 시선을 고정하고 그 사실을 직면하도록 촉구한다. 따라서, 원죄를 지고 태어난 우리 인간들은 각자의 가슴 속에 뱀을 탄생시킬 조건을 갖추고 있는 것이고, 그 뱀이 엘리스톤의 것만큼 괴물로 클 것인가는 각자가 마음과 영혼을 다스리기에 따른 것이라는 것이다.

모두의 가슴 속에 있는 뱀의 존재는 인간들로 하여금 겸허하게 이 사실을 인정하고 상대방에게 사랑과 연민으로 대할 것을 촉구하기도 한다. 인간은 누구나 죄인이기 때문에 상대방을 판단하고 비난하기에 앞서 자신을 다스리고 상대방을 품어 따뜻한 사회를 이루어야 한다는 것이다.

<반점 “The Birth-mark”>은 최초의 성형 스토리다. <반점>은 <미의 예술가 “The Artist of the Beautiful”>나 마찬가지로 완벽한 아름다움의 추구를 주제로 하고 있다. 한 가지 더 추가된 것은 아름다움의 추구에 사용된 방법론이다. 주인공은 과학자요, 자연과학의 모든 분야에서 저명한 학자다. 과학의 연구에 지나치게 헌신해 온 이 스토리의 주인공 에일머(Aylmer)는 과학·의학의 힘을 빌어서 매력이랄 수도 있는 뺨의 반점을 제거하여 아내를 결함이 없는 완벽한 미인으로 만들고자 한다. 작품의 포인트는 몇 가지로 볼 수 있다. 첫째는, 호손의 주요 주제 중 하나인 감성과 지성의 균형 파괴다. 에일머는 반점을 없앤다는 목표에 열중한 나머지 더 소중한 아내의 생명에 대한 경외심을

잃는다. 즉 지적인 목표에 과중한 노력을 기울인 나머지 감성이 결핍하게 된다. 그에게는 과학의 탐구가 제일 중요한 과제가 된 것이다.

둘째는, 과학·의학의 생명파괴 우려다. 혼신하는 지식의 탐구는 자칫 인간성의 파멸을 초래한다는 것이다. 과학기술이 박차를 가하고 있는 현 21세기에서 돌아볼 때, 인류는 19세기에 제기한 호손의 예지를 겸허히 받아들여야 할 것이다. 인간의 외적 조건과 환경을 개선·개량한다는 미명하에 자행되는 각종 실험과 시행은 인간성의 한계를 인식하는 것에서 출발하여야한다. 무지몽매한 과학적 탐구는 인류의 멸망을 가져올 수도 있다는 것이다. 에일머의 지식추구는 아내 조지아나(Georgiana)의 생명을 경시한 미시적 차원의 개인 만족에서 이루어진 것이다.

셋째는, 미의 상대적 평가 문제다. 조지아나의 뺨에 있는 반점은 조지아나가 순진하게 말하듯이 매력 포인트로 여겨지기도 했었다. 그러나 에일머의 눈에 불완전한 인간의 가시적 상징으로 일단 비추어지자, 그 반점은 점점 더 또렷해지고 흉측한 모습으로 강조되어 에일머를 견디기 힘들게 한다. 동일한 현상에 대한 주관적 평가는 극과 극으로 다를 수 있음을 호손의 <반점>은 이야기하고 있다. 이는 밀톤의 <실낙원 *Paradise Lost*>에서 사탄이 지옥에 떨어져서 "행 불행은 마음 먹기에 달린 것"이라고 토로하는 것과도 상통한다.

<미의 예술가 "The Artist of the Beautiful">는 대조되는 두 타입의 匠人을 등장시켜 "평범함"(mediocrity)를 비판한다. 시계 제조공 오웬(Owen)은 최고의 예술품 제작에 주야로 노력을 기울인다. 어릴 적부터 세밀한 솜씨를 보였고, 실용성에는 관심이 없이, 꽃이며 새 등 자연의 아름다운 움직임을 포착하려고 심혈을 기울인다. 또 다른 기술자 대장장이 로벗(Robert)은 오웬과는 대조적으로 거칠고 신체가 강

인하며 실생활에 사용가능한 물건들을 만든다. 오웬이 섬세함, 미스테리, 이상, 영혼, 정신적 천상의 가치와 미를 상징한다면, 로벗은 이와는 대조적인 가치 즉 강인함, 육체, 실용성, 현실, 지상적 가치와 상식, 힘(strength)을 상징한다 할 것이다.

이 둘을 바라보는 어른 피터(Peter Hovenden)의 시선은 대중의 시선을 대표한다 할 수 있다. 피터는 견습생이었던 오웬을 잘 알고 있으며, 그 청년의 성향이 시계공 본래의 역할을 벗어남을 우려하고 있다. 오웬 같은 예술가는 아름다움을 자기 혼자 속으로 감상하고 즐기는 것에 만족하지 않고, 스쳐지나가는 미스테리를 구태여 실체로 만들어서, 보이는 것에 치중하는 자들에게 보여주려고 한다. 오웬이 피터 앞에서 위축되고 생기를 잃는 것은 예술적 가치를 하찮게 여기는 피터와 로벗같은 대중 앞에서 예술가가 빛을 잃음을 나타낸다. 오웬이 현실적 어려움을 극복하고 마침내 자연의 최상 형태로 인간들을 위해 완벽한 나비를 만들어 낸다. 나비는 인간의 손에서 곧 번쩍이는 파편으로 망가지지만, 예술가는 이미 아름다움을 성취하였으므로 개의치 않는다. 호손은 그의 작품을 대중의 눈에 맞게 펴내지만, 일반 독자가 이를 이해하지 못하여 외면하여도, 보통수준의 것을 거부하는 자신의 정신세계는 만족되었으므로 개의치 않는다는 뜻으로 풀이된다. <미의 예술가>는 호손의 a poetic apology인 셈이다.

<라파치니의 딸 "Dr Rappaccini's Daughter">은 <미의 예술가>와 <반점>의 연장선상에 있다. 즉 이 단편은 전자에서 본 과학기술의 극치와 후자에서 본 미의 완성 소재를 결합한 이야기다. 의사 라파치니는 딸 베아트리스(Beatrice)가 어렸을 때부터 그를 공동체와 격리시키고 초목의 독을 주입하여 키운다. 혹시라도 딸이 여성으로서 피해자가 되는 일을 예방하기 위함이다. 라파치니는 창조주의 자리에 서서 한 인간

을 그의 철학에 따라 창조한 것이다. 이 이야기는 현대의 우리에게 많은 것을 생각하게 한다.

첫째, 호손이 자주 그리듯이, 이 소설은 기독교적인 주제를 다루고 있다. 창조주의 자리를 범한 라파치니, 인간은 공동체를 이루어 서로 죄를 다스리며 살아야하는데, 인간사회를 등진 라파치니 부녀, 그리고 지성과 감성이 균형을 이루어야하는데, 라파치니의 지성이 감성을 파괴한 주제 등이다. 라파치니는 창조주 하나님의 자리를 찬탈하여 인간의 한계를 넘어서는 오만을 범한 용서하지 못할 죄인이다. 그의 범죄로 인하여 그의 딸은 죽음을 맞이하고, 그 또한 과학자·의사로서의 비극적 실패를 경험한다. 라파치니의 또 다른 죄는 인간의 연쇄사슬을 절단한 것이다. 라파치니는 자신의 실험을 위하여 자신의 딸을 실험대상으로 삼았으며 딸과 스스로를 주변의 삶으로부터 철저하게 차단함으로써 인간성을 스스로 말살하였다.

둘째, 일반 독자의 시각에서 볼 때, 라파치니는 결손가정의 가부장으로서 과잉보호의 화신이다. 베아트리스를 과보호함으로써 딸 스스로 인간관계를 성립시키는 방법을 깨칠 기회가 없었다. 따라서 베아트리스는 그녀에게 관심을 보이는 이웃청년 조바니(Geovanni)를 어떻게 파악해야하는지 알지 못한다. 라파치니는 또한 철저한 가부장으로서 딸이자 여성인 베아트리스의 인생을 이기적으로 조작한, 여성의 적이 되는 남성이다.

셋째, <라파치니의 딸>은 그 제목이 암시하듯이, 주인공은 딸이다. 베아트리스는 철저하게 가부장적 부친 하에서 억압적 삶을 살았으나, 자연의 초목들과 연대하여 조화를 이룰 뿐 아니라, 타고난 지혜로 상황의 위급성을 파악하고는 죽음으로 부친의 억압에 항거하여 부친에게 일생의 패배와 좌절을 안겨준다.

넷째, <라파치니의 딸>에서는 작품의 화자 조바니의 모호성이 흥미

롭다. 해가 질 무렵이나 밤의 그림자 가운데 혹은 다소 불확실한 달빛 아래서는 조바니가 관찰하여 서술하는 내용에 진실여부가 불분명한 경우가 생긴다. 조바니가 이층 자기 방의 창을 통하여 이웃 라파치니 정원에서 일어나는 일—지나가던 도마뱀이 베아트리스가 꺾어 든 꽃의 진액을 한 방울 맞고 경련하다가 죽는다든가, 베아트리스에게 자신이 던져준 꽃다발이 그녀의 손에 쥐어지자마자 시들기 시작했다든가—등은 실제로 관찰하기가 어려운 것으로 여겨진다. 그러나 이런 이미지들이 반복되면서 베아트리스의 몸에 흐르고 있는 독성을 확인시키고 있는 것이다.

이 선집에 마지막으로 실린 <이선 브랜드 "Ethan Brand">는 호손의 홀마크 스토리다. 자주 등장하는 주제—용서받지 못할 죄—에 대한 호기심을 이기지 못하여 가마쟁이 이선 브랜드는 길을 떠난다. 도대체 용서받지 못할 죄는 어디에 있는 것인가? 여정 중에 학식을 쌓으면서 명성도 올라가지만, 상대적으로 잃어버리는 것이 있다. 이선은 이 특별한 죄성을 규명하는 데 몰입한 나머지 인간생활에 기본이 되는 모든 것을 내려놓는다. 사람들 간의 만남과 교류를 마다하고 세상을 홀로 떠돌아다니면서 마침내 마을로 돌아온 그는 그 여정 중에 자신이 바로 그 죄를 범하였다는 사실을 깨닫고 가마에 몸을 던진다.

이선은 추상적인 개념에 몸과 마음을 바쳤지만, 현대 독자들에게 용서 못할 죄는 자신들이 만사를 젖히고 추구하는 무엇이든지 될 수 있다. 예컨대, 물질의 축적이나 명예, 권력의 추구 등 현세적인 목표를 위해 기본적인 가치인 인간관계, 사랑, 동정, 연민 등을 도외시할 때 범하게 되는 죄가 바로 현대인의 용서 못할 죄인 것이다.

Suggested Readings:

"My Kinsman, Major Molineux":

Evans, Robert C. "That Evening of Ambiguity and Weariness': Readerly Exploration in Hawthorne's 'My Kinsman, Major Molineux'." *Exploration and Colonization* (2010): 115-122.

Herbert, T. Walter, Jr. "Doing Cultural Work: 'My Kinsman Major Molineux' and the Construction of the Self-Made Man." *Studies in the Novel* 23.2 (1991): 20-27.

Saunders, Judith P. "Nepotism in Hawthorne's 'My Kinsman, Major Molineux': A Darwinian Approach to a Classic Text." *Telling Stories: Literature and Evolution* (2012): 296-309.

"Roger Malvin's Burial":

Mackenzie, Manfred. "Hawthorne's 'Roger Malvin's Burial': A Postcolonial Reading." *New Literary History: A Journal of Theory and Interpretation* 27.3 (1996): 459-72.

Ortolano, Guy. "The Role of Dorcas in 'Roger Malvin's Burial'." *Nathaniel Hawthorne Review* 25.2 (1999): 89-100, 167-68.

"The Ambitious Guest":

Edgren, C. Hobart, Clarence L. Branton, William G. Lane and B. R. McElderry, Jr. "Hawthorne's 'The Ambitious Guest': An Interpretation." *Nineteenth-Century Fiction* 10. 2 (1955), 151-168.

Sears, John F. "Hawthorne's 'The Ambitious Guest' and the Significance of the Willey Disaster." *American Literature.*

54.3 (1982), 354-367.

"The Grey Champion":

Orians, G. Harrison. "The Angel of Hadley in Fiction: A Study of the Sources of Hawthorne's 'The Grey Champion.'" *American Literature* 4.3 (1932), 257-269.

"The Minister's Black Veil":

Boone, N. S. "'The Minister's Black Veil' and Hawthorne's Ethical Refusal of Reciprocity: A Levinasian Parable." *Renascence: Essays on Values in Literature* 57.3 (2005) : 165-76.

Freedman, William. "The Artist's Symbol and Hawthorne's Veil: 'The Minister's Black Veil' Resartus." *Studies in Short Fiction.* 29.3 (1992): 353-62.

"Egotism, or The Bosom Serpent":

Paryz, Marek. "The Ridiculed Reason: The Presentation of the Insane Asylum in Nathaniel Hawthorne's 'Egotism; or, the Bosom Serpent' and Edgar Allan Poe's 'The System of Doctor Tarr and Professor Fether'." *American Studies* 18 (1999): 87-104.

Wohlpart, A. James. "Allegories of Art, Allegories of Heart: Hawthorne's 'Egotism' and 'The Christmas Banquet'." *Studies in Short Fiction.* 31.3 (1994): 449-60.

"The Birth-Mark":

Shakinovsky, Lynn. "The Return of the Repressed: Illiteracy and the Death of the Narrative in Hawthorne's 'The Birthmark'." *American Transcendental Quarterly* 9.4 (1995): 269-81.

Weinstein, Cindy. "The Invisible Hand Made Visible: 'The Birth-Mark'." *Nineteenth-Century Literature* 48.1 (1993): 44-73.

"The Artist of the Beautiful":

Newberry, Frederick. "'The Artist of the Beautiful': Crossing the Transcendent Divide in Hawthorne's Fiction." *Nineteenth-Century Literature* 50.1 (1995) : 78-96.

Urban, David V. "Evasion of the Finite in Hawthorne's 'The Artist of the Beautiful'." *Christianity and Literature* 54.3 (2005): 343-58.

"Rappaccini's Daughter":

Medoro, Dana. "'Looking into Their Inmost Nature': The Speculum and Sexual Selection in 'Rappaccini's Daughter'." *Nathaniel Hawthorne Review* 35.1 (2009): 70-86.

Wilson-Jordan, Jacqueline. "'Paint It Black': Teaching Hawthorne's 'Rappaccini's Daughter' as a Gothic." *Eureka Studies in Teaching Short Fiction*. 7.1 (2006): 17-35.

"Ethan Brand":

Eisen, Kurt. "The Tragical History of Ethan Brand." *Essays in Literature*, 19.1 (1992) : 55-60.

Harris, Mark. "A New Reading of 'Ethan Brand': The Failed Quest." *Studies in Short Fiction* 31.1 (1994) : 69-77.

기타:

Bromell, Nicholas K. "'The Bloody Hand' of Labor: Work, Class, and Gender in Three Stories by Hawthorne." *American Quarterly* 42.4 (1990) : 542-564.

Goldman, Eric. "Explaining Mental Illness: Theology and Pathology in Nathaniel Hawthorne's Short Fiction." *Nineteenth-Century Literature* 59.1 (2004): 27-52.

Kevorkian, Martin. "'Within the Domain of Chaos'" Nathaniel Hawthorne, Lucretian Physics, and Martial Logic." *Studies in the Novel* 31.2 (1999): 178-201.

Nathaniel Hawthorne 연보

July 4, 1804: 매서추세츠 주 세일럼(Salem)에서 New England 명문가의 후손으로 태어남.

January 1808: 여동생(Maria Louise) 출생.

April 1808: 수리남(Surinam, New Guinea)에서 부친, 열병으로 사망. 가족은 가난으로 인하여 친척에 의존하게 됨.

August-September 1820: 뉴스잡지, *The Spectator*, 발간.

1821: 보든 컬리지(Bowdoin College) 입학. 여기서 만난 급우들 중 미래의 미국대통령 피어스(Franklin Pierce)와 당대의 유명한 시인 롱펠로우(Henry Wadsworth Longfellow)가 있음.

1825: 보든 졸업과 동시에 온 가족, 세일럼으로 이사.

1828: 첫 소설『팬쇼』(*Fanshawe: A Tale*)를 익명, 자비로 출간. 독자의 관심을 별로 끌지 못함.

October-November 1830: 본명 Hathorne으로 단편 2편 출간. 이후 사적으로나 작가로서 "w"를 추가한 이름 사용.

1837: *Twice-Told Tales* 출간.

1839-1840: 보스톤 세관(the Boston Custom House)에 surveyor로 취업.

April-November, 1841: 매서추세츠 주 록스베리(West Roxbury, Massachusetts)에 소재한 브룩크 팜(Brook Farm) 이상공동체 합류. 일 천 불 투자.

July 9, 1842-1845: 3년간 약혼자였던 화가 소피아(Sophia Peabody)와 결혼하여 콩코드의 셋집(Old Manse)으로 이사. 에머슨, 소로, 마가렛 풀러 등 철학자와 문인들을 이웃하며 지냄.

March 3, 1844: 장녀 우나 (Una) 출생.

June 2, 1846: 장남 출생. 수 개월간 이름을 지어주지 못하고 있다가 마침내 부모가 "Julian"으로 부르기로 합의.

1846: 단편집 *Mosses from an Old Manse* 발표.

July 1846-1849: 세일럼 세관의 surveyor로 취업. 세일럼으로 이사.

1849: 정치적 이유로 해고됨. 호손 분노. 간통과 위선을 다루는 소설 집필.

July 31, 1849: 모친 (Elizabeth Hathorne) 사망. 우울함 속에 『주홍글자』(*The Scarlet Letter*) 집필 계속.

March 1850: 『주홍글자』 출간.

May 1850: 가족들 레녹스 (Lenox, Massachusetts) 근교의 농가로 이사.

1851: *The House of the Seven Gables* 출간. 멜빌 (Herman Melville)은 『모비 딕』을 같은 해에 출간하면서 호손에게 헌정함.

*The Snow Image and Other Twice-Told Tales*와 *True Stories from History and Biography* 출간. 차녀 (Rose) 출생(May 20, 1851); Boston 근교의 West Newton으로 이사.

1852: Brook Farm에서의 이상적 공동체 체험을 기초로 한 *The Blithedale Romance*와 *A Wonder-Book for Girls and Boys* 외, 피어스(Franklin Pierce)의 선거용 전기(傳記) 출간.

1852: 콩코드에 올콧 (Alcott)가 (家)가 소유하던 집을 사서 Wayside라 명명함.

1853: 피어스가 대통령으로 당선되면서 호손을 영국 리버풀의 영사로의 미 영사로 지명. 가족을 데리고 영국으로 건너감.

1857: 피어스가 민주당에서의 지명권 획득에 실패하자 영사로서의 지위 상실.

1857-1859: 로마와 플로렌스, 영국의 동북부에 위치한 Redcar에 거주.

1859: 미국행 승선. 콩코드의 Wayside에 재정착.

1860: *The Marble Faun* 출간.

1863: *Our Old Home* 출간. 유럽 경험을 다룬 non-fiction.

May 19, 1864: 피어스 전 대통령을 비롯한 친구들과 휴가를 즐기던 중 플리머스 (Plymouth, New Hampshire)에서 사망. 5월 23일, 콩코드의 슬리피 할로우 묘지(Sleepy Hollow Cemetery)에 매장됨.

遺作: *The Ancestral Footstep;*
Dr. Grimshawe's Secret;
Septimius Felton;
The Dolliver Romance 등.

Feb 26, 1871: 부인 소피아, 런던서 사망하여 그곳에 매장됨.

June 26, 2006: 일백 주기가 지난 후, 호손의 부인 소피아와 딸 우나는 런던에서 콩코드의 묘지로 이장됨.

The Text

My Kinsman, Major Molineux

AFTER the kings of Great Britain had assumed the right of appointing the colonial governors,[1] the measures of the latter[2] seldom met with the ready and generous approbation which had been paid to those of their predecessors, under the original charters.[3] The people looked with most jealous scrutiny to the exercise of power which did not emanate from themselves, and they usually rewarded their rulers with slender gratitude for the compliances by which, in softening their instructions from beyond the sea,[4] they had incurred the reprehension of those who gave them. The annals of Massachusetts Bay[5] will inform us, that of six governors[6] in the space of about forty years from the surrender of the old charter, under James II., two were imprisoned by a popular insurrection; a third, as Hutchinson[7]

---

1) 영국의 Charles II세의 헌장(charter) 폐지(1684) 이후 40여 년 간 영국의 왕 James II(1685-1688 재위), William III of Orange 등은 식민지 주민들의 생각과는 관계없이 식민지 총독들을 직접 임명했다.

2) the latter는 식민지 총독들을 가리킴.

3) Charles I세: 1628/9-Charles II세: 1684까지 55년 동안 식민지는 헌장 체제 하에 주민들이 총독을 선출해 옴.

4) from beyond the sea, 본국 즉 영국.

5) the Massachusetts Bay Colony: 1630년 영국인 John Winthrop이 대서양을 건너 신대륙에 건설한 식민지.

6) of six governors=out of six governors.

7) Hutchinson, Thomas(1711-1780). 영국왕의 임명을 받은 매서추세츠 식민지 주지사(1771-1774). 막강한 권력자로 군림하여 주민들의 원망을 받음. Boston Tea Party 이후 Thomas Gage 장군에게 주지사를 양도하고 영국으로 건너감. 역사가로, 매우 정확하고 유용한 식민사(*The History of the Colony and Province of Massachusetts*

inclines to believe, was driven from the province[8)] by the whizzing of a musket-ball; a fourth, in the opinion of the same historian,[9)] was hastened to his grave by continual bickerings with the House of Representatives; and the remaining two, as well as their successors, till the Revolution,[10)] were favored with few and brief intervals of peaceful sway. The inferior members of the court party, in times of high political excitement, led scarcely a more desirable life. These remarks may serve as a preface to the following adventures, which chanced upon[11)] a summer night, not far from a hundred years ago. The reader, in order to avoid a long and dry detail of colonial affairs, is requested to dispense with an account of the train of circumstances that had caused much temporary inflammation of the popular mind.

It was near nine o'clock of a moonlight evening, when a boat crossed the ferry with a single passenger, who had obtained his conveyance at that unusual hour by the promise of an extra fare. While he stood on the landing-place, searching in either pocket for the means of fulfilling his agreement,[12)] the ferryman lifted a lantern, by the aid of which, and the newly risen moon, he took a very accurate survey of the stranger's figure. He was a youth of barely eighteen years, evidently country-bred, and now, as it should seem, upon his first visit to town. He was clad in a coarse gray coat, well worn, but in excellent repair; his under

---

Bay)의 저자.

8) the province=the Massachusetts Bay Colony.

9) Thomas Hutchinson

10) American Revolution: 1776.

11) to chance upon=to come upon accidentally.

12) in either pocket··· agreement. 내기로 한 배 값을 지불하려고 양쪽 주머니를 뒤져 찾는 중.

garments were durably constructed of leather, and fitted tight to a pair of serviceable and well-shaped limbs; his stockings of blue yarn were the incontrovertible work of a mother or a sister; and on his head was a three-cornered hat, which in its better days had perhaps sheltered the graver brow of the lad's father.[13] Under his left arm was a heavy cudgel formed of an oak sapling, and retaining a part of the hardened root; and his equipment was completed by a wallet, not so abundantly stocked as to incommode[14] the vigorous shoulders on which it hung. Brown, curly hair, well-shaped features, and bright, cheerful eyes were nature's gifts, and worth all that art could have done for his adornment.

The youth, one of whose names was Robin, finally drew from his pocket the half of a little province bill of five shillings,[15] which, in the depreciation in that sort of currency, did but satisfy the ferryman's demand, with the surplus of a sexangular[16] piece of parchment, valued at three pence. He then walked forward into the town, with as light a step as if his day's journey had not already exceeded thirty miles, and with as eager an eye as if he were entering London city, instead of the little metropolis of a New England colony.[17] Before Robin had proceeded far, however, it occurred to him that he knew not whither to direct his steps; so he paused, and looked up and down the narrow street, scrutinizing the small and mean wooden buildings that

---

13) the three-cornered hat··· father. 아버지에게서 물려받은 삼각모자.

14) incommode [라틴어] =to cause to be inconvenienced.

15) 식민기에 쓰인 화폐는 영국과 동일한 파운드, 실링, 펜스 등이었음.

16) sexangular=Having six angles; hexagonal.

17) light ··· and eager ··· 마치 먼 여행길을 오지 않은 듯 경쾌한 걸음과 런던같은 큰 도시에 온 듯 궁금한 눈초리로.

were scattered on either side.

"This low hovel cannot be my kinsman's dwelling," thought he, "nor yonder old house, where the moonlight enters at the broken casement; and truly I see none hereabouts that might be worthy of him. It would have been wise to inquire my way of the ferryman, and doubtless he would have gone with me, and earned a shilling from the Major for his pains. But the next man I meet will do as well."[18)]

He resumed his walk, and was glad to perceive that the street now became wider, and the houses more respectable in their appearance. He soon discerned a figure moving on moderately in advance, and hastened his steps to overtake it. As Robin drew nigh, he saw that the passenger was a man in years, with a full periwig of gray hair, a wide-skirted coat of dark cloth, and silk stockings rolled above his knees. He carried a long and polished cane, which he struck down perpendicularly before him at every step; and at regular intervals he uttered two successive hems, of a peculiarly solemn and sepulchral intonation. Having made these observations, Robin laid hold of the skirt of the old man's coat just when the light from the open door and windows of a barber's shop fell upon both their figures.

"Good evening to you, honored sir," said he, making a low bow, and still retaining his hold of the skirt. "I pray you tell me whereabouts is the dwelling of my kinsman, Major Molineux."

The youth's question was uttered very loudly; and one of the barbers, whose razor was descending on a well-soaped

---

18) 소년의 순진하고 낙천적인 자세를 엿볼 수 있다.

chin, and another who was dressing a Ramillies wig,[19] left their occupations,[20] and came to the door. The citizen, in the mean time, turned a long-favored countenance upon Robin, and answered him in a tone of excessive anger and annoyance. His two sepulchral hems, however, broke into the very centre of his rebuke, with most singular effect, like a thought of the cold grave obtruding among wrathful passions.

"Let go my garment, fellow! I tell you, I know not the man you speak of. What! I have authority, I have — hem, hem — authority; and if this be the respect you show for your betters, your feet shall be brought acquainted with the stocks[21] by daylight, tomorrow morning!"

Robin released the old man's skirt, and hastened away, pursued by an ill-mannered roar of laughter from the barber's shop. He was at first considerably surprised by the result of his question, but, being a shrewd youth, soon thought himself able to account for the mystery.

"This is some country representative," was his conclusion,

19) Ramillies wig: 래밀리즈 가발. 길게 땋은 꼬리머리. 머리 꼭대기와 끝에 각각 검은색 리본을 맨 땋은 머리. 18세기에는 온갖 변발에 밀가루나 흰 가루를 묻혀 백발 흉내를 낸 것이 유행이었음. [아래 그림 참조 : www.americanrevolution.org]

20) left their occupations. 하던 일을 놓고.

21) stocks. 뚫린 구멍에 손목이나 발목을 넣는 형벌기구. 차꼬.

"who has never seen the inside of my kinsman's door, and lacks the breeding[22)] to answer a stranger civilly. The man is old, or verily — I might be tempted to turn back and smite him on the nose. Ah, Robin, Robin! even the barber's boys laugh at you for choosing such a guide! You will be wiser in time, friend Robin."

He now became entangled in a succession of crooked and narrow streets, which crossed each other, and meandered at no great distance from the water-side. The smell of tar was obvious to his nostrils, the masts of vessels pierced the moonlight above the tops of the buildings, and the numerous signs, which Robin paused to read, informed him that he was near the centre of business. But the streets were empty, the shops were closed, and lights were visible only in the second stories of a few dwelling-houses. At length, on the corner of a narrow lane, through which he was passing, he beheld the broad countenance of a British hero swinging before the door of an inn, whence proceeded the voices of many guests. The casement of one of the lower windows was thrown back, and a very thin curtain permitted Robin to distinguish a party[23)] at supper, round a well-furnished table. The fragrance of the good cheer steamed forth into the outer air, and the youth could not fail to recollect that the last remnant of his travelling stock of provision had yielded to his morning appetite, and that noon had found and left him dinnerless.

"Oh, that a parchment three-penny might give me a right to sit down at yonder table!" said Robin, with a sigh. "But the Major

---

22) lacks the breeding. 가정교육 부족.

23) a party=a group of people.

will make me welcome to the best of his victuals; so I will even step boldly in, and inquire my way to his dwelling."

He entered the tavern, and was guided by the murmur of voices and the fumes of tobacco to the public-room. It was a long and low apartment, with oaken walls, grown dark in the continual smoke, and a floor which was thickly sanded, but of no immaculate purity. A number of persons — the larger part of whom appeared to be mariners, or in some way connected with the sea — occupied the wooden benches, or leather-bottomed chairs, conversing on various matters, and occasionally lending their attention to some topic of general interest. Three or four little groups were draining as many bowls of punch, which the West India trade had long since made a familiar drink in the colony. Others, who had the appearance of men who lived by regular and laborious handicraft, preferred the insulated bliss of an unshared potation, and became more taciturn under its influence. Nearly all, in short, evinced a predilection for the Good Creature[24)] in some of its various shapes, for this is a vice to which, as Fast Day sermons of a hundred years ago will testify, we have a long hereditary claim. The only guests to whom Robin's sympathies inclined him were two or three sheepish countrymen, who were using the inn somewhat after the fashion of a Turkish caravansary[25)]; they had gotten themselves into the darkest corner of the room, and heedless

24) Good Creature. 즉 술.

25) a Turkish caravansary(혹은 caravansarai). 12세기 경 Silk Road를 따라 근동을 여행하는 낙타와 상인들에게 안전과 편의를 위해 생겨난 길가 숙박시설로 세계가 현대화하면서 20세기 초에 쇠락하였다. 한 가운데 큰 마당을 두고 둘러선 시설로서 상인들이 그들의 물품과 낙타들과 함께 단위 단위로 사용하였다. 터키의 caravansarai는 석조건물인 것이 특징이다.

of the Nicotian atmosphere, were supping on the bread of their own ovens, and the bacon cured[26] in their own chimney-smoke. But though Robin felt a sort of brotherhood with these strangers, his eyes were attracted from them to a person who stood near the door, holding whispered conversation with a group of ill-dressed associates. His features were separately striking almost to grotesqueness, and the whole face left a deep impression on the memory. The forehead bulged out into a double prominence, with a vale between; the nose came boldly forth in an irregular curve, and its bridge was of more than a finger's breadth; the eyebrows were deep and shaggy, and the eyes glowed beneath them like fire in a cave.

While Robin deliberated[27] of whom to inquire respecting[28] his kinsman's dwelling, he was accosted by the innkeeper, a little man in a stained white apron, who had come to pay his professional welcome to the stranger.[29] Being in the second generation from a French Protestant,[30] he seemed to have inherited the courtesy of his parent nation[31]; but no variety of circumstances was ever known to change his voice from the one

---

26) to cure=to prepare

27) deliberate: to consider carefully, as by weighing alternatives.

28) respecting: concerning

29) to pay his professional welcome to the stranger. 즉 여관주인이 the stranger 즉 Robin에게 직업적으로 손님을 환영하는 일.

30) Being in the generation from a French Protestant: 여관주인은 프랑스 신교도 2세가 되므로. 일명 위그노 (Huguenots)라고 불리는 프랑스의 신교도들은 1530년대 John Calvin의 영향을 받아 교회를 개혁하고자 하였으며, 박해를 받게 되자, 17세기 말, 대략 20만 명의 위그노들이 조국을 떠나 유럽 각지로 흩어졌는데 일부는 북미, 당시 영국의 식민지로 건너왔다.

31) his parent nation: 즉 프랑스. 프랑스는 사교술이 발달되어 있어 사람들이 예절에 밝다고 볼 수 있다.

shrill note in which he now addressed Robin.

"From the country, I presume, sir?" said he, with a profound bow. "Beg leave[32] to congratulate you on your arrival, and[33] trust you intend a long stay with us. Fine town here, sir, beautiful buildings, and much that may interest a stranger. May I hope for the honor of your commands[34] in respect to supper?"

"The man sees a family likeness![35] the rogue[36] has guessed that I am related to the Major!" thought Robin, who had hitherto experienced little superfluous civility.

All eyes were now turned on the country lad, standing at the door, in his worn three-cornered hat, gray coat, leather breeches, and blue yarn stockings, leaning on an oaken cudgel, and bearing a wallet on his back.

Robin replied to the courteous innkeeper, with such an assumption of confidence as befitted the Major's relative. "My honest friend," he said, "I shall make it a point to patronize your house on some occasion, when" — here he could not help lowering his voice — "when I may have more than a parchment three-pence in my pocket. My present business," continued he, speaking with lofty confidence, "is merely to inquire my way to

---

32) [I] beg [your] leave: 허락해 주시오. 공손한 인사말투.

33) and 다음에 I가 생략되었다. 즉 I trust. 오래 머무실거지요?

34) commands: 주문.

35) The man sees a family likeness!: the man=the innkeeper. "a family likeness" 집안 내(內) 닮은 걸 알아보는구먼! 이는 로빈은 여관주인의 친절이 곧 그 유명한 친척과 자신이 닮았다는 것을 알아본데서 연유한다고 생각한다.

36) the rogue: 불한당. 즉 여관주인.

the dwelling of my kinsman, Major Molineux.[37)]"

There was a sudden and general movement in the room, which Robin interpreted as expressing the eagerness of each individual to become his guide. But the innkeeper turned his eyes to a written paper on the wall, which he read, or seemed to read, with occasional recurrences to the young man's figure.

"What have we here?" said he, breaking his speech into little dry fragments. "'Left the house of the subscriber, bounden servant,[38)] Hezekiah Mudge, — had on, when he went away, gray coat, leather breeches, master's third-best hat. One pound currency reward to whosoever shall lodge him in any jail of the providence.' Better trudge, boy; better trudge!"

Robin had begun to draw his hand towards the lighter end of the oak cudgel, but a strange hostility in every countenance induced him to relinquish his purpose of breaking the courteous innkeeper's head. As he turned to leave the room, he encountered a sneering glance from the bold-featured personage whom he had before noticed; and no sooner was he beyond the door, than he heard a general laugh, in which the innkeeper's voice might be distinguished, like the dropping of small stones into a kettle.

"Now, is it not strange," thought Robin, with his usual shrewdness, — "is it not strange that the confession of an empty pocket should outweigh the name of my kinsman, Major

---

37) Molineux. 발음 /ˈmɒlɨnju:/ 멀리뉴

38) Left the house of the subscriber, bounden servant: bounden=under obligation, obliged. the subscriber: 광고주. 곧 주인. Left의 주어는 servant. 이하의 had on과 연결됨. 이어서 도망간 자의 인상착의를 설명하고 있음. servant를 주어로 함.

Molineux? Oh, if I had one of those grinning rascals in the woods, where I and my oak sapling grew up together, I would teach him that my arm is heavy though my purse be light!"

On turning the corner of the narrow lane, Robin found himself in a spacious street, with an unbroken line of lofty houses on each side, and a steepled building at the upper end, whence the ringing of a bell announced the hour of nine. The light of the moon, and the lamps from the numerous shop-windows, discovered people promenading on the pavement, and amongst them Robin had hoped to recognize his hitherto inscrutable relative.[39] The result of his former inquiries made him unwilling to hazard another, in a scene of such publicity, and he determined to walk slowly and silently up the street, thrusting his face close to that of every elderly gentleman, in search of the Major's lineaments. In his progress, Robin encountered many gay and gallant figures. Embroidered garments of showy colors, enormous periwigs, gold-laced hats, and silver-hilted swords glided past him and dazzled his optics. Travelled youths, imitators of the European fine gentlemen of the period, trod jauntily along, half dancing to the fashionable tunes which they hummed, and making poor Robin ashamed of his quiet and natural gait. At length, after many pauses to examine the gorgeous display of goods in the shop-windows, and after suffering some rebukes for the impertinence of his scrutiny into people's faces, the Major's kinsman found himself near the steepled building, still unsuccessful in his search. As yet, however, he had seen only one side of the thronged street; so Robin crossed, and continued the same sort of inquisition down

---

39) his hitherto(=until this time) inscrutable relative: 즉 멀리뉴 소령.

the opposite pavement, with stronger hopes than the philosopher seeking an honest man, but with no better fortune. He had arrived about midway towards the lower end, from which his course began, when he overheard the approach of some one who struck down a cane on the flag-stones at every step, uttering at regular intervals, two sepulchral hems.

"Mercy on us!" quoth Robin, recognizing the sound.

Turning a corner, which chanced to be close at his right hand, he hastened to pursue his researches in some other part of the town. His patience now was wearing low, and he seemed to feel more fatigue from his rambles since he crossed the ferry, than from his journey of several days on the other side. Hunger also pleaded loudly within him, and Robin began to balance the propriety of demanding, violently, and with lifted cudgel, the necessary guidance from the first solitary passenger whom he should meet. While a resolution to this effect was gaining strength, he entered a street of mean appearance, on either side of which a row of ill-built houses was straggling towards the harbor. The moonlight fell upon no passenger along the whole extent, but in the third domicile which Robin passed there was a half-opened door, and his keen glance detected a woman's garment within.

"My luck may be better here," said he to himself.

Accordingly, he approached the doors and beheld it shut closer as he did so; yet an open space remained, sufficing for the fair occupant[40] to observe the stranger, without a corresponding

40) the fair occupant: 안에 있는 여성.

display on her part. All that Robin could discern was a strip of scarlet petticoat, and the occasional sparkle of an eye, as if the moonbeams were trembling on some bright thing.

"Pretty mistress," for I may call her so[41)] with a good conscience thought the shrewd youth, since I know nothing to the contrary, — "my sweet pretty mistress, will you be kind enough to tell me whereabouts I must seek the dwelling of my kinsman, Major Molineux?"

Robin's voice was plaintive and winning, and the female, seeing nothing to be shunned in the handsome country youth, thrust open the door, and came forth into the moonlight. She was a dainty little figure with a white neck, round arms, and a slender waist, at the extremity of which her scarlet petticoat jutted out over a hoop, as if she were standing in a balloon. Moreover, her face was oval and pretty, her hair dark beneath the little cap, and her bright eyes possessed a sly freedom, which triumphed over those of Robin.

"Major Molineux dwells here," said this fair woman.

Now, her voice was the sweetest Robin had heard that night, yet he could not help doubting whether that sweet voice spoke Gospel truth.[42)] He looked up and down the mean street, and then surveyed the house before which they stood. It was a small, dark edifice of two stories, the second of which projected over the lower floor, and the front apartment had the aspect of a shop

---

41) so: 'pretty mistress'라고.

42) Gospel truth: 복음같은 수준의 진실.

for petty commodities.

"Now, truly, I am in luck," replied Robin, cunningly, "and so indeed is my kinsman, the Major, in having so pretty a housekeeper. But I prithee trouble[43] him to step to the door; I will deliver him a message from his friends in the country, and then go back to my lodgings at the inn."

"Nay, the Major has been abed[44] this hour or more," said the lady of the scarlet petticoat; "and it would be to little purpose to disturb him to-night, seeing his evening draught was of the strongest. But he is a kind-hearted man, and it would be as much as my life's worth to let a kinsman of his turn away from the door. You are the good old gentleman's very picture, and I could swear that was his rainy-weather hat. Also he has garments very much resembling those leather small-clothes. But come in, I pray, for I bid you hearty welcome in his name.

So saying, the fair and hospitable dame took our hero by the hand; and the touch was light, and the force was gentleness, and though Robin read in her eyes what he did not hear in her words, yet the slender-waisted woman in the scarlet petticoat proved stronger than the athletic country youth. She had drawn his half-willing footsteps nearly to the threshold, when the opening of a door in the neighborhood startled the Major's housekeeper, and, leaving the Major's kinsman, she vanished speedily into her own domicile. A heavy yawn preceded the appearance of a man, who, like the Moonshine of Pyramus and Thisbe,[45] carried a lantern,

43) I prithee trouble him: I pray you to trouble him. 수고스럽지만 … 해주세요.

44) abed: in bed.

45) the Moonshine of Pyramus and Thisbe: 셰익스피어의 작품 『한 여름 밤의 꿈』 5막1

needlessly aiding his sister luminary[46) in the heavens. As he walked sleepily up the street, he turned his broad, dull face on Robin, and displayed a long staff, spiked at the end.

"Home, vagabond, home!" said the watchman, in accents that seemed to fall asleep as soon as they were uttered. "Home, or we'll set you in the stocks by peep of day!"

"This is the second hint of the kind," thought Robin. "I wish they would end my difficulties, by setting me there to-night."

Nevertheless, the youth felt an instinctive antipathy towards the guardian of midnight order, which at first prevented him from asking his usual question.[47) But just when the man was about to vanish behind the corner, Robin resolved not to lose the opportunity, and shouted lustily after him, —

"I say, friend! will you guide me to the house of my kinsman, Major Molineux?"

The watchman made no reply, but turned the corner and was gone; yet Robin seemed to hear the sound of drowsy laughter stealing along the solitary street. At that moment, also, a pleasant titter saluted him from the open window above his head; he looked up, and caught the sparkle of a saucy eye; a round arm beckoned to him, and next he heard light footsteps descending the staircase within. But Robin, being of the household of a New

---

장에서 작중인물들이 벌이는 연극 장면. 두 주인공 연인들, 피라무스와 티스베에게 비추는 등을 들고 달빛 역할을 하는 등장인물을 로빈이 연상하고 있음.

46) his sister luminary: 즉 천체의 달.

47) his usual question: 그의 친척 멀리뉴 소령의 집을 가리켜 달라는 질문.

England clergyman, was a good youth, as well as a shrewd one; so he resisted temptation, and fled away.

He now roamed desperately, and at random, through the town, almost ready to believe that a spell was on him, like that by which a wizard of his country had once kept three pursuers wandering, a whole winter night, within twenty paces of the cottage which they sought. The streets lay before him, strange and desolate, and the lights were extinguished in almost every house. Twice, however, little parties of men, among whom Robin distinguished individuals in outlandish attire, came hurrying along; but, though on both occasions, they paused to address him such intercourse did not at all enlighten his perplexity. They did but utter a few words in some language of which Robin knew nothing, and perceiving his inability to answer, bestowed a curse upon him in plain English and hastened away. Finally, the lad determined to knock at the door of every mansion that might appear worthy to be occupied by his kinsman, trusting that perseverance would overcome the fatality that had hitherto thwarted him. Firm in this resolve, he was passing beneath the walls of a church, which formed the corner of two streets, when, as he turned into the shade of its steeple, he encountered a bulky stranger muffled in a cloak. The man was proceeding with the speed of earnest business, but Robin planted himself full before him, holding the oak cudgel with both hands across his body as a bar to further passage

"Halt, honest man, and answer me a question," said he, very resolutely Tell me, this instant, whereabouts is the dwelling of my kinsman, Major Molineux!"

"Keep your tongue between your teeth, fool, and let me pass!" said a deep, gruff voice, which Robin partly remembered. "Let me pass, or I'll strike you to the earth!"

"No, no, neighbor!" cried Robin, flourishing his cudgel, and then thrusting its larger end close to the man's muffled face. "No, no, I'm not the fool you take me for, nor do you pass till I have an answer to my question. Whereabouts is the dwelling of my kinsman, Major[48] Molineux?" The stranger, instead of attempting to force his passage, stepped back into the moonlight, unmuffled his face, and stared full into that of Robin.

"Watch here an hour, and Major Molineux will pass by," said he.

Robin gazed with dismay and astonishment on the unprecedented physiognomy of the speaker. The forehead with its double prominence the broad hooked nose, the shaggy eyebrows, and fiery eyes were those which he had noticed at the inn, but the man's complexion had undergone a singular, or, more properly, a twofold change. One side of the face blazed an intense red, while the other was black as midnight, the division line being in the broad bridge of the nose; and a mouth which seemed to extend from ear to ear was black or red, in contrast to the color of the cheek. The effect was as if two individual devils, a fiend of fire and a fiend of darkness, had united themselves to form this infernal visage. The stranger grinned in Robin's face, muffled his party-colored features, and was out of sight in a moment.

48) unmuffle: to free from something that covers

"Strange things we travellers see!" ejaculated Robin.

He seated himself, however, upon the steps of the church-door, resolving to wait the appointed time for his kinsman. A few moments were consumed in philosophical speculations upon the species of man who had just left him; but having settled this point shrewdly, rationally, and satisfactorily, he was compelled to look elsewhere for his amusement. And first he threw his eyes along the street. It was of more respectable appearance than most of those into which he had wandered, and the moon, creating, like the imaginative power, a beautiful strangeness in familiar objects, gave something of romance to a scene that might not have possessed it in the light of day. The irregular and often quaint architecture of the houses, some of whose roofs were broken into numerous little peaks, while others ascended, steep and narrow, into a single point, and others again were square; the pure snow-white of some of their complexions, the aged darkness of others, and the thousand sparklings, reflected from bright substances in the walls of many; these matters engaged Robin's attention for a while, and then began to grow wearisome. Next he endeavored to define the forms of distant objects, starting away, with almost ghostly indistinctness, just as his eye appeared to grasp them, and finally he took a minute survey of an edifice which stood on the opposite side of the street, directly in front of the church-door, where he was stationed. It was a large, square mansion, distinguished from its neighbors by a balcony, which rested on tall pillars, and by an elaborate Gothic window, communicating therewith.

"Perhaps this is the very house I have been seeking," thought Robin.

Then he strove to speed away the time, by listening to a murmur which swept continually along the street, yet was scarcely audible, except to an unaccustomed ear like his; it was a low, dull, dreamy sound, compounded of many noises, each of which was at too great a distance to be separately heard. Robin marvelled at this snore of a sleeping town, and marvelled more whenever its continuity was broken by now and then a distant shout, apparently loud where it originated. But altogether it was a sleep-inspiring sound, and, to shake off its drowsy influence, Robin arose, and climbed a window-frame, that he might view the interior of the church. There the moonbeams came trembling in, and fell down upon the deserted pews, and extended along the quiet aisles. A fainter yet more awful radiance was hovering around the pulpit, and one solitary ray had dared to rest upon the open page of the great Bible. Had nature, in that deep hour, become a worshipper in the house which man had builded? Or was that heavenly light the visible sanctity of the place,—visible because no earthly and impure feet were within the walls? The scene made Robin's heart shiver with a sensation of loneliness stronger than he had ever felt in the remotest depths of his native woods; so he turned away and sat down again before the door. There were graves around the church, and now an uneasy thought obtruded into Robin's breast. What if the object of his search, which had been so often and so strangely thwarted, were all the time mouldering in his shroud? What if his kinsman should glide through yonder gate, and nod and smile to him in dimly passing by?

"Oh that any breathing thing were here with me!" said Robin.

Recalling his thoughts from this uncomfortable track, he sent them over forest, hill, and stream, and attempted to imagine how that evening of ambiguity and weariness had been spent by his father's household. He pictured them assembled at the door, beneath the tree, the great old tree, which had been spared for its huge twisted trunk and venerable shade, when a thousand leafy brethren fell. There, at the going down of the summer sun, it was his father's custom to perform domestic worship that the neighbors might come and join with him like brothers of the family, and that the wayfaring man might pause to drink at that fountain, and keep his heart pure by freshening the memory of home. Robin distinguished the seat of every individual of the little audience; he saw the good man in the midst, holding the Scriptures in the golden light that fell from the western clouds; he beheld him close the book and all rise up to pray. He heard the old thanksgivings for daily mercies, the old supplications for their continuance to which he had so often listened in weariness, but which were now among his dear remembrances. He perceived the slight inequality of his father's voice when he came to speak of the absent one[49]; he noted how his mother turned her face to the broad and knotted trunk; how his elder brother scorned, because the beard was rough upon his upper lip[50]; to permit his features to be moved; how the younger sister drew down a low hanging branch before her eyes; and how the little one of all, whose sports had hitherto broken the decorum of the scene, understood the prayer for her playmate,[51] and burst into clamorous grief. Then he saw them go in at the door; and when Robin would have entered also, the latch tinkled into its

49) the absent one: 자리에 없는 식구, 즉 집을 떠난 로빈 자신을 가리킴.

50) the beard was rough upon his upper lip: 형이 어른으로 성장한 모습을 드러냄.

51) her[the baby sister's] playmate: 자신[어린 여동생]과 놀아주던 Robin.

place, and he was excluded from his home.

"Am I here, or there?" cried Robin, starting; for all at once, when his thoughts had become visible and audible in a dream, the long, wide, solitary street shone out before him.

He aroused himself, and endeavored to fix his attention steadily upon the large edifice which he had surveyed before. But still his mind kept vibrating between fancy and reality; by turns, the pillars of the balcony lengthened into the tall, bare stems of pines, dwindled down to human figures, settled again into their true shape and size, and then commenced a new succession of changes. For a single moment, when he deemed himself awake, he could have sworn that a visage — one which he seemed to remember, yet could not absolutely name as his kinsman's — was looking towards him from the Gothic window. A deeper sleep wrestled with and nearly overcame him, but fled at the sound of footsteps along the opposite pavement. Robin rubbed his eyes, discerned a man passing at the foot of the balcony, and addressed him a loud, peevish, and lamentable cry.

"Hallo, friend! must I wait here all night for my kinsman, Major Molineux?"

The sleeping echoes awoke, and answered the voice; and the passenger, barely able to discern a figure sitting in the oblique shade of the steeple, traversed the street[52] to obtain a nearer view. He was himself a gentleman in his prime, of open, intelligent, cheerful, and altogether pre-possessing countenance.

52) pre-possessing: pleasing.

Perceiving a country youth,[53)] apparently homeless and without friends, he accosted him in a tone of real kindness, which had become strange to Robin's ears.

"Well, my good lad, why are you sitting here?" inquired he. "Can I be of service to you in any way?"

"I am afraid not, sir," replied Robin, despondingly; "yet I shall take it kindly, if you'll answer me a single question. I've been searching, half the night, for one Major Molineux, now, sir, is there really such a person in these parts, or am I dreaming?"

"Major Molineux! The name is not altogether strange to me," said the gentleman, smiling. "Have you any objection to telling me the nature of your business with him?"

Then Robin briefly related that his father was a clergyman, settled on a small salary, at a long distance back in the country, and that he[54)] and Major Molineux were brothers' children. The Major, having inherited riches, and acquired civil and military rank, had visited his cousin, in great pomp, a year or two before; had manifested much interest in Robin and an elder brother,[55)] and, being childless himself, had thrown out hints respecting the future establishment of one of them in life. The elder brother was destined to succeed to the farm which his father cultivated in the interval of sacred duties; it was therefore determined that Robin should profit by his kinsman's generous intentions, especially as

---

53) Perceiving a country youth: 시골 청년임을 알아보고.

54) he: 로빈의 아버지. 로빈의 아버지와 멀리뉴 소령은 사촌간이다.

55) an elder brother: 로빈의 형.

he seemed to be rather the favorite, and was thought to possess other necessary endowments.

"For I have the name of being a shrewd youth,"[56] observed Robin, in this part of his story.

"I doubt not you deserve it," replied his new friend, good-naturedly; "but pray proceed."[57]

"Well, sir, being nearly eighteen years old, and well grown, as you see," continued Robin, drawing himself up to his full height, "I thought it high time to begin in the world. So my mother and sister put me in handsome trim, and my father gave me half the remnant of his last year's salary, and five days ago I started for this place, to pay the Major a visit. But, would you believe it, sir! I crossed the ferry a little after dark, and have yet found nobody that would show me the way to his dwelling; only, an hour or two since, I was told to wait here, and Major Molineux would pass by."

"Can you describe the man who told you this?" inquired the gentleman.

"Oh, he was a very ill-favored fellow, sir," replied Robin, "with two great bumps on his forehead, a hook nose, fiery eyes; and, what struck me as the strangest, his face was of two different colors. Do you happen to know such a man, sir?"

56) For I have . . . a shrewd youth: 똑똑한 젊은이로 알려져 있기 때문이죠.
57) pray proceed: 그래서. 더 말해보렴.

"Not intimately," answered the stranger, "but I chanced to meet him a little time previous to your stopping me. I believe you may trust his word, and that the Major will very shortly pass through this street. In the mean time, as I have a singular curiosity to witness your meeting, I will sit down here upon the steps and bear you company."

He seated himself accordingly, and soon engaged his companion in animated discourse. It was but of brief continuance, however, for a noise of shouting, which had long been remotely audible, drew so much nearer that Robin inquired its cause.

"What may be the meaning of this uproar?" asked he. "Truly, if your town be always as noisy, I shall find little sleep while I am an inhabitant."

"Why, indeed, friend Robin, there do appear to be three or four riotous fellows abroad to-night," replied the gentleman. "You must not expect all the stillness of your native woods here in our streets. But the watch will shortly be at the heels of these lads and"—

"Ay, and set them in the stocks by peep of day," interrupted Robin recollecting his own encounter with the drowsy lantern-bearer. "But, dear sir, if I may trust my ears, an army of watchmen would never make head against[58)] such a multitude of rioters. There were at least a thousand voices went up to make that one shout."

58) make head against: to resist with success.

"May not a man have several voices, Robin, as well as two complexions? said his friend.

"Perhaps a man may; but Heaven forbid that a woman should!" responded the shrewd youth, thinking of the seductive tones of the Major's housekeeper.

The sounds of a trumpet in some neighboring street now became so evident and continual, that Robin's curiosity was strongly excited. In addition to the shouts, he heard frequent bursts from many instruments of discord, and a wild and confused laughter filled up the intervals. Robin rose from the steps, and looked wistfully towards a point whither[59)] people seemed to be hastening.

"Surely some prodigious merry-making is going on," exclaimed he "I have laughed very little since I left home, sir, and should be sorry to lose an opportunity. Shall we step round the corner by that darkish house and take our share of the fun?"

"Sit down again, sit down, good Robin," replied the gentleman, laying his hand on the skirt[60)] of the gray coat. "You forget that we must wait here for your kinsman; and there is reason to believe that he will pass by, in the course of a very few moments."

The near approach of the uproar had now disturbed the neighborhood; windows flew open on all sides; and many heads, in the attire of the pillow, and confused by sleep suddenly

59) whither: to what place.

60) the skirt: 여기서는 옷자락을 가리킴.

broken, were protruded to the gaze of whoever had leisure to observe them. Eager voices hailed each other from house to house, all demanding the explanation, which not a soul[61] could give. Half-dressed men hurried towards the unknown commotion stumbling as they went over the stone steps that thrust themselves into the narrow foot-walk. The shouts, the laughter, and the tuneless bray[62] the antipodes of music, came onwards with increasing din, till scattered individuals, and then denser bodies,[63] began to appear round a corner at the distance of a hundred yards

"Will you recognize your kinsman, if he passes in this crowd?" inquired the gentleman

"Indeed, I can't warrant it, sir; but I'll take my stand here, and keep a bright lookout," answered Robin, descending to the outer edge of the pavement.

A mighty stream of people now emptied into the street, and came rolling slowly towards the church. A single horseman wheeled the corner in the midst of them, and close behind him came a band of fearful wind-instruments, sending forth a fresher discord now that no intervening buildings kept it from the ear. Then a redder light disturbed the moonbeams, and a dense multitude of torches shone along the street, concealing, by their glare, whatever object they illuminated. The single horseman, clad in a military dress, and bearing a drawn sword, rode onward as the leader, and, by his fierce and variegated countenance,

61) not a soul: nobody.

62) bray: to sound loudly and harshly.

63) scattered individuals, and then denser bodies: 처음에는 흐트러진 대열로, 나중에는 대오를 짜고 행진하는 모습.

appeared like war personified; the red of one cheek was an emblem of fire and sword; the blackness of the other betokened the mourning that attends them. In his train[64] were wild figures in the Indian dress, and many fantastic shapes without a model, giving the whole march a visionary air, as if a dream had broken forth from some feverish brain, and were sweeping visibly through the midnight streets. A mass of people, inactive, except as applauding spectators, hemmed the procession in; and several women ran along the sidewalk, piercing the confusion of heavier sounds with their shrill voices of mirth or terror.

"The double-faced fellow has his eye upon me," muttered Robin, with an indefinite but an uncomfortable idea that he was himself to bear a part in the pageantry.

The leader turned himself in the saddle, and fixed his glance full upon the country youth, as the steed went slowly by. When Robin had freed his eyes from those fiery ones, the musicians were passing before him, and the torches were close at hand; but the unsteady brightness of the latter formed a veil which he could not penetrate. The rattling of wheels over the stones sometimes found its way to his ear, and confused traces of a human form appeared at intervals, and then melted into the vivid light. A moment more, and the leader thundered a command to halt: the trumpets vomited a horrid breath, and then held their peace; the shouts and laughter of the people died away, and there remained only a universal hum, allied to silence. Right before Robin's eyes was an uncovered cart. There the torches blazed the brightest, there the moon shone out like day, and there, in tar-

64) in his train: 그의 뒤를 이어.

and-feathery dignity,[65] sat his kinsman, Major Molineux!

He was an elderly man, of large and majestic person, and strong, square features, betokening a steady soul; but steady as it was, his enemies had found means to shake it. His face was pale as death, and far more ghastly; the broad forehead was contracted in his agony, so that his eyebrows formed one grizzled line; his eyes were red and wild, and the foam hung white upon his quivering lip. His whole frame was agitated by a quick and continual tremor, which his pride strove to quell, even in those circumstances of overwhelming humiliation. But perhaps the bitterest pang of all was when his eyes met those of Robin; for he evidently knew him on the instant, as the youth stood witnessing the foul disgrace of a head grown gray in honor. They stared at each other in silence, and Robin's knees shook, and his hair bristled, with a mixture of pity and terror. Soon, however, a bewildering excitement began to seize upon his mind; the preceding adventures of the night, the unexpected appearance of the crowd, the torches, the confused din and the hush that followed, the spectre of his kinsman reviled by that great multitude,—all this, and, more than all, a perception of tremendous ridicule in the whole scene, affected him with a sort of mental inebriety. At that moment a voice of sluggish merriment saluted Robin's ears; he turned instinctively, and just behind the corner of the church stood the lantern-bearer, rubbing his eyes, and drowsily enjoying the lad's amazement. Then he heard a peal of laughter like the ringing of silvery bells; a woman twitched his arm, a saucy eye met his, and he saw the lady of the scarlet petticoat. A sharp, dry cachinnation

---

65) in tar-and-feathery dignity: 수치와 형벌의 상징인 검은 기름과 깃털을 뒤집어 쓰고 서도 위엄을 부리며.

appealed to his memory, and, standing on tiptoe in the crowd, with his white apron over his head, he beheld the courteous little innkeeper. And lastly, there sailed over the heads of the multitude a great, broad laugh, broken in the midst by two sepulchral hems; thus, "Haw, haw, haw, — hem, hem, — haw, haw, haw, haw!"

The sound proceeded from the balcony of the opposite edifice, and thither Robin turned his eyes. In front of the Gothic window stood the old citizen, wrapped in a wide gown, his gray periwig exchanged for a nightcap, which was thrust back from his forehead, and his silk stockings hanging about his legs. He supported himself on his polished cane in a fit of convulsive merriment, which manifested itself on his solemn old features like a funny inscription on a tombstone. Then Robin seemed to hear the voices of the barbers, of the guests of the inn, and of all who had made sport of him that night. The contagion was spreading among the multitude, when all at once, it seized upon Robin, and he sent forth a shout of laughter that echoed through the street, — every man shook his sides, every man emptied his lungs, but Robin's shout was the loudest there. The cloud-spirits peeped from their silvery islands, as the congregated mirth went roaring up the sky! The Man in the Moon heard the far bellow. "Oho," quoth he, "the old earth is frolicsome to-night!"

When there was a momentary calm in that tempestuous sea of sound, the leader gave the sign, the procession resumed its march. On they went, like fiends that throng in mockery around some dead potentate,[66)] mighty no more, but majestic still in his

---

66) potentate: a powerful person, a ruler, or monarch.

agony. On they went, in counterfeited pomp, in senseless uproar, in frenzied merriment, trampling all on an old man's heart. On swept the tumult, and left a silent street behind.

....

"Well, Robin, are you dreaming?" inquired the gentleman, laying his hand on the youth's shoulder.

Robin started, and withdrew his arm from the stone post to which he had instinctively clung, as the living stream rolled by him. His cheek was somewhat pale, and his eye not quite as lively as in the earlier part of the evening.

"Will you be kind enough to show me the way to the ferry?" said he, after a moment's pause.

"You have, then, adopted a new subject of inquiry?" observed his companion, with a smile.

"Why, yes, sir," replied Robin, rather dryly. "Thanks to you, and to my other friends, I have at last met my kinsman, and he will scarce desire to see my face again. I begin to grow weary of a town life, sir. Will you show me the way to the ferry?"

"No, my good friend Robin, — not to-night, at least," said the gentleman. "Some few days hence, if you wish it, I will speed you on your journey. Or, if you prefer to remain with us, perhaps, as you are a shrewd youth, you may rise in the world without the help of your kinsman, Major Molineux."

Roger Malvin's Burial

ONE of the few incidents of Indian warfare naturally susceptible of the moonlight of romance was that expedition undertaken for the defence of the frontiers in the year 1725, which resulted in the well-remembered "Lovell's Fight."[1)] Imagination, by casting certain circumstances judicially into the shade, may see much to admire in the heroism of a little band who gave battle to twice their number[2)] in the heart of the enemy's country.[3)] The open bravery displayed by both parties was in accordance with civilized ideas of valor; and chivalry itself might not blush to record the deeds of one or two individuals. The battle, though so fatal to those who fought, was not unfortunate in its consequences to the country; for it broke the strength of a tribe and conduced to the peace which subsisted during several ensuing years. History and tradition are unusually minute[4)] in their memorials of their affair; and the captain of a scouting party of frontier men has acquired as actual a military renown as many a victorious leader of thousands. Some of the incidents contained in the following pages will be recognized, notwithstanding the substitution of fictitious names, by such as

1) Lovewell's Fight: John Lovewell(1691-1725)이 인디언 격퇴에 성공함으로써, Maine, New Hampshire, Massachusetts 등지에서의 백인과 인디언 적대관계에 종지부를 찍게 된 중요한 전투. 호손, 포우, 소로의 작품에 "Lovell's Fight"로 등장함.

2) twice their number: 그들의 군세보다 두 배나 되는.

3) the enemy's country: 인디언들이 점령하고 있는 敵地.

4) minute: 세심한, 상세한.

have heard, from old men's lips, the fate of the few combatants who were in a condition to retreat after "Lovell's Fight."

....

The early sunbeams hovered cheerfully upon the tree-tops, beneath which two weary and wounded men had stretched their limbs the night before. Their bed of withered oak leaves was strewn upon the small level space, at the foot of a rock, situated near the summit of one of the gentle swells[5)] by which the face of the country is there diversified. The mass of granite, rearing its smooth, flat surface fifteen or twenty feet above their heads, was not unlike a gigantic gravestone, upon which the veins seemed to form an inscription in forgotten characters. On a tract of several acres around this rock, oaks and other hard-wood trees had supplied the place of the pines, which were the usual growth of the land; and a young and vigorous sapling stood close beside the travellers.

The severe wound of the elder man had probably deprived him of sleep; for, so soon as the first ray of sunshine rested on the top of the highest tree, he reared himself painfully from his recumbent[6)] posture and sat erect. The deep lines of his countenance and the scattered gray of his hair marked him as past the middle age; but his muscular frame would, but for the effect of his wound, have been as capable of sustaining fatigue as in the early vigor of life. Languor and exhaustion now sat upon his haggard features; and the despairing glance which he

5) swell: a rounded hill.

6) recumbent: reclining, resting.

sent forward through the depths of the forest proved his own conviction that his pilgrimage was at an end. He next turned his eyes to the companion who reclined by his side. The youth — for he had scarcely attained the years of manhood — lay, with his head upon his arm, in the embrace of an unquiet sleep, which a thrill of pain from his wounds seemed each moment on the point of breaking. His right hand grasped a musket; and, to judge from the violent action of his features, his slumbers were bringing back a vision of the conflict of which he was one of the few survivors. A shout — deep and loud in his dreaming fancy — found its way in an imperfect murmur to his lips; and, starting even at the slight sound of his own voice, he suddenly awoke. The first act of reviving recollection was to make anxious inquiries respecting[7] the condition of his wounded fellow-traveller. The latter shook his head.

"Reuben,[8] my boy," said he, "this rock beneath which we sit will serve for an old hunter's gravestone. There is many and many a long mile of howling wilderness before us yet; nor would it avail me anything if the smoke of my own chimney were but on the other side of that swell of land. The Indian bullet was deadlier than I thought."

"You are weary with our three days' travel," replied the youth, "and a little longer rest will recruit you. Sit you here while I search the woods for the herbs and roots that must be our sustenance; and, having eaten, you shall lean on me, and we will turn our faces homeward. I doubt not that, with my help, you

7) respecting: with respect to; as regards.

8) Reuben: 루번

can attain to some one of the frontier garrisons."

"There is not two days' life in me, Reuben," said the other, calmly, "and I will no longer burden you with my useless body, when you can scarcely support your own. Your wounds are deep and your strength is failing fast; yet, if you hasten onward alone, you may be preserved. For me there is no hope, and I will await death here."

"If it must be so, I will remain and watch by you," said Reuben, resolutely

"No, my son, no," rejoined his companion. "Let the wish of a dying man have weight with you; give me one grasp of your hand, and get[9] you hence. Think you[10] that my last moments will be eased by the thought that I leave you to die a more lingering death? I have loved you like a father, Reuben; and at a time like this I should have something of a father's authority. I charge[11] you to be gone that I may die in peace."

"And because you have been a father to me, should I therefore leave you to perish and to lie unburied in the wilderness?" exclaimed the youth. "No; if your end be in truth approaching, I will watch by you and receive your parting words. I will dig a grave here by the rock, in which, if my weakness overcome me, we will rest together; or, if Heaven gives me strength, I will seek my way home."

---

9) get: start or come to be doing something.

10) Think you: Do you think. . .

11) charge: give orders.

"In the cities and wherever men dwell," replied the other, "they bury their dead in the earth; they hide them from the sight of the living; but here, where no step may pass perhaps for a hundred years, wherefore should I not rest beneath the open sky, covered only by the oak leaves when the autumn winds shall strew them? And for a monument, here is this gray rock, on which my dying hand shall carve the name of Roger Malvin, and the traveller in days to come[12] will know that here sleeps a hunter and a warrior. Tarry not, then, for a folly like this, but hasten away, if not for your own sake, for hers[13] who will else[14] be desolate."

Malvin spoke the last few words in a faltering voice, and their effect upon his companion was strongly visible. They[15] reminded him that there were other and less questionable duties than that of sharing the fate of a man whom his death could not benefit. Nor can it be affirmed that no selfish feeling strove to enter Reuben's heart, though the consciousness made him more earnestly resist his companion's entreaties

"How terrible to wait the slow approach of death in this solitude!" exclaimed he. "A brave man does not shrink in the battle; and, when friends stand round the bed, even women may die composedly; but here"—

"I shall not shrink even here, Reuben Bourne," interrupted Malvin.

---

12) in days to come: in future days; some day.
13) for hers: for her own sake. 즉 맬빈의 딸.
14) else: 그렇지 않으면.
15) They: 맬빈의 마지막 몇 마디 말.

I am a man of no weak heart, and, if I were, there is a surer support than that of earthly friends.[16] You are young, and life is dear to you. Your last moments will need comfort far more than mine; and when you have laid me in the earth, and are alone, and night is settling on the forest, you will feel all the bitterness of the death that may now be escaped. But I will urge no selfish motive to your generous nature. Leave me for my sake, that, having said a prayer for your safety, I may have space[17] to settle my account undisturbed by worldly sorrows."

"And your daughter, — how shall I dare to meet her eye?" exclaimed Reuben. "She will ask the fate of her father, whose life I vowed to defend with my own. Must I tell her that he travelled three days' march with me from the field of battle and that then I left him to perish in the wilderness? Were it not better to lie down and die by your side than to return safe and say this to Dorcas?"

"Tell my daughter," said Roger Malvin, "that, though yourself sore wounded,[18] and weak, and weary, you led my tottering footsteps many a mile, and left me only at my earnest entreaty, because I would not have your blood upon my soul.[19] Tell her that through pain and danger you were faithful, and that, if your lifeblood[20] could have saved me, it would have flowed to its last drop; and tell her that you will be something dearer than a father,

16) a surer support than that of earthly friends: 즉 인간으로부터가 아닌 하늘이 내리는 힘.

17) space: (일생을 정리할) 시간.

18) sore(ly) wounded: wounded greatly.

19) upon my soul: 맹세코, 확실히.

20) lifeblood: (생명을 유지하는데 필요한) 혈액, 생피.

and that my blessing is with you both, and that my dying eyes can see a long and pleasant path in which you will journey together."

As Malvin spoke he almost raised himself from the ground, and the energy of his concluding words seemed to fill the wild and lonely forest with a vision of happiness; but, when he sank exhausted upon his bed of oak leaves, the light which had kindled in Reuben's eye was quenched. He felt as if it were both sin and folly to think of happiness at such a moment. His companion watched his changing countenance, and sought with generous art to wile him to his own good.

"Perhaps I deceive myself in regard to the time I have to live," he resumed. "It may be that, with speedy assistance, I might recover of my wound. The foremost fugitives[21)] must, ere[22)] this, have carried tidings of our fatal battle to the frontiers, and parties[23)] will be out to succor[24)] those in like[25)] condition with ourselves. Should you meet one of these and guide them hither, who can tell[26)] but that I may sit by my own fireside again?"

A mournful smile strayed across the features of the dying man as he insinuated that unfounded hope, — which, however, was not without its effect on Reuben. No merely selfish motive, nor even the desolate condition of Dorcas, could have induced him to desert his companion at such a moment — but his wishes

21) The foremost fugitives: 최초로 달아난 병사들
22) ere: before.
23) parties: a selected group of soldiers.
24) succor: to give assistance to in time of distress.
25) like: similar.
26) who can tell: who knows?

seized on the thought that Malvin's life might be preserved, and his sanguine nature heightened almost to certainty the remote possibility of procuring human aid.

"Surely there is reason, weighty reason, to hope that friends are not far distant," he said, half aloud. "There fled one coward, unwounded, in the beginning of the fight, and most probably he made good speed. Every true man on the frontier would shoulder his musket at the news; and, though no party may range so far into the woods as this, I shall perhaps encounter them in one day's march. Counsel me faithfully," he added, turning to Malvin, in distrust of his own motives. "Were your situation mine,[27)] would you desert me while life remained?"

"It is now twenty years," replied Roger Malvin, — sighing, however, as he secretly acknowledged the wide dissimilarity between the two cases, — "it is now twenty years since I escaped with one dear friend from Indian captivity near Montreal. We journeyed many days through the woods, till at length overcome with hunger and weariness, my friend lay down and besought me to leave him; for he knew that, if I remained, we both must perish; and, with but little hope of obtaining succor, I heaped a pillow of dry leaves beneath his head and hastened on."

"And did you return in time to save him?" asked Reuben, hanging on Malvin's words as if they were to be prophetic of his own success.[28)]

---

27) Were your situation mine (=If your situation were mine …) 내가 어르신의 입장에 있다 해도.

28) 루번의 마음은 이미 어르신을 두고 떠나는 쪽으로 기울어있음을 보인다.

"I did," answered the other. "I came upon the camp of a hunting party before sunset of the same day. I guided them to the spot where my comrade was expecting death; and he is now a hale and hearty man upon his own farm, far within the frontiers, while I lie wounded here in the depths of the wilderness."

This example, powerful in affecting Reuben's decision, was aided, unconsciously to himself, by the hidden strength of many another motive. Roger Malvin perceived that the victory was nearly won.[29)]

"Now, go, my son[30)], and Heaven prosper you!" he said. "Turn not back with your friends when you meet them, lest your wounds and weariness overcome you; but send hitherward two or three, that may be spared, to search for me; and believe me, Reuben, my heart will be lighter with every step you take towards home." Yet there was, perhaps, a change both in his countenance and voice as he spoke thus; for, after all, it was a ghastly fate to be left expiring[31)] in the wilderness.

Reuben Bourne, but half convinced that he was acting rightly, at length raised himself from the ground and prepared himself for his departure. And first, though contrary to Malvin's wishes, he collected a stock of roots and herbs, which had been their only food during the last two days. This useless supply he placed within reach of the dying man, for whom, also, he swept together a bed of dry oak leaves. Then climbing to the summit of the rock, which on one side was rough and broken,

29) 맬빈이 드디어 청년을 떠나도록 설득했음을 감지하고 있다.
30) 청년을 친근하게 부르는 호칭.
31) expiring: dying.

he bent the oak sapling downward, and bound his handkerchief to the topmost branch. This precaution was not unnecessary to direct any who might come in search of Malvin; for every part of the rock, except its broad, smooth front, was concealed at a little distance by the dense undergrowth of the forest. The handkerchief had been the bandage of a wound upon Reuben's arm; and, as he bound it to the tree, he vowed by the blood that stained it that he would return, either to save his companion's life or to lay his body in the grave.[32)] He then descended, and stood, with downcast eyes, to receive Roger Malvin's parting words.

The experience of the latter[33)] suggested much and minute advice respecting the youth's journey through the trackless forest. Upon this subject he spoke with calm earnestness, as if he were sending Reuben to the battle or the chase while he himself remained secure at home, and not as if the human countenance[34)] that was about to leave him[35)] were the last[36)] he would ever behold. But his firmness was shaken before he concluded.

"Carry my blessing to Dorcas, and say that my last prayer shall be for her and you. Bid her to have no hard thoughts because you left me here," — Reuben's heart smote him, — "for that[37)] your life would not have weighed with you[38)] if[39)] its sacrifice could

32) to lay his body in the grave. 장례를 치러주러.

33) the latter: 맬빈.

34) the human countenance: the human face, 즉 루번.

35) him: 맬빈.

36) the last countenance로 읽을 것.

37) for that: 그로 인해서.

38) your life would not have weighed with you: 자네의 생명을 경시한 것이 되었을 것이다.

39) if: even if로 이해할 것.

have done me good. She will marry you after she has mourned a little while[40] for her father; and Heaven grant you long and happy days, and may your children's children stand round your death bed! And, Reuben," added he, as the weakness of mortality made its way at last, "return, when your wounds are healed and your weariness refreshed,—return to this wild rock, and lay my bones in the grave, and say a prayer over them."

An almost superstitious regard, arising perhaps from the customs of the Indians, whose war was with the dead as well as the living, was paid by the frontier inhabitants to the rites of sepulture; and there are many instances of the sacrifice of life in the attempt to bury those who had fallen by the "sword of the wilderness.[41]" Reuben, therefore, felt the full importance of the promise which he most solemnly made to return and perform Roger Malvin's obsequies.[42] It was remarkable that the latter, speaking his whole heart in his parting words, no longer endeavored to persuade the youth that even the speediest succor might avail to the preservation of his life. Reuben was internally convinced that he should see Malvin's living face no more. His generous nature would fain have delayed him, at whatever risk, till the dying scene were past; but the desire of existence and the hope of happiness had strengthened in his heart, and he was unable to resist them.

"It is enough," said Roger Malvin, having listened to Reuben's

40) a little while: for some time.

41) "the sword of the wilderness": 성경의 哀歌 (Lamentations) 5장9절: "We get our bread at the risk of our lives / Because of the sword in the wilderness."에서 나옴. "광야에 칼이 있으므로," 즉 여기서는 인디언의 칼에 쓰러진 군인들.

42) obsequies: pl. a funeral rite or ceremony.

promise. "Go, and God speed you![43)]"

The youth pressed his hand in silence, turned, and was departing. His slow and faltering steps, however, had borne him but a little way before Malvin's voice recalled him.

"Reuben, Reuben," said he, faintly; and Reuben returned and knelt down by the dying man.

"Raise me, and let me lean against the rock," was his last request. "My face will be turned towards home, and I shall see you a moment longer as you pass among the trees."

Reuben, having made the desired alteration in his companion's posture, again began his solitary pilgrimage. He walked more hastily at first than was consistent with his strength; for[44)] a sort of guilty feeling, which sometimes torments men in their most justifiable acts, caused him to seek concealment from Malvin's eyes; but after he had trodden far upon the rustling forest leaves he crept back, impelled by a wild and painful curiosity, and, sheltered by the earthy roots of an uptorn tree, gazed earnestly at the desolate man. The morning sun was unclouded, and the trees and shrubs imbibed the sweet air of the month of May; yet there seemed a gloom on Nature's face, as if she sympathized with mortal pain and sorrow Roger Malvin's hands were uplifted in a fervent prayer, some of the words of which stole through the stillness of the woods and entered Reuben's heart, torturing it with an unutterable pang. They were the broken accents of a petition for

---

43) God speed you!: 성공을 빕니다.

44) for: 왜냐하면.

his own happiness and that of Dorcas; and, as the youth listened, conscience, or something in its similitude, pleaded strongly with him to return and lie down again by the rock. He felt how hard was the doom of the kind and generous being[45] whom he had deserted in his extremity. Death would come like the slow approach of a corpse, stealing gradually towards him through the forest, and showing its ghastly and motionless features from behind a nearer and yet a nearer tree. But such must have been Reuben's own fate had he tarried another sunset; and who shall impute blame to him if he shrink from so useless a sacrifice? As he gave a parting look, a breeze waved the little banner upon the sapling oak and reminded Reuben of his vow.

....

Many circumstances combined to retard the wounded traveller in his way to the frontiers. On the second day the clouds, gathering densely over the sky, precluded the possibility of regulating his course by the position of the sun; and he knew not but that every effort of his almost exhausted strength was removing him farther from the home he sought. His scanty sustenance was supplied by the berries and other spontaneous products of the forest. Herds of deer, it is true, sometimes bounded past him, and partridges frequently whirred up before his footsteps; but his ammunition had been expended in the fight, and he had no means of slaying them. His wounds, irritated by the constant exertion in which lay the only hope of life, wore away his strength and at intervals confused his reason. But, even in the wanderings of intellect, Reuben's young heart clung

45) the kind and generous being: 맬빈.

strongly to existence; and it was only through absolute incapacity of motion that he at last sank down beneath a tree, compelled there to await death.

In this situation he was discovered by a party who, upon the first intelligence of the fight, had been despatched to the relief of the survivors. They conveyed him to the nearest settlement, which chanced to be that of his own residence.

Dorcas, in the simplicity of the olden time, watched by the bedside of her wounded lover, and administered all those comforts that are in the sole gift of woman's heart and hand. During several days Reuben's recollection strayed drowsily among the perils and hardships through which he had passed, and he was incapable of returning definite answers to the inquiries with which many were eager to harass him. No authentic particulars of the battle had yet been circulated; nor could mothers, wives, and children tell whether their loved ones were detained by captivity or by the stronger chain of death. Dorcas nourished her apprehensions in silence till one afternoon when Reuben awoke from an unquiet sleep, and seemed to recognize her more perfectly than at any previous time. She saw that his intellect had become composed, and she could no longer restrain her filial anxiety.

"My father, Reuben?" she began; but the change in her lover's countenance made her pause.

The youth shrank as if with a bitter pain, and the blood gushed vividly into his wan and hollow cheeks. His first impulse was to cover his face; but, apparently with a desperate effort, he half raised himself and spoke vehemently, defending himself against an imaginary accusation.

"Your father was sore wounded in the battle, Dorcas; and he bade me not burden myself with him, but only to lead him to the lakeside, that he might quench his thirst and die. But I would not desert the old man in his extremity, and, though bleeding myself, I supported him; I gave him half my strength, and led him away with me. For three days we journeyed on together, and your father was sustained beyond my hopes, but, awaking at sunrise on the fourth day, I found him faint and exhausted; he was unable to proceed; his life had ebbed away fast; and"—

"He died!" exclaimed Dorcas, faintly.

Reuben felt it impossible to acknowledge that his selfish love of life had hurried him away before her father's fate was decided. He spoke not; he only bowed his head; and, between shame and exhaustion, sank back and hid his face in the pillow. Dorcas wept when her fears were thus confirmed; but the shock, as it had been long anticipated. was on that account the less violent.

"You dug a grave for my poor father in the wilderness, Reuben?" was the question by which her filial piety manifested itself.

"My hands were weak; but I did what I could," replied the youth in a smothered tone. "There stands a noble tombstone above his head; and I would to Heaven I slept as soundly as he!"

Dorcas, perceiving the wildness of his latter words, inquired no further at the time; but her heart found ease in the thought that Roger Malvin had not lacked such funeral rites as it was possible to bestow. The tale of Reuben's courage and fidelity lost nothing when she communicated it to her friends; and the poor youth, tottering from his sick chamber to breathe the sunny air, experienced from every tongue[46)] the miserable and humiliating torture of unmerited praise. All acknowledged that he might worthily demand the hand of the fair maiden to whose father he had been "faithful unto death;" and, as my tale is not of love, it shall suffice to say that in the space of a few months Reuben became the husband of Dorcas Malvin. During the marriage ceremony the bride was covered with blushes, but the bridegroom's face was pale.

There was now in the breast of Reuben Bourne an incommunicable thought—something which he was to conceal most heedfully from her whom he most loved and trusted. He regretted, deeply and bitterly, the moral cowardice that had restrained his words when he was about to disclose the truth to Dorcas; but pride, the fear of losing her affection, the dread of universal scorn, forbade him to rectify this falsehood. He felt that for leaving Roger Malvin he deserved no censure. His presence, the gratuitous sacrifice of his own life, would have added only another and a needless agony to the last moments of the dying man; but concealment had imparted to a justifiable act much of the secret effect of guilt;[47)] and Reuben, while reason told him that he had done right, experienced in no small

46) every tongue: 모든 사람들.

47) much of the secret effect of guilt: impart의 목적어.

degree the mental horrors which punish the perpetrator of undiscovered crime. By a certain association of ideas, he at times almost imagined himself a murderer. For years, also, a thought would occasionally recur, which, though he perceived all its folly and extravagance, he had not power to banish from his mind. It was a haunting and torturing fancy that his father-in-law was yet sitting at the foot of the rock, on the withered forest leaves, alive, and awaiting his pledged assistance. These mental deceptions, however, came and went, nor did he ever mistake them for realities: but in the calmest and clearest moods of his mind he was conscious that he had a deep vow unredeemed, and that an unburied corpse was calling to him out of the wilderness. Yet such was the consequence of his prevarication that he could not obey the call. It was now too late to require the assistance of Roger Malvin's friends in performing his long-deferred sepulture; and superstitious fears, of which none were more susceptible than the people of the outward settlements,[48)] forbade Reuben to go alone. Neither did he know where in the pathless and illimitable forest to seek that smooth and lettered rock at the base of which the body lay: his remembrance of every portion of his travel thence was indistinct, and the latter part had left no impression upon his mind. There was, however, a continual impulse, a voice audible only to himself, commanding him to go forth and redeem his vow; and he had a strange impression that, were he to make the trial, he would be led straight to Malvin's bones. But year after year that summons, unheard but felt, was disobeyed. His one secret thought became like a chain binding down his spirit and like a serpent gnawing into his heart; and he

48) of which none were more susceptible than the people of the outward settlements: 외곽 정착지 주민들은 미신적 두려움에 매우 취약했다.

was transformed into a sad and downcast yet irritable man.

In the course of a few years after their marriage changes began to be visible in the external prosperity of Reuben and Dorcas. The only riches of the former had been his stout heart and strong arm; but the latter, her father's sole heiress, had made her husband master of a farm, under older cultivation, larger, and better stocked than most of the frontier establishments. Reuben Bourne, however, was a neglectful husbandman; and, while the lands of the other settlers became annually more fruitful, his[49] deteriorated in the same proportion. The discouragements to agriculture were greatly lessened by the cessation of Indian war, during which men held the plough in one hand and the musket in the other, and were fortunate if the products of their dangerous labor were not destroyed, either in the field or in the barn, by the savage enemy. But Reuben did not profit by the altered condition of the country; nor can it be denied that his intervals of industrious attention to his affairs were but scantily rewarded with success. The irritability by which he had recently become distinguished was another cause of his declining prosperity, as it occasioned frequent quarrels in his unavoidable intercourse with the neighboring settlers. The results of these were innumerable lawsuits; for the people of New England, in the earliest stages and wildest circumstances of the country, adopted, whenever attainable, the legal mode of deciding their differences. To be brief, the world did not go well with Reuben Bourne; and, though not till many years after his marriage, he was finally a ruined man, with but one remaining expedient against the evil fate that had pursued him. He was to throw sunlight into some

49) his: his land.

deep recess of the forest, and seek subsistence from the virgin bosom of the wilderness.

The only child of Reuben and Dorcas was a son, now arrived at the age of fifteen years, beautiful in youth, and giving promise of a glorious manhood. He was peculiarly qualified for, and already began to excel in, the wild accomplishments of frontier life. His foot was fleet, his aim true, his apprehension quick, his heart glad and high; and all who anticipated the return of Indian war spoke of Cyrus Bourne as a future leader in the land. The boy was loved by his father with a deep and silent strength, as if whatever was good and happy in his own nature had been transferred to his child, carrying his affections with it. Even Dorcas, though loving and beloved, was far less dear to him; for Reuben's secret thoughts and insulated emotions had gradually made him a selfish man, and he could no longer love deeply except where he saw or imagined some reflection or likeness of his own mind. In Cyrus he recognized what he had himself been in other days; and at intervals he seemed to partake of the boy's spirit, and to be revived with a fresh and happy life. Reuben was accompanied by his son in the expedition, for the purpose of selecting a tract of land and felling and burning the timber, which necessarily preceded the removal of the household gods. Two months of autumn were thus occupied, after which Reuben Bourne and his young hunter returned to spend their last winter in the settlements.

....

It was early in the month of May that the little family snapped asunder whatever tendrils of affections had clung to inanimate objects, and bade farewell to the few who, in the blight of fortune, called themselves their friends. The sadness of the parting moment had, to each of the pilgrims,[50)] its peculiar alleviations. Reuben, a moody man, and misanthropic because unhappy, strode onward with his usual stern brow and downcast eye, feeling few regrets and disdaining to acknowledge any.[51)] Dorcas, while she wept abundantly over the broken ties by which her simple and affectionate nature had bound itself to everything, felt that the inhabitants of her inmost heart moved on with her, and that all else would be supplied wherever she might go. And the boy dashed one tear-drop from his eye, and thought of the adventurous pleasures of the untrodden forest.

Oh, who, in the enthusiasm of a daydream, has not wished that he were a wanderer in a world of summer wilderness, with one fair and gentle being hanging lightly on his arm? In youth his free and exulting step would know no barrier but the rolling ocean or the snow-topped mountains; calmer manhood would choose a home where Nature had strewn a double wealth in the vale of some transparent stream; and when hoary age, after long, long years of that pure life, stole on and found him there, it would find him the father of a race, the patriarch of a people, the founder of a mighty nation yet to be. When death, like the sweet sleep which we welcome after a day of happiness, came over him, his far descendants would mourn over the venerated dust.[52)] Enveloped by tradition in mysterious attributes, the men of future generations would call him godlike; and remote posterity

---

50) to each of the pilgrims: 여정에 오르는 루번 가족 한 사람 한 사람.

51) any: any regrets. 루번은 [떠나는 것에 대한] 아무런 후회나 유감이 없다.

52) the venerated dust: 존경스러운 시신.

would see him standing, dimly glorious, far up the valley of a hundred centuries.

The tangled and gloomy forest through which the personages of my tale[53] were wandering differed widely from the dreamer's land of fantasy; yet there was something in their way of life that Nature asserted as her own, and the gnawing cares which went with them from the world were all that now obstructed their happiness. One stout and shaggy steed,[54] the bearer of all their wealth, did not shrink from the added weight of Dorcas; although her hardy breeding sustained her, during the latter part of each day's journey, by her husband's side. Reuben and his son, their muskets on their shoulders and their axes slung behind them, kept an unwearied pace, each watching with a hunter's eye for the game that supplied their food. When hunger bade, they halted and prepared their meal on the bank of some unpolluted forest brook, which, as they knelt down with thirsty lips to drink, murmured a sweet unwillingness, like a maiden at love's first kiss. They slept beneath a hut of branches, and awoke at peep of light refreshed for the toils of another day. Dorcas and the boy went on joyously, and even Reuben's spirit shone at intervals with an outward gladness; but inwardly there was a cold cold sorrow, which he compared to the snowdrifts lying deep in the glens and hollows of the rivulets while the leaves were brightly green above.

Cyrus Bourne was sufficiently skilled in the travel of the woods to observe that his father did not adhere to the course

53) the personages of my tale: 내 이야기의 주인공들.

54) steed: a spirited horse. (Dorcas가 말에 타고 있음을 표현.)

they had pursued in their expedition of the preceding autumn. They were now keeping farther to the north, striking out more directly from the settlements, and into a region of which savage beasts and savage men were as yet the sole possessors. The boy sometimes hinted his opinions upon the subject, and Reuben listened attentively, and once or twice altered the direction of their march in accordance with his son's counsel; but, having so done, he seemed ill at ease.[55)] His quick and wandering glances were sent forward apparently in search of enemies lurking behind the tree trunks, and, seeing nothing there, he would car gradually resumed the old direction, forbore to interfere; nor, though something began to weigh upon his heart, did his adventurous nature permit him to regret the increased length and the mystery of their way.

On the afternoon of the fifth day they halted, and made their simple encampment nearly an hour before sunset. The face of the country, for the last few miles, had been diversified by swells of land resembling huge waves of a petrified sea; and in one of the corresponding hollows, a wild and romantic spot, had the family reared their hut and kindled their fire. There is something chilling, and yet heart-warming, in the thought of these three, united by strong bands of love and insulated from all that breathe beside. The dark and gloomy pines looked down upon them, and, as the wind swept through their tops, a pitying sound was heard in the forest; or did those old trees groan in fear that men were come to lay the axe to their roots at last? Reuben and his son, while Dorcas made ready their meal, proposed to wander out in search of game, of which that day's march had

55) ill at ease: uncomfortable, nervous.

afforded no supply. The boy, promising not to quit the vicinity of the encampment, bounded off with a step as light and elastic as that of the deer he hoped to slay; while his father, feeling a transient happiness as he gazed after him, was about to pursue an opposite direction. Dorcas in the meanwhile, had seated herself near their fire of fallen branches upon the mossgrown and mouldering trunk of a tree uprooted years before. Her employment, diversified by an occasional glance at the pot, now beginning to simmer over the blaze, was the perusal of the current year's Massachusetts Almanac, which, with the exception of an old black-letter Bible, comprised all the literary wealth of the family. None pay a greater regard to arbitrary divisions of time than those who are excluded from society; and Dorcas mentioned, as if the information were of importance, that it was now the twelfth of May. Her husband started.

"The twelfth of May! I should remember it well," muttered he, while many thoughts occasioned a momentary confusion in his mind. "Where am I? Whither am I wandering? Where did I leave him?"

Dorcas, too well accustomed to her husband's wayward moods to note any peculiarity of demeanor, now laid aside the almanac and addressed him in that mournful tone which the tender hearted appropriate to griefs long cold and dead.[56)]

"It was near this time of the month, eighteen years ago, that my poor father left this world for a better. He had a kind arm to hold his head and a kind voice to cheer him, Reuben, in his

---

56) griefs long cold and dead: 식어지고 잊혀진 오래 전 슬픔.

last moments; and the thought of the faithful care you took of him has comforted me many a time since. Oh, death would have been awful to a solitary man in a wild place like this!"

"Pray Heaven, Dorcas," said Reuben, in a broken voice,— "pray Heaven that neither of us three dies solitary and lies unburied in this howling wilderness!" And he hastened away, leaving her to watch the fire beneath the gloomy pines.

Reuben Bourne's rapid pace gradually slackened as the pang, unintentionally inflicted by the words of Dorcas, became less acute. Many strange reflections, however, thronged upon him; and, straying onward rather like a sleep walker than a hunter, it was attributable to no care of his own that his devious course kept him in the vicinity of the encampment. His steps were imperceptibly led almost in a circle; nor did he observe that he was on the verge of a tract of land heavily timbered, but not with pine-trees. The place of the latter was here supplied by oaks and other of the harder woods; and around their roots clustered a dense and bushy under-growth, leaving, however, barren spaces between the trees, thick strewn with withered leaves. Whenever the rustling of the branches or the creaking of the trunks made a sound, as if the forest were waking from slumber, Reuben instinctively raised the musket that rested on his arm, and cast a quick, sharp glance on every side; but, convinced by a partial observation that no animal was near, he would again give himself up to his thoughts. He was musing on the strange influence that had led him away from his premeditated course, and so far into the depths of the wilderness. Unable to penetrate to the secret place of his soul where his motives lay hidden, he believed that a supernatural voice had called him onward, and that a supernatural power had obstructed his retreat. He trusted that it was Heaven's intent to afford him an opportunity of expiating his sin; he hoped that he might find the bones so long unburied; and that, having laid the earth over them, peace would throw its sunlight into the sepulture of his heart. From these thoughts he was aroused by a rustling in the forest at some distance from the spot to which he had wandered. Perceiving the motion of some object behind a thick veil of undergrowth, he fired, with the instinct of a hunter and the aim of a practised marksman. A low moan, which told his success, and by which even animals cars express their dying agony, was unheeded by Reuben Bourne. What were the recollections now breaking upon him?

The thicket into which Reuben had fired was near the summit of a swell of land, and was clustered around the base of a rock, which, in the shape and smoothness of one of its surfaces, was not unlike a gigantic gravestone. As if reflected in a mirror, its likeness was in Reuben's memory. He even recognized the veins which seemed to form an inscription in forgotten characters: everything remained the same, except that a thick covert of bushes shrouded the lower part of the rock, and would have hidden Roger Malvin had he still been sitting there. Yet in the next moment Reuben's eye was caught by another change that time had effected since he last stood where he was now standing again behind the earthy roots of the uptorn tree. The sapling to which he had bound the bloodstained symbol of his vow had increased and strengthened into an oak, far indeed from its maturity, but with no mean spread of shadowy branches. There was one singularity observable in this tree which made Reuben tremble.

The middle and lower branches were in luxuriant life, and an excess of vegetation had fringed the trunk almost to the ground; but a blight had apparently stricken the upper part of the oak, and the very topmost bough was withered, sapless, and utterly dead. Reuben remembered how the little banner had fluttered on that topmost bough, when it was green and lovely, eighteen years before. Whose guilt had blasted it?

....

Dorcas, after the departure of the two hunters, continued her preparations for their evening repast. Her sylvan table was the moss-covered trunk of a large fallen tree, on the broadest part of which she had spread a snow-white cloth and arranged what were left of the bright pewter vessels that had been her pride in the settlements. It had a strange aspect that one little spot of homely comfort in the desolate heart of Nature. The sunshine yet lingered upon the higher branches of the trees that grew on rising ground; but the shadows of evening had deepened into the hollow where the encampment was made, and the firelight began to redden as it gleamed up the tall trunks of the pines or hovered on the dense and obscure mass of foliage that circled round the spot. The heart of Dorcas was not sad; for she felt that it was better to journey in the wilderness with two whom she loved than to be a lonely woman in a crowd that cared not for her. As she busied herself in arranging seats of mouldering wood, covered with leaves, for Reuben and her son, her voice danced through the gloomy forest in the measure of a song that she had learned in youth. The rude melody, the production of a bard who won no name, was descriptive of a winter evening in a frontier cottage, when, secured from savage inroad by the high-piled snow-drifts, the family rejoiced by their own fireside. The whole song possessed the nameless charm peculiar to unborrowed thought, but four continually-recurring lines shone out from the rest like the blaze of the hearth whose joys they celebrated. Into them, working magic with a few simple words, the poet had instilled the very essence of domestic love and household happiness, and they were poetry and picture joined in one. As Dorcas sang, the walls of her forsaken home seemed to encircle her; she no longer saw the gloomy pines, nor heard the wind which still, as she began each verse, sent a heavy breath through the branches, and died away in a hollow moan from the burden of the song. She was aroused by the report[57)] of a gun in the vicinity of the encampment; and either the sudden sound, or her loneliness by the glowing fire, caused her to tremble violently. The next moment she laughed in the pride of a mother's heart.

"My beautiful young hunter! My boy has slain a deer!" she exclaimed, recollecting that in the direction whence the shot proceeded Cyrus had gone to the chase.

She waited a reasonable time to hear her son's light step bounding over the rustling leaves to tell of his success. But he did not immediately appear; and she sent her cheerful voice among the trees in search of him.

"Cyrus! Cyrus!"

His coming was still delayed; and she determined, as the report had apparently been very near, to seek for him in person.

---

57) the report: an explosive noise.

Her assistance, also, might be necessary in bringing home the venison which she flattered herself he had obtained. She therefore set forward, directing her steps by the long-past sound, and singing as she went, in order that the boy might be aware of her approach and run to meet her. From behind the trunk of every tree, and from every hiding-place in the thick foliage of the undergrowth, she hoped to discover the countenance of her son, laughing with the sportive mischief that is born of affection. The sun was now beneath the horizon, and the light that came down among the leaves was sufficiently dim to create many illusions in her expecting fancy. Several times she seemed indistinctly to see his face gazing out from among the leaves; and once she imagined that he stood beckoning to her at the base of a craggy rock. Keeping her eyes on this object, however, it proved to be no more than the trunk of an oak fringed to the very ground with little branches, one of which, thrust out farther than the rest, was shaken by the breeze. Making her way round the foot of the rock, she suddenly found herself close to her husband, who had approached in another direction. Leaning upon the butt of his gun, the muzzle of which rested upon the withered leaves, he was apparently absorbed in the contemplation of some object at his feet.

"How is this, Reuben? Have you slain the deer and fallen asleep over him?" exclaimed Dorcas, laughing cheerfully, on her first slight observation of his posture and appearance.

He stirred not, neither did he turn his eyes towards her; and a cold, shuddering fear, indefinite in its source and object, began to creep into her blood. She now perceived that her husband's face was ghastly pale, and his features were rigid, as if incapable of assuming any other expression than the strong despair which had hardened upon them. He gave not the slightest evidence that he was aware of her approach.

"For the love of Heaven, Reuben, speak to me!" cried Dorcas; and the strange sound of her own voice affrighted[58)] her even more than the dead silence.

Her husband started, stared into her face, drew her to the front of the rock, and pointed with his finger.

Oh, there lay the boy, asleep, but dreamless, upon the fallen forest leaves! His cheek rested upon his arm — his curled locks were thrown back from his brow — his limbs were slightly relaxed. Had a sudden weariness overcome the youthful hunter? Would his mother's voice arouse him? She knew that it was death.

"This broad rock is the gravestone of your near kindred, Dorcas," said her husband. "Your tears will fall at once over your father and your son."

She heard him not. With one wild shriek, that seemed to force its way from the sufferer's inmost soul, she sank insensible by the side of her dead boy. At that moment the withered topmost bough of the oak loosened itself in the stilly air, and fell in soft, light fragments upon the rock, upon the leaves, upon Reuben, upon his wife and child, and upon Roger Malvin's bones. Then Reuben's heart was stricken, and the tears gushed out like water

58) affright: to arouse fear in; terrify.

from a rock. The vow that the wounded youth[59] had made the blighted man[60] had come to redeem. His sin was expiated,—the curse was gone from him; and in the hour when he had shed blood dearer to him than his own,[61] a prayer, the first for years, went up to Heaven from the lips of Reuben Bourne.

59) the wounded youth: 젊은 부상병 루번.

60) the blighted(=ruined) man: 세월을 삭여 병들어 시들은 루번.

61) blood dearer to him than his own: 자신의 피보다 그에게 더 귀한 피, 즉 아들 Cyrus의 희생.

The Ambitious Guest

ONE September night a family had gathered round their hearth, and piled it high with the driftwood of mountain streams, the dry cones of the pine, and the splintered ruins of great trees that had come crashing down the precipice. Up the chimney roared the fire, and brightened the room with its broad blaze. The faces of the father and mother had a sober gladness; the children laughed; the eldest daughter was the image of Happiness at seventeen; and the aged grandmother, who sat knitting in the warmest place, was the image of Happiness grown old. They had found the "herb, heart's-ease,[1)]" in the bleakest spot of all New England. This family were situated in the Notch[2)] of the White Hills, where the wind was sharp throughout the year, and pitilessly cold in the winter, — giving their cottage all its fresh inclemency before it descended on the valley of the Saco.[3)] They dwelt in a cold spot and a dangerous one; for a mountain towered above their heads, so steep, that the stones would often rumble down its sides and startle them at midnight.

The daughter had just uttered some simple jest that filled them all with mirth, when the wind came through the Notch

---

1) heart's-ease (also heartsease): peace of mind; a Eurasian plant, *Viola tricolor*, bearing small, spurred, various colored flowers.

2) Notch: 골짜기, 협곡.

3) The Saco River: a river in northeastern New Hampshire and southwestern Maine in the United States.

and seemed to pause before their cottage — rattling the door, with a sound of wailing and lamentation, before it passed into the valley. For a moment it saddened them, though there was nothing unusual in the tones. But the family were glad again when they perceived that the latch was lifted by some traveller, whose footsteps had been unheard amid the dreary blast which heralded his approach, and wailed as he was entering, and went moaning away from the door.

Though they dwelt in such a solitude, these people held daily converse with the world. The romantic pass of the Notch is a great artery, through which the life-blood of internal commerce is continually throbbing between Maine, on one side, and the Green Mountains and the shores of the St. Lawrence, on the other. The stage-coach always drew up before the door of the cottage. The wayfarer, with no companion but his staff, paused here to exchange a word, that the sense of loneliness might not utterly overcome him ere he could pass through the cleft of the mountain, or reach the first house in the valley. And here the teamster, on his way to Portland market, would put up for the night; and, if a bachelor, might sit an hour beyond the usual bedtime, and steal a kiss from the mountain maid at parting. It was one of those primitive taverns where the traveller pays only for food and lodging, but meets with a homely kindness beyond all price. When the footsteps were heard, therefore, between the outer door and the inner one, the whole family rose up, grandmother, children and all, as if about to welcome some one who belonged to them, and whose fate was linked with theirs.

The door was opened by a young man. His face at first wore the melancholy expression, almost despondency, of one who travels a wild and bleak road, at nightfall and alone, but soon brightened up when he saw the kindly warmth of his reception. He felt his heart spring forward to meet them all, from the old woman, who wiped a chair with her apron, to the little child that held out its arms to him.[4)] One glance and smile placed the stranger on a footing of innocent familiarity with the eldest daughter.

"Ah, this fire is the right thing!" cried he; "especially when there is such a pleasant circle round it. I am quite benumbed; for the Notch is just like the pipe of a great pair of bellows; it has blown a terrible blast in my face all the way from Bartlett."

"Then you are going towards Vermont?" said the master of the house, as he helped to take a light knapsack off the young man's shoulders.

"Yes; to Burlington, and far enough beyond," replied he. "I meant to have been at Ethan Crawford's[5)] to-night; but a pedestrian lingers along such a road as this. It is no matter; for, when I saw this good fire, and all your cheerful faces, I felt as if you had kindled it on purpose for me, and were waiting my arrival. So I shall sit down among you, and make myself at home."

The frank-hearted stranger had just drawn his chair to the fire when something like a heavy footstep was heard without,[6)]

---

4) from … to … : 이 주막을 찾아온 객이 주막식구들을 둘러보고 있다.

5) Ethan (Allen) Crawford: 19세기 초 크로포드는 White Mountains 여행객들에게 숙박을 제공하였다.

6) without: outside.

rushing down the steep side of the mountain, as with long and rapid strides, and taking such a leap in passing the cottage as to strike the opposite precipice. The family held their breath, because they knew the sound, and their guest held his[7)] by instinct.

"The old mountain has thrown a stone at us, for fear we should forget him,[8)]" said the landlord, recovering himself. "He sometimes nods his head and threatens to come down; but we are old neighbors, and agree together pretty well upon the whole. Besides we have a sure place of refuge hard by[9)] if he should be coming in good earnest."

Let us now suppose the stranger to have finished his supper of bear's meat; and, by his natural felicity of manner, to have placed himself on a footing of kindness with the whole family, so that they talked as freely together as if he belonged to their mountain brood. He was of a proud, yet gentle spirit—haughty and reserved among the rich and great; but ever ready to stoop his head to the lowly cottage door, and be like a brother or a son at the poor man's fireside. In the household of the Notch he found warmth and simplicity of feeling, the pervading intelligence of New England, and a poetry of native growth, which they had gathered when they little thought of it from the mountain peaks and chasms, and at the very threshold of their romantic and dangerous abode. He had travelled far and alone; his whole life, indeed, had been a solitary path; for, with the

---

7) his: his breath. 손님도 본능적으로 숨을 죽임.
8) him: the old mountain의 의인화.
9) hard by: close by. 바로 옆에.

lofty caution of his nature, he had kept himself apart from those who might otherwise have been his companions. The family, too, though so kind and hospitable, had that consciousness of unity among themselves, and separation from the world at large, which, in every domestic circle, should still keep a holy place where no stranger may intrude. But this evening a prophetic sympathy impelled the refined and educated youth to pour out his heart before the simple mountaineers, and constrained them to answer him with the same free confidence. And thus it should have been. Is not the kindred of a common fate a closer tie than that of birth?

The secret of the young man's character was a high and abstracted ambition. He could have borne to live an undistinguished life, but not to be forgotten in the grave. Yearning desire had been transformed to hope; and hope, long cherished, had become like certainty, that, obscurely as he journeyed now, a glory was to beam on all his pathway,—though not, perhaps, while he was treading it. But when posterity should gaze back into the gloom of what was now the present, they would trace the brightness of his footsteps, brightening as meaner glories faded, and confess that a gifted one had passed from his cradle to his tomb with none to recognize him.

"As yet," cried the stranger—his cheek glowing and his eye flashing with enthusiasm—"as yet, I have done nothing. Were I to vanish from the earth to-morrow, none would know so much of me as you: that a nameless youth came up at nightfall from the valley of the Saco, and opened his heart to you in the evening, and passed through the Notch by sunrise, and was seen no more. Not a soul would ask, 'Who was he? Whither did the wanderer go?' But I cannot die till I have achieved my destiny. Then, let Death come! I shall have built my monument!"

There was a continual flow of natural emotion, gushing forth amid abstracted reverie, which enabled the family to understand this young man's sentiments, though so foreign from their own. With quick sensibility of the ludicrous, he blushed at the ardor into which he had been betrayed.

"You laugh at me," said he, taking the eldest daughter's hand, and laughing himself. "You think my ambition as nonsensical as if I were to freeze myself to death on the top of Mount Washington, only that people might spy at me from the country round about. And, truly, that would be a noble pedestal for a man's statue!"

"It is better to sit here by this fire," answered the girl, blushing, "and be comfortable and contented, though nobody thinks about us."

"I suppose," said her father, after a fit of musing, "there is something natural in what the young man says; and if my mind had been turned that way, I might have felt just the same. It is strange, wife, how his talk has set my head running on things that are pretty certain never to come to pass."

"Perhaps they may," observed the wife. "Is the man thinking what he will do when he is a widower?"

"No, no!" cried he, repelling the idea with reproachful kindness. "When I think of your death, Esther, I think of mine, too. But I was wishing we had a good farm in Bartlett, or Bethlehem, or Littleton,[10] or some other township round the White Mountains; but not where they could tumble on our heads. I should want to stand well with my neighbors and be called Squire, and sent to General Court for a term or two; for a plain, honest man may do as much good there as a lawyer. And when I should be grown quite an old man, and you an old woman, so as not to be long apart, I might die happy enough in my bed, and leave you all crying around me. A slate gravestone would suit me as well as a marble one—with just my name and age, and a verse of a hymn, and something to let people know that I lived an honest man and died a Christian."

"There now!" exclaimed the stranger; "it is our nature to desire a monument, be it slate or marble, or a pillar of granite, or a glorious memory in the universal heart of man."

"We're in a strange way, to-night," said the wife, with tears in her eyes. "They say it's a sign of something, when folks' minds go a wandering so. Hark to the children!"

They listened accordingly. The younger children had been put to bed in another room, but with an open door between, so that they could be heard talking busily among themselves. One and all seemed to have caught the infection from the fireside circle, and were outvying[11] each other in wild wishes, and childish projects of what they would do when they came to be men and

10) Bartlett, or Bethlehem, or Littleton: 모두 New Hampshire주 White Mountains 주변에 있는 작은 도시들.

11) outvie: outrival; be more of a rival than.

women. At length a little boy, instead of addressing his brothers and sisters, called out to his mother.

"I'll tell you what I wish, mother," cried he. "I want you and father and grandma'm, and all of us, and the stranger too, to start right away, and go and take a drink out of the basin of the Flume![12)]"

Nobody could help laughing at the child's notion of leaving a warm bed, and dragging them from a cheerful fire, to visit the basin of the Flume,—a brook, which tumbles over the precipice, deep within the Notch. The boy had hardly spoken when a wagon rattled along the road, and stopped a moment before the door. It appeared to contain two or three men, who were cheering their hearts with the rough chorus of a song, which resounded, in broken notes, between the cliffs, while the singers hesitated whether to continue their journey or put up here for the night."

"Father," said the girl, "they are calling you by name."

But the good man doubted whether they had really called him, and was unwilling to show himself too solicitous of gain by inviting people to patronize his house. He therefore did not hurry to the door; and the lash being soon applied, the travellers plunged into the Notch, still singing and laughing, though their music and mirth came back drearily from the heart of the mountain.

---

12) the Flume: 자연적으로 형성된 New Hampshire의 협곡. 깎아지른 화강암 절벽의 높이가 20~30미터에 이르고 3~6미터 넓이 사이로 계곡물이 240여 미터에 걸쳐 흐르고 있음. 1808년에 우연히 발견됨.

"There, mother!" cried the boy, again. "They'd have given us a ride to the Flume."

Again they laughed at the child's pertinacious fancy for a night ramble. But it happened that a light cloud passed over the daughter's spirit; she looked gravely into the fire, and drew a breath that was almost a sigh. It forced its way, in spite of a little struggle to repress it. Then starting and blushing, she looked quickly round the circle, as if they had caught a glimpse into her bosom. The stranger asked what she had been thinking of.

"Nothing," answered she, with a downcast smile. "Only I felt lonesome just then."

"Oh, I have always had a gift of feeling what is in other people's hearts," said he, half seriously. "Shall I tell the secrets of yours? For I know what to think when a young girl shivers by a warm hearth, and complains of lonesomeness at her mother's side. Shall I put these feelings into words?"

"They would not be a girl's feelings any longer if they could be put into words," replied the mountain nymph, laughing, but avoiding his eye.

All this was said apart. Perhaps a germ of love was springing in their hearts, so pure that it might blossom in Paradise, since it could not be matured on earth; for women worship such gentle dignity as his; and the proud, contemplative, yet kindly soul is oftenest[13)] captivated by simplicity like hers. But while

13) oftenest: many times, frequently.

they spoke softly, and he was watching the happy sadness, the lightsome shadows, the shy yearnings of a maiden's nature, the wind through the Notch took a deeper and drearier sound. It seemed, as the fanciful stranger said, like the choral strain of the spirits of the blast, who in old Indian times had their dwelling among these mountains, and made their heights and recesses a sacred region. There was a wail along the road, as if a funeral were passing. To chase away the gloom, the family threw pine branches on their fire, till the dry leaves crackled and the flame arose, discovering once again a scene of peace and humble happiness. The light hovered about them fondly, and caressed them all. There were the little faces of the children, peeping from their bed apart and here the father's frame of strength, the mother's subdued and careful mien, the high-browed youth, the budding girl, and the good old grandam, still knitting in the warmest place. The aged woman looked up from her task, and, with fingers ever busy, was the next to speak.

"Old folks have their notions," said she, "as well as young ones. You've been wishing and planning; and letting your heads run on one thing and another, till you've set my mind a wandering too. Now what should an old woman wish for, when she can go but a step or two before she comes to her grave? Children, it will haunt me night and day till I tell you."

"What is it, mother?" cried the husband and wife at once.

Then the old woman, with an air of mystery which drew the circle closer round the fire, informed them that she had provided her grave-clothes some years before,—a nice linen shroud, a cap with a muslin ruff, and everything of a finer sort than she had worn since her wedding day. But this evening an old superstition had strangely recurred to her. It used to be said, in her younger days, that if anything were amiss with a corpse, if only the ruff were not smooth, or the cap did not set right, the corpse in the coffin and beneath the clods would strive to put up its cold hands and arrange it. The bare thought made her nervous.

"Don't talk so, grandmother!" said the girl, shuddering.

"Now," — continued the old woman, with singular earnestness, yet smiling strangely at her own folly, — "I want one of you, my children — when your mother is dressed and in the coffin — I want one of you to hold a looking-glass over my face. Who knows but I may take a glimpse at myself, and see whether all's right?"

"Old and young, we dream of graves and monuments," murmured the stranger youth. "I wonder how mariners feel when the ship is sinking, and they, unknown and undistinguished, are to be buried together in the ocean — that wide and nameless sepulchre?"

For a moment, the old woman's ghastly conception so engrossed the minds of her hearers that a sound abroad in the night, rising like the roar of a blast, had grown broad, deep, and terrible, before the fated group were conscious of it. The house and all within it trembled; the foundations of the earth seemed to be shaken, as if this awful sound were the peal of the last trump. Young and old exchanged one wild glance, and remained an instant, pale, affrighted, without utterance, or power to move. Then the same shriek burst simultaneously from all their lips.

"The Slide! The Slide!"[14)]

The simplest words must intimate, but not portray, the unutterable horror of the catastrophe. The victims rushed from their cottage, and sought refuge in what they deemed a safer spot — where, in contemplation of such an emergency, a sort of barrier had been reared. Alas! they had quitted their security, and fled right into the pathway of destruction. Down came the whole side of the mountain, in a cataract of ruin. Just before it reached the house, the stream broke into two branches — shivered not a window there, but overwhelmed the whole vicinity, blocked up the road, and annihilated everything in its dreadful course. Long ere the thunder of the great Slide had ceased to roar among the mountains, the mortal agony had been endured, and the victims were at peace. Their bodies were never found.

The next morning, the light smoke was seen stealing from the cottage chimney up the mountain side. Within, the fire was yet smouldering on the hearth, and the chairs in a circle round it, as if the inhabitants had but gone forth to view the devastation of the Slide, and would shortly return, to thank Heaven for their miraculous escape. All had left separate tokens, by which those who had known the family were made to shed a tear for each. Who has not heard their name? The story has been told far and wide, and will forever be a legend of these mountains. Poets have sung their fate.

There were circumstances which led some to suppose that a stranger had been received into the cottage on this awful night,

---

14) The Slide: 산사태, landslide.

and had shared the catastrophe of all its inmates. Others denied that there were sufficient grounds for such a conjecture. Woe for the high-souled youth, with his dream of Earthly Immortality! His name and person utterly unknown; his history, his way of life, his plans, a mystery never to be solved, his death and his existence equally a doubt! Whose was the agony of that death moment?

The Gray Champion

THERE was once a time when New England groaned under the actual pressure of heavier wrongs than those threatened ones which brought on the Revolution.[1] James II.,[2] the bigoted successor of Charles the Voluptuous,[3] had annulled the charters of all the colonies, and sent a harsh and unprincipled soldier to take away our liberties and endanger our religion. The administration of Sir Edmund Andros[4] lacked scarcely a single characteristic of tyranny: a Governor and Council, holding office from the King, and wholly independent of the country; laws made and taxes levied without concurrence of the people immediate or by their representatives; the rights of private citizens violated, and the titles of all landed property declared void; the voice of complaint stifled by restrictions on the press; and, finally, disaffection overawed by the first band of mercenary troops that ever marched on our free soil. For two years our

---

1) Revolution: The American Revolution (1765-1783).

2) James II: (재위 1685-1688), 제임스 2세. 영국, 애란, 스콧트란드를 통치하였으나, 왕권신수설과 카톨릭을 옹호하여 의회에 배척당함.

3) Charles the Voluptuous: (재위 1649-1651; 1660-1685), 의회를 4번이나 해산한 경력이 있는 등, 정치, 사회적으로 사건과 사고를 많이 일으킨 찰스 2세. 종교의 자유를 추진하고 예술가를 지원함. 서자를 12명 남기었으나 적자가 없어 동생이 제임스 2세로 왕위 계승. John Wilmot의 찰스 2세 평은 다음과 같다: "We have a pretty witty king / And whose word no man relies on / He never said a foolish thing / And never did a wise one"

4) Sir Edmund Andros: (1637-1714) 식민지에서 수차 통치권을 행사한 인물로 대체로 전횡적이고 문제가 많았던 인물. 그의 악행이 작품 속에 여러 행에 걸쳐 나열되어 있다.

ancestors were kept in sullen submission by that filial love which had invariably secured their allegiance to the mother country, whether its head chanced to be a Parliament, Protector, or Popish Monarch. Till these evil times, however, such allegiance had been merely nominal, and the colonists had ruled themselves, enjoying far more freedom than is even yet the privilege of the native subjects of Great Britain.

At length a rumor reached our shores that the Prince of Orange[5)] had ventured on an enterprise, the success of which would be the triumph of civil and religious rights and the salvation of New England. It was but a doubtful whisper: it might be false, or the attempt might fail; and, in either case, the man that stirred against King James would lose his head. Still the intelligence produced a marked effect. The people smiled mysteriously in the streets, and threw bold glances at their oppressors; while far and wide there was a subdued and silent agitation, as if the slightest signal would rouse the whole land from its sluggish despondency. Aware of their danger, the rulers resolved to avert it by an imposing display of strength, and perhaps to confirm their despotism by yet harsher measures. One afternoon in April, 1689, Sir Edmund Andros and his favorite councillors, being warm with wine, assembled the red-coats[6)] of the Governor's Guard, and made their appearance in the streets of Boston. The sun was near setting when the march commenced.

---

5) Prince of Orange: King William III. 카톨릭주의를 선호하는 James 2세와 대전하여 영국에 종교의 자유라는 헌법체계를 세운 최초의 군주. 그의 관용적이고 현명한 정책 하에 신교가 탄탄한 토대 위에 설 수 있게 되었다.

6) the red-coats: British soldiers during the American Revolution.

The roll of the drum at that unquiet crisis seemed to go through the streets, less as the martial music of the soldiers, than as a muster-call to the inhabitants themselves. A multitude, by various avenues, assembled in King Street, which was destined to be the scene, nearly a century afterwards, of another encounter[7)] between the troops of Britain, and a people struggling against her tyranny. Though more than sixty years had elapsed since the pilgrims[8)] came, this crowd of their descendants still showed the strong and sombre features of their character perhaps more strikingly in such a stern emergency than on happier occasions. There were the sober garb, the general severity of mien, the gloomy but undismayed expression, the scriptural forms of speech, and the confidence in Heaven's blessing on a righteous cause, which would have marked a band of the original Puritans, when threatened by some peril of the wilderness. Indeed, it was not yet time for the old spirit to be extinct; since there were men in the street that day who had worshipped there beneath the trees, before a house was reared to the God for whom they had become exiles.[9)] Old soldiers of the Parliament were here, too, smiling grimly at the thought that their aged arms might strike another blow against the house of Stuart.[10)] Here, also, were the veterans of King Philip's war, who had burned villages and slaughtered young and old, with pious fierceness, while the godly souls throughout the land were helping them with prayer.

---

7) another encounter: 식민통치국인 영국과 신대륙 식민지가 대치하는 1세기 이후의 상황.

8) since the pilgrims came: 청교도 이주가 시작된 이래.

9) they had become exiles: 신앙을 위해 고국을 떠나 이방인이 됨.

10) the house of Stuart: 14세기에 스콧트란드 왕조를 시작으로 17세기까지 스콧트란드는 물론, 아일랜드와 잉글런드 등 전체 영국 섬들을 통치한 영국 왕조, 즉 여기서는 영국 식민정부를 뜻함.

Several ministers were scattered among the crowd, which, unlike all other mobs, regarded them with such reverence, as if there were sanctity in their very garments. These holy men exerted their influence to quiet the people, but not to disperse them. Meantime, the purpose of the Governor, in disturbing the peace of the town at a period when the slightest commotion might throw the country into a ferment, was almost the universal subject of inquiry, and variously explained.

"Satan will strike his master-stroke presently," cried some, "because he knoweth that his time is short. All our godly pastors are to be dragged to prison! We shall see them at a Smithfield fire[11)] in King Street!"

Hereupon the people of each parish gathered closer round their minister, who looked calmly upwards and assumed a more apostolic dignity, as well befitted a candidate for the highest honor of his profession, the crown of martyrdom.[12)] It was actually fancied, at that period, that New England might have a John Rogers[13)] of her own to take the place of that worthy in the Primer.[14)]

---

11) a Smithfield fire: 12세기에 장터 및 처형 등이 행해진 런던의 한 지역. 매리 여왕 재위시(1553-58)에는 신교도들이 여기서 처형됨. 이러한 순교 화형을 가리킴.

12) 성직자의 최고의 영예는 순교라는 뜻.

13) John Rogers (c. 1500-1555): 목사, 성경번역 및 해설가. 카톨릭 교도인 Mary 1세 여왕 통치기간 중 순교한 최초 영국인 개신교 목사. 캠브리지 출신. 1537년 신구약을 영어로 번역, 출간한 William Tyndale의 영향으로 Roman Catholicism을 버렸으며, 카톨릭교의 우상화와 미신과 함께 급진적 신교활동도 비판. 1555년 1월, 이교도 식으로 로마교회의 기독교적 특성과 성례를 부인한 죄목으로 투옥되어 사형선고를 받고 그 해 2월 Smithfield에서 화형에 처해져 순교함.

14) the Primer: 기도서의 통칭. 13세기부터 16세기에 걸쳐서 일반신도들이 사용한 보통 기도서.

"The Pope of Rome has given orders for a new St. Bartholomew![15)]" cried others. "We are to be massacred, man and male child!"

Neither was this rumor wholly discredited, although the wiser class believed the Governor's object somewhat less atrocious. His predecessor under the old charter, Bradstreet,[16)] a venerable companion of the first settlers, was known to be in town. There were grounds for conjecturing, that Sir Edmund Andros intended at once to strike terror by a parade of military force, and to confound the opposite faction by possessing himself of their chief.

"Stand firm for the old charter Governor!" shouted the crowd, seizing upon the idea. "The good old Governor Bradstreet!"

While this cry was at the loudest, the people were surprised by the well-known figure of Governor Bradstreet himself, a patriarch of nearly ninety, who appeared on the elevated steps of a door, and, with characteristic mildness, besought them to submit to the constituted authorities.

---

15) St. Bartholomew: A.D. 1세기. 그리스도 열 두 제자 중 하나로 요한복음에서는 나타니엘로 언급되고 있음. 아르메니아에서 포교하다가 순교함. 일설에는 산채로 껍질이 벗겨지고 십자가에 거꾸로 매달려 죽었다함. 이 성도와 관련한 그림에 큰 칼이 등장하는 것은 이 때문.

16) Royal Governor Simon Bradstreet (1604-1697): Colonial Governor. 캠브리지 학사, 석사. 미국 최초의 여성 청교도 시인 Anne Dudley Bradstreet의 남편. 1661년 영국 왕 찰스 즉위 시, 식민지 특사로 식민지 헌장 재확인. 1679년에 주지사로 선임, 식민지 헌장하의 마지막 주지사가 됨. 1686년 식민지의 자주통치 기득권이 부인되고 영국은 Edmund Andros를 주지사로 임명. 그러나 그는 곧 퇴출되고 Bradstreet가 다시 1689년부터 1692년까지 주지사로 지냄.

"My children," concluded this venerable person, "do nothing rashly. Cry not aloud, but pray for the welfare of New England, and expect patiently what the Lord will do in this matter!"

The event was soon to be decided. All this time, the roll of the drum had been approaching through Cornhill,[17] louder and deeper, till with reverberations from house to house, and the regular tramp of martial footsteps, it burst into the street. A double rank of soldiers made their appearance, occupying the whole breadth of the passage, with shouldered matchlocks,[18] and matches burning, so as to present a row of fires in the dusk. Their steady march was like the progress of a machine, that would roll irresistibly over everything in its way. Next, moving slowly, with a confused clatter of hoofs on the pavement, rode a party of mounted gentlemen, the central figure being Sir Edmund Andros, elderly, but erect and soldier-like. Those around him were his favorite councillors, and the bitterest foes of New England. At his right hand rode Edward Randolph,[19] our arch-enemy, that "blasted wretch," as Cotton Mather[20] calls him, who achieved the downfall of our ancient government, and was followed with a sensible curse, through life and to his grave.

---

17) Cornhill: Boston 시청 플라자 인근의 거리 이름.

18) matchlock: 화승총.

19) Edward Randolph (1632-1703): 17세기 후반기에 영국의 식민지 관할에 큰 변화를 가져온 인물. Charles 2세를 설득하여 매서추세츠 베이 식민지의 헌장을 폐지하고 뉴잉글런드 자치령(New England Dominion)으로 대체함. 본국정부의 통제를 강화함으로써 대영제국의 식민행정 하부구조 발전에는 기여했으나 식민지 주민들의 거센 반발을 불러일으켰으며, 1689년 안드로스를 축출하고 자치령을 전복시킨 보스톤 폭동 시 투옥됨.

20) Cotton Mather (1663-1728): 사회적으로나 정치적으로 영향력을 발휘한 뉴 잉글런드 청교도 목사. 방대한 저술로도 유명. Salem 마녀재판에 가담.

On the other side was Bullivant,[21)] scattering jests and mockery as he rode along. Dudley[22)] came behind, with a downcast look, dreading, as well he might, to meet the indignant gaze of the people, who beheld him, their only countryman by birth, among the oppressors of his native land. The captain of a frigate in the harbor, and two or three civil officers under the Crown, were also there. But the figure which most attracted the public eye, and stirred up the deepest feeling, was the Episcopal clergyman of King's Chapel, riding haughtily among the magistrates in his priestly vestments, the fitting representatives of prelacy and persecution, the union of church and state, and all those abominations which had driven the Puritans to the wilderness. Another guard of soldiers, in double rank, brought up the rear.

The whole scene was a picture of the condition of New England, and its moral, the deformity of any government that does not grow out of the nature of things and the character of the people. On one side the religious multitude, with their sad visages and dark attire, and on the other, the group of despotic rulers, with the high churchman in the midst, and here and there a crucifix at their bosoms, all magnificently clad, flushed with wine, proud of unjust authority, and scoffing at the universal groan. And the mercenary soldiers, waiting but the word to deluge the street with blood, showed the only means by which obedience could be secured.

"O Lord of Hosts," cried a voice among the crowd, "provide a

21) Benjamin Bullivant: "bon enfant" (=good infant)라는 프랑스 어원의 단어. 더들리가 지명한 뉴잉글런드 자치령 초대 검찰총장.
22) Joseph Dudley (1647-1720): 뉴잉글런드 의회 의장.

Champion for thy people!"

This ejaculation was loudly uttered, and served as a herald's cry, to introduce a remarkable personage. The crowd had rolled back, and were now huddled together nearly at the extremity of the street, while the soldiers had advanced no more than a third of its length. The intervening space was empty—a paved solitude, between lofty edifices, which threw almost a twilight shadow over it. Suddenly, there was seen the figure of an ancient man, who seemed to have emerged from among the people, and was walking by himself along the centre of the street, to confront the armed band. He wore the old Puritan dress, a dark cloak and a steeple-crowned hat, in the fashion of at least fifty years before, with a heavy sword upon his thigh, but a staff in his hand to assist the tremulous gait of age.

When at some distance from the multitude, the old man turned slowly round, displaying a face of antique majesty, rendered doubly venerable by the hoary beard that descended on his breast. He made a gesture at once of encouragement and warning, then turned again, and resumed his way.

"Who is this gray patriarch?" asked the young men of their sires.

"Who is this venerable brother?" asked the old men among themselves.

But none could make reply. The fathers of the people,[23)] those

23) The fathers of the people: 대중의 어르신들.

of four-score years and upwards,[24] were disturbed, deeming it strange that they should forget one of such evident authority, whom they must have known in their early days, the associate of Winthrop,[25] and all the old councillors, giving laws, and making prayers, and leading them against the savage.[26] The elderly men ought to have remembered him, too, with locks as gray in their youth, as their own were now. And the young![27] How could he have passed so utterly from their[28] memories — that hoary sire, the relic of long-departed times, whose awful benediction had surely been bestowed on their uncovered heads, in childhood?

"Whence did he come? What is his purpose? Who can this old man be?" whispered the wondering crowd.

Meanwhile, the venerable stranger, staff in hand, was pursuing his solitary walk along the centre of the street. As he drew near the advancing soldiers, and as the roll of their drum came full upon his ears, the old man raised himself to a loftier mien, while the decrepitude of age seemed to fall from his shoulders, leaving him in gray but unbroken dignity. Now, he marched onward with a warrior's step, keeping time to the military music. Thus the aged form advanced on one side, and the whole parade of soldiers and magistrates on the other, till, when scarcely twenty yards remained between, the old man grasped his staff by the

---

24) four-score years and upwards: 80세 이상되신.

25) 윈스롭의 동기. John Winthrop(1587/8-1649): 매서추세츠 베이 식민지 건설에 기여한 청교도. 1630년에 최초의 영국 이민단을 이끌고 신대륙에 왔으며 십여 년 간 식민지 주지사를 지냄.

26) the savage: 아메리칸 인디언, 즉 원주민을 말함.

27) the young: 앞서 나온 The elderly men과 대응함. 즉 the young ought to have remembered him, too가 생략됨.

28) their: 젊은이들의

middle, and held it before him like a leader's truncheon.

"Stand!" cried he.

The eye, the face, and attitude of command; the solemn, yet warlike peal of that voice, fit either to rule a host in the battle-field or be raised to God in prayer, were irresistible. At the old man's word and outstretched arm, the roll of the drum was hushed at once, and the advancing line stood still. A tremulous enthusiasm seized upon the multitude. That stately form, combining the leader and the saint, so gray, so dimly seen, in such an ancient garb, could only belong to some old champion of the righteous cause, whom the oppressor's drum had summoned from his grave. They raised a shout of awe and exultation, and looked for the deliverance of New England.

The Governor, and the gentlemen of his party, perceiving themselves brought to an unexpected stand,[29)] rode hastily forward, as if they would have pressed their snorting and affrighted horses right against the hoary apparition. He, however, blenched[30)] not a step, but glancing his severe eye round the group, which half encompassed him, at last bent it sternly on Sir Edmund Andros. One would have thought that the dark old man was chief ruler there, and that the Governor and Council, with soldiers at their back, representing the whole power and authority of the Crown,[31)] had no alternative but obedience.

"What does this old fellow here?" cried Edward Randolph,

29) stand: standstill.

30) blench: 뒷걸음치다.

31) the Crown: 영국왕.

fiercely. "On, Sir Edmund! Bid the soldiers forward, and give the dotard the same choice that you give all his countrymen — to stand aside or be trampled on!"

"Nay, nay, let us show respect to the good grandsire," said Bullivant, laughing. "See you not, he is some old round-headed dignitary, who hath lain asleep these thirty years, and knows nothing o'[32] the change of times? Doubtless, he thinks to put us down with a proclamation in Old Noll's[33] name!"

"Are you mad, old man?" demanded Sir Edmund Andros, in loud and harsh tones. "How dare you stay[34] the march of King James's Governor?"

"I have stayed the march of a King himself, ere now," replied the gray figure, with stern composure. "I am here, Sir Governor, because the cry of an oppressed people hath disturbed me in my secret place; and beseeching this favor earnestly of the Lord, it was vouchsafed me to appear once again on earth, in the good old cause of his saints. And what speak ye[35] of James? There is no longer a Popish tyrant[36] on the throne of England, and by to-morrow noon, his name shall be a byword in this very street, where ye would make it a word of terror. Back, thou wast a Governor, back! With this night thy power is ended — to-morrow, the prison! — back, lest I foretell the scaffold!"

The people had been drawing nearer and nearer, and drinking

---

32) o': of.

33) Old Noll: a disparaging nickname for Oliver Cromwell.

34) stay: 멈추다.

35) what speak ye of: what do you say about ~ 제임스라니?

36) a Popish tyrant: 카톨릭교도였던 James 2세를 말함.

in the words of their champion, who spoke in accents long disused, like one unaccustomed to converse, except with the dead of many years ago. But his voice stirred their souls. They confronted the soldiers, not wholly without arms, and ready to convert the very stones of the street into deadly weapons. Sir Edmund Andros looked at the old man; then he cast his hard and cruel eye over the multitude, and beheld them burning with that lurid wrath, so difficult to kindle or to quench; and again he fixed his gaze on the aged form, which stood obscurely in an open space, where neither friend nor foe had thrust himself. What were his thoughts, he uttered no word which might discover. But whether the oppressor were overawed by the Gray Champion's look, or perceived his peril in the threatening attitude of the people, it is certain that he gave back, and ordered his soldiers to commence a slow and guarded retreat. Before another sunset, the Governor, and all that rode so proudly with him, were prisoners, and long ere it was known that James had abdicated, King William[37)] was proclaimed throughout New England.

But where was the Gray Champion? Some reported that, when the troops had gone from King Street, and the people were thronging tumultuously in their rear, Bradstreet, the aged Governor, was seen to embrace a form more aged than his own. Others soberly affirmed, that while they marvelled at the venerable grandeur of his aspect, the old man had faded from their eyes, melting slowly into the hues of twilight, till, where he stood, there was an empty space. But all agreed that the hoary shape was gone. The men of that generation watched for his reappearance, in sunshine and in twilight, but never saw

---

37) King William of Orange.

him more, nor knew when his funeral passed, nor where his gravestone was.

And who was the Gray Champion? Perhaps his name might be found in the records of that stern Court of Justice, which passed a sentence, too mighty for the age, but glorious in all after-times, for its humbling lesson to the monarch and its high example to the subject. I have heard, that whenever the descendants of the Puritans are to show the spirit of their sires, the old man appears again. When eighty years had passed, he walked once more in King Street. Five years later, in the twilight of an April morning, he stood on the green, beside the meeting-house, at Lexington,[38)] where now the obelisk of granite, with a slab of slate inlaid, commemorates the first fallen[39)] of the Revolutions And when our fathers were toiling at the breastwork on Bunker's Hill,[40)] all through that night the old warrior walked his rounds. Long, long may it be, ere he comes again! His hour is one of darkness, and adversity, and peril. But should domestic tyranny oppress us, or the invader's step pollute our soil, still may the Gray Champion come, for he is the type of New England's hereditary spirit; and his shadowy march, on the eve of danger, must ever be the pledge, that New England's sons will vindicate their ancestry.

---

38) Lexington: 1775년 4월 19일, 렉싱톤 전투에서 미국 독립전쟁의 시작을 알리는 최초의 총성이 울린 곳으로 유명함.

39) the first fallen: 혁명 초기에 전사한 이들.

40) Bunker's Hill: 1775년 6월 17일. 미국 독립전쟁 시 The Battle of Bunker Hill의 전쟁터. 2,400명의 영국 정규군을 1,500명의 미숙련된 식민지인들이 대처하였음에도, 영국군에게 큰 손실을 입힘.

The Minister's Black Veil

THE sexton stood in the porch of Milford[1] meeting-house, pulling busily at the bell-rope. The old people of the village came stooping along the street. Children, with bright faces, tripped merrily beside their parents, or mimicked a graver gait, in the conscious dignity of their Sunday clothes.[2] Spruce bachelors looked sidelong at the pretty maidens, and fancied that the Sabbath[3] sunshine made them prettier than on week days. When the throng had mostly streamed into the porch, the sexton began to toll the bell, keeping his eye on the Reverend Mr. Hooper's door. The first glimpse of the clergyman's figure was the signal for the bell to cease its summons.

“But what has good Parson Hooper got upon his face?” cried the sexton in astonishment.

All within hearing[4] immediately turned about, and beheld the semblance of Mr. Hooper,[5] pacing slowly his meditative way towards the meeting-house. With one accord they started,

---

1) Milford: 1639년에 정착된 Connecticut주 New Haven 남서 방향에 위치한 해안 도시. 19세기까지 선박 건조지였음.

2) Sunday clothes: 당시에는 일요일, 곧 주일에 예배를 보러갈 때는 제일 좋은 옷을 입었다.

3) Sabbath: 안식일.(유대교, 토요일; 기독교, 일요일; 이슬람교, 금요일)

4) all within hearing: 교회지기가 뱉는 말을 들은 자마다 모두.

5) the semblance of Mr. Hooper: 후퍼 목사 비슷한 사람.

expressing more wonder than if some strange minister were coming to dust the cushions of Mr. Hooper's pulpit.

"Are you sure it is our parson?" inquired Goodman Gray of the sexton.

"Of a certainty[6] it is good Mr. Hooper," replied the sexton. "He was to have exchanged pulpits with Parson Shute, of Westbury; but Parson Shute sent to excuse himself yesterday, being to preach a funeral sermon."

The cause of so much amazement may appear sufficiently slight. Mr. Hooper, a gentlemanly person, of about thirty, though still a bachelor, was dressed with due clerical neatness, as if a careful wife had starched his band, and brushed the weekly dust from his Sunday's garb. There was but one thing remarkable in his appearance. Swathed about his forehead, and hanging down over his face, so low as to be shaken by his breath, Mr. Hooper had on a black veil. On a nearer view it seemed to consist of two folds of crape, which entirely concealed his features, except the mouth and chin, but probably did not intercept his sight, further than to give a darkened aspect to all living and inanimate things. With this gloomy shade before him, good Mr. Hooper walked onward, at a slow and quiet pace, stooping somewhat, and looking on the ground, as is customary with abstracted men, yet nodding kindly to those of his parishioners who still waited on the meeting-house steps. But so wonder-struck were they[7] that his greeting hardly met with a return.

---

6) Of a certainty: (古) certainly.

7) so wonder-struck were they: they were so wonder-struck.

"I can't really feel as if good Mr. Hooper's face was behind that piece of crape," said the sexton.

"I don't like it," muttered an old woman, as she hobbled into the meeting-house. "He has changed himself into something awful, only by hiding his face."

"Our parson has gone mad!" cried Goodman Gray, following him across the threshold.

A rumor of some unaccountable phenomenon had preceded Mr. Hooper into the meeting-house, and set all the congregation astir.[8)] Few could refrain from twisting their heads towards the door; many stood upright, and turned directly about; while several little boys clambered upon the seats, and came down again with a terrible racket. There was a general bustle, a rustling of the women's gowns and shuffling of the men's feet, greatly at variance with[9)] that hushed repose which should attend the entrance of the minister. But Mr. Hooper appeared not to notice the perturbation of his people. He entered with an almost noiseless step, bent his head mildly to the pews on each side, and bowed as he passed his oldest parishioner, a white-haired great grandsire,[10)] who occupied an arm-chair in the centre of the aisle. It was strange to observe how slowly this venerable man became conscious of something singular in the appearance of his pastor. He seemed not fully to partake of the prevailing wonder,[11)] till Mr. Hooper had ascended the stairs, and showed himself in the

---

8) astir: moving or stirring especially with much activity or excitement.

9) at variance with: 일치하지 않는.

10) grandsire: =grandfather.

11) partake of the prevailing wonder: 교인들을 휩쓸고 있는 놀라움을 같이 느끼지는.

pulpit, face to face with his congregation, except for the black veil. That mysterious emblem was never once withdrawn. It shook with his measured breath, as he gave out the psalm; it threw its obscurity between him and the holy page, as he read the Scriptures; and while he prayed, the veil lay heavily on his uplifted countenance. Did he seek to hide it from the dread Being whom he was addressing?

Such was the effect of this simple piece of crape, that more than one woman of delicate nerves was forced to leave the meeting-house. Yet perhaps the pale-faced congregation was almost as fearful a sight to the minister, as his black veil to them.

Mr. Hooper had the reputation of a good preacher, but not an energetic one: he strove to win his people heavenward by mild, persuasive influences, rather than to drive them thither by the thunders of the Word.[12)] The sermon which he now delivered was marked by the same characteristics of style and manner as the general series of his pulpit oratory. But there was something, either in the sentiment of the discourse itself, or in the imagination of the auditors, which made it greatly the most powerful effort that they had ever heard from their pastor's lips. It was tinged, rather more darkly than usual, with the gentle gloom of Mr. Hooper's temperament. The subject had reference to secret sin, and those sad mysteries which we hide from our nearest and dearest, and would fain conceal from our own consciousness, even forgetting that the Omniscient[13)] can detect them. A subtle power was breathed into his words. Each

---

12) the Word: 하나님의 말씀.

13) the Omniscient: 전지전능하신 하나님.

member of the congregation, the most innocent girl, and the man of hardened breast, felt as if the preacher had crept upon them, behind his awful veil, and discovered their hoarded iniquity of deed or thought. Many spread their clasped hands on their bosoms. There was nothing terrible in what Mr. Hooper said, at least, no violence; and yet, with every tremor of his melancholy voice, the hearers quaked.[14)]An unsought pathos came hand in hand with awe. So sensible were the audience of some unwonted attribute[15)] in their minister, that they longed for a breath of wind to blow aside the veil, almost believing that a stranger's visage would be discovered, though the form, gesture, and voice were those of Mr. Hooper.

At the close of the services, the people hurried out with indecorous confusion, eager to communicate their pent-up amazement, and conscious of lighter spirits[16)] the moment they lost sight of[17)] the black veil. Some gathered in little circles, huddled closely together, with their mouths all whispering in the centre; some went homeward alone, wrapt[18)] in silent meditation; some talked loudly, and profaned the Sabbath day with ostentatious laughter. A few shook their sagacious heads, intimating that they could penetrate the mystery; while one or two affirmed that there was no mystery at all, but only that Mr. Hooper's eyes were so weakened by the midnight lamp, as to

14) quake: shake, tremble.

15) So sensible were the audience of some unwonted attribute: =the audience were so sensible of some unwonted attribute가 도치된 문장으로 that they longed for로 연결된다. unwonted attribute: 낯선 소지물.

16) lighter spirits: 가벼워진 기분.

17) lost sight of: to lose sight of: =be no longer able to see.

18) wrapt: wrapped.

require a shade. After a brief interval, forth came[19] good Mr. Hooper also, in the rear of his flock. Turning his veiled face from one group to another, he paid due reverence to the hoary[20] heads, saluted the middle aged with kind dignity as their friend and spiritual guide, greeted the young with mingled authority and love, and laid his hands on the little children's heads to bless them. Such was always his custom on the Sabbath day. Strange and bewildered looks[21] repaid him for his courtesy. None,[22] as on former occasions, aspired to the honor of walking by their pastor's side. Old Squire Saunders, doubtless by an accidental lapse of memory, neglected to invite Mr. Hooper to his table,[23] where the good clergyman had been wont to bless the food, almost every Sunday since his settlement. He returned, therefore, to the parsonage, and, at the moment of closing the door, was observed to look back upon the people, all of whom had their eyes fixed upon the minister. A sad smile gleamed faintly from beneath the black veil, and flickered about his mouth, glimmering as he disappeared.

"How strange," said a lady, "that a simple black veil, such as any woman might wear on her bonnet, should become such a terrible thing on Mr. Hooper's face!"

"Something must surely be amiss with Mr. Hooper's intellects," observed her husband, the physician of the village. "But

---

19) forth came: (Mr Hooper) came forth.

20) hoary: 백발의.

21) Strange and bewildered looks: 달라진 후퍼목사의 모습 때문에 기이해하고 당황하고 있는 신도들의 표정.

22) None: nobody, no one. aspired에 연결됨.

23) to his table: 점심식사 초대.

the strangest part of the affair is the effect of this vagary,[24] even on a sober-minded man like myself. The black veil, though it covers only our pastor's face, throws its influence over his whole person, and makes him ghostlike from head to foot. Do you not feel it so?"

"Truly do I," replied the lady; "and I would not be alone with him for the world. I wonder he is not afraid to be alone with himself!"

"Men sometimes are so,[25]" said her husband.

The afternoon service was attended with similar circumstances. At its conclusion, the bell tolled for the funeral of a young lady. The relatives and friends were assembled in the house, and the more distant acquaintances stood about the door, speaking of the good qualities of the deceased, when their talk was interrupted by the appearance of Mr. Hooper, still covered with his black veil. It was now an appropriate emblem. The clergyman stepped into the room where the corpse was laid, and bent over the coffin, to take a last farewell of his deceased parishioner. As he stooped, the veil hung straight down from his forehead, so that, if her eye-lids had not been closed forever, the dead maiden might have seen his face. Could Mr. Hooper be fearful of her glance, that he so hastily caught back the black veil? A person who watched the interview between the dead and living, scrupled not to affirm, that, at the instant when the clergyman's features were disclosed, the corpse had slightly shuddered, rustling the

24) vagary: an erratic notion or action.

25) so: afraid.

shroud and muslin cap, though the countenance retained the composure of death. A superstitious old woman was the only witness of this prodigy. From the coffin Mr. Hooper passed into the chamber of the mourners, and thence to the head of the staircase, to make the funeral prayer. It was a tender and heart-dissolving prayer, full of sorrow, yet so imbued with celestial hopes, that the music of a heavenly harp, swept by the fingers of the dead, seemed faintly to be heard among the saddest accents of the minister. The people trembled, though they but darkly understood him when he prayed that they, and himself, and all of mortal race, might be ready, as he trusted this young maiden had been, for the dreadful hour that should snatch the veil from their faces. The bearers[26)] went heavily forth, and the mourners followed, saddening all the street, with the dead before them, and Mr. Hooper in his black veil behind.

"Why do you look back?" said one in the procession to his partner.

"I had a fancy," replied she, "that the minister and the maiden's spirit were walking hand in hand."

"And so had I, at the same moment," said the other.

That night, the handsomest couple in Milford village were to be joined in wedlock. Though reckoned a melancholy man, Mr. Hooper had a placid cheerfulness for such occasions, which often excited a sympathetic smile where livelier merriment would have been thrown away. There was no quality of his disposition which

---

26) bearer: pallbearer. A person who carries or attends a coffin at a funeral.

made him more beloved than this. The company at the wedding awaited his arrival with impatience, trusting that the strange awe, which had gathered over him throughout the day, would now be dispelled. But such was not the result. When Mr. Hooper came, the first thing that their eyes rested on was the same horrible black veil, which had added deeper gloom to the funeral, and could portend[27)] nothing but evil to the wedding. Such was its immediate effect on the guests that a cloud seemed to have rolled duskily from beneath the black crape, and dimmed the light of the candles. The bridal pair stood up before the minister. But the bride's cold fingers quivered in the tremulous hand of the bridegroom, and her deathlike paleness caused a whisper that the maiden who had been buried a few hours before was come from her grave to be married. If ever another wedding were so dismal, it was that famous one where they tolled the wedding knell. After performing the ceremony, Mr. Hooper raised a glass of wine to his lips, wishing happiness to the new-married couple in a strain of mild pleasantry that ought to have brightened the features of the guests, like a cheerful gleam from the hearth. At that instant, catching a glimpse of his figure in the looking-glass, the black veil involved[28)] his own spirit in the horror with which it overwhelmed all others. His frame shuddered, his lips grew white, he spilt the untasted wine upon the carpet, and rushed forth into the darkness. For the Earth, too, had on her Black Veil.

The next day, the whole village of Milford talked of little else than[29)] Parson Hooper's black veil. That, and the mystery

27) portend: to serve as a sign or warning of.
28) involve: to engross, to wrap.
29) little else than: almost only.

concealed behind it, supplied a topic for discussion between acquaintances meeting in the street, and good women gossiping at their open windows. It was the first item of news that the tavern-keeper told to his guests. The children babbled of it on their way to school. One imitative little imp[30)] covered his face with an old black handkerchief, thereby so affrighting[31)] his playmates that the panic seized himself, and he well-nigh[32)] lost his wits by his own waggery.[33)]

It was remarkable that all of the busybodies[34)] and impertinent people in the parish, not one ventured to put the plain question to Mr. Hooper, wherefore he did this thing. Hitherto, whenever there appeared the slightest call for such interference, he had never lacked advisers, nor shown himself averse to be guided by their judgment. If he erred at all, it was by so painful a degree of self-distrust, that even the mildest censure would lead him to consider an indifferent action as a crime. Yet, though so well acquainted with this amiable weakness, no individual among his parishioners chose to make the black veil a subject of friendly remonstrance. There was a feeling of dread, neither plainly confessed nor carefully concealed, which caused each to shift the responsibility upon another, till at length it was found expedient to send a deputation[35)] of the church, in order to deal with Mr. Hooper about the mystery, before it should grow into a scandal. Never did an embassy so ill[36)] discharge its duties. The

30) imp: a mischievous child.
31) affright: to arouse fear in.
32) well-nigh: nearly, almost.
33) waggery: playfully humorous spirit or behavior.
34) busybody: a nosy, meddlesome person.
35) deputation: delegation.
36) so ill: in such an ill manner.

minister received then with friendly courtesy, but became silent, after they were seated, leaving to his visitors the whole burden of introducing their important business. The topic, it might be supposed, was obvious enough. There was the black veil swathed round Mr. Hooper's forehead, and concealing every feature above his placid mouth, on which, at times, they could perceive the glimmering of a melancholy smile. But that piece of crape, to their imagination, seemed to hang down before his heart, the symbol of a fearful secret between him and them. Were the veil but cast aside,[37] they might speak freely of it, but not till then. Thus they sat a considerable time, speechless, confused, and shrinking uneasily from Mr. Hooper's eye, which they felt to be fixed upon them with an invisible glance. Finally, the deputies returned abashed to their constituents, pronouncing the matter too weighty to be handled, except by a council of the churches, if, indeed, it might not require a general synod.

But there was one person in the village unappalled by the awe with which the black veil had impressed all beside herself. When the deputies returned without an explanation, or even venturing to demand one, she, with the calm energy of her character, determined to chase away the strange cloud that appeared to be settling round Mr. Hooper, every moment more darkly than before. As his plighted[38] wife, it should be her privilege to know what the black veil concealed. At the minister's first visit, therefore, she entered upon the subject with a direct simplicity, which made the task easier both for him and her. After he had seated himself, she fixed her eyes steadfastly upon the veil,

---

37) Were the veil but cast aside: If only the veil were cast aside.

38) plighted: 약혼한.(plight가 곤경의 뜻도 있음에 유의.)

but could discern nothing of the dreadful gloom that had so overawed the multitude: it was but a double fold of crape, hanging down from his forehead to his mouth, and slightly stirring with his breath.

"No," said she aloud, and smiling, "there is nothing terrible in this piece of crape, except that it hides a face which I am always glad to look upon. Come, good sir, let the sun shine from behind the cloud. First lay-aside your black veil: then tell me why you put it on."

Mr. Hooper's smile glimmered faintly.

"There is an hour to come," said he, "when all of us shall cast aside our veils. Take it not amiss,[39] beloved friend, if I wear this piece of crape till then."

"Your words are a mystery, too," returned the young lady. "Take away the veil from them, at least."

"Elizabeth, I will," said he, "so far as my vow may suffer me. Know, then, this veil is a type and a symbol, and I am bound to wear it ever, both in light and darkness, in solitude and before the gaze of multitudes, and as with strangers, so with my familiar friends. No mortal eye will see it withdrawn. This dismal shade must separate me from the world: even you, Elizabeth, can never come behind it!"

"What grievous affliction hath befallen you," she earnestly

39) amiss: in a wrong way.

inquired, "that you should thus darken your eyes forever?"

"If it be a sign of mourning," replied Mr. Hooper, "I, perhaps, like most other mortals, have sorrows dark enough to be typified by a black veil."

"But what if the world will not believe that it is the type of an innocent sorrow?" urged Elizabeth. "Beloved and respected as[40] you are, there may be whispers that you hide your face under the consciousness of secret sin. For the sake of your holy office, do away[41] this scandal!"

The color rose into her cheeks as she intimated the nature of the rumors that were already abroad in the village. But Mr. Hooper's mildness did not forsake him. He even smiled again—that same sad smile, which always appeared like a faint glimmering of light, proceeding from the obscurity beneath the veil.

"If I hide my face for sorrow, there is cause enough," he merely replied; "and if I cover it for secret sin, what mortal might not do the same?"

And with this gentle, but unconquerable obstinacy did he resist all her entreaties. At length Elizabeth sat silent. For a few moments she appeared lost in thought, considering, probably, what new methods might be tried to withdraw her lover from so dark a fantasy, which, if it had no other meaning, was perhaps a

40) as: though.

41) do away: to put an end to.

symptom of mental disease. Though of a firmer character than his own,[42] the tears rolled down her cheeks. But, in an instant, as it were, a new feeling took the place of sorrow: her eyes were fixed insensibly on the black veil, when, like a sudden twilight in the air, its terrors fell around her. She arose, and stood trembling before him.

"And do you feel it then, at last?" said he mournfully.

She made no reply, but covered her eyes with her hand, and turned to leave the room. He rushed forward and caught her arm.

"Have patience with me, Elizabeth!" cried he, passionately. "Do not desert me, though this veil must be between us here on earth. Be mine, and hereafter there shall be no veil over my face, no darkness between our souls! It is but a mortal veil — it is not for eternity! O! you know not how lonely I am, and how frightened, to be alone behind my black veil. Do not leave me in this miserable obscurity forever!"

"Lift the veil but once, and look me in the face," said she.

"Never! It cannot be!" replied Mr. Hooper.

"Then farewell!" said Elizabeth.

She withdrew her arm from his grasp, and slowly departed, pausing at the door, to give one long shuddering gaze, that seemed almost to penetrate the mystery of the black veil. But,

42) Though of a firmer character than his own: Hooper목사보다 강한 성격이었으나.

even amid his grief, Mr. Hooper smiled to think that only a material emblem had separated him from happiness, though the horrors, which it shadowed forth, must be drawn darkly between the fondest of lovers.

From that time no attempts were made to remove Mr. Hooper's black veil, or, by a direct appeal, to discover the secret which it was supposed to hide. By persons who claimed a superiority to popular prejudice, it was reckoned merely an eccentric whim, such as often mingles with the sober actions of men otherwise[43] rational, and tinges them all with its own semblance of insanity. But with the multitude, good Mr. Hooper was irreparbly a bugbear.[44] He could not walk the street with any peace of mind, so conscious was he that the gentle and timid would turn aside to avoid him, and that others would make it a point of hardihood[45] to throw themselves in his way. The impertinence of the latter class compelled him to give up his customary walk at sunset to the burial ground; for when he leaned pensively over the gate, there would always be faces behind the gravestones, peeping at his black veil. A fable went the rounds[46] that the stare of the dead people drove him thence. It grieved him, to the very depth of his kind heart, to observe how the children fled from his approach, breaking up their merriest sports, while his melancholy figure was yet afar off. Their instinctive dread caused him to feel more strongly than aught[47] else, that a preternatural horror was

43) otherwise: in another way; under different circumstances.
44) bugbear: an object of obsessive dread. 공포의 근원.
45) hardihood: boldness.
46) go [make] the rounds: (of information, rumor, etc) to be passed around, so as to be generally known.
47) aught: anything whatever.

interwoven with the threads of the black crape. In truth, his own antipathy to the veil was known to be so great, that he never willingly passed before a mirror, nor stooped to drink at a still fountain, lest, in its peaceful bosom, he should be affrighted by himself. This was what gave plausibility to the whispers, that Mr. Hooper's conscience tortured him for some great crime too horrible to be entirely concealed, or otherwise than so obscurely intimated. Thus, from beneath the black veil, there rolled a cloud into the sunshine, an ambiguity of sin or sorrow, which enveloped the poor minister, so that love or sympathy could never reach him. It was said that ghost and fiend consorted with him there. With self-shudderings and outward terrors, he walked continually in its shadow, groping darkly within his own soul, or gazing through a medium that saddened the whole world. Even the lawless wind, it was believed, respected his dreadful secret, and never blew aside the veil. But still good Mr. Hooper sadly smiled at the pale visages of the worldly throng as he passed by.

Among all its bad influences, the black veil had the one desirable effect, of making its wearer a very efficient clergyman. By the aid of his mysterious emblem[48] — for there was no other apparent cause — he became a man of awful power over souls that were in agony for sin. His converts always regarded him with a dread peculiar to themselves, affirming, though but figuratively, that, before he brought them to celestial light, they had been with him behind the black veil. Its gloom, indeed, enabled him to sympathize with all dark affections. Dying sinners cried aloud for Mr. Hooper, and would not yield their breath till he appeared; though ever, as he stooped to whisper

48) his mysterious emblem: his black veil.

consolation, they shuddered at the veiled face so near their own. Such were the terrors of the black veil, even when Death had bared his visage! Strangers came long distances to attend service at his church, with the mere idle purpose of gazing at his figure, because it was forbidden them to behold his face. But many were made to quake ere[49] they departed! Once, during Governor Belcher's administration, Mr. Hooper was appointed to preach the election sermon. Covered with his black veil, he stood before the chief magistrate, the council, and the representatives, and wrought so deep an impression, that the legislative measures of that year were characterized by all the gloom and piety of our earliest ancestral sway.

In this manner Mr. Hooper spent a long life, irreproachable in outward act, yet shrouded in dismal suspicions; kind and loving, though unloved, and dimly feared; a man apart from men, shunned in their health and joy, but ever summoned to their aid in mortal anguish. As years wore on, shedding their snows above his sable veil, he acquired a name throughout the New England churches, and they called him Father Hooper. Nearly all his parishioners, who were of mature age when he was settled, had been borne away by many a funeral: he had one congregation in the church, and a more crowded one in the churchyard; and having wrought so late into the evening, and done his work so well, it was now good Father Hooper's turn to rest.

Several persons were visible by the shaded candlelight, in the death chamber of the old clergyman. Natural connections[50] he

49) ere: before.
50) Natural connections: families and relatives.

had none. But there was the decorously grave, though unmoved physician, seeking only to mitigate the last pangs[51)] of the patient whom he could not save. There were the deacons, and other eminently pious members of his church. There, also, was the Reverend Mr. Clark, of Westbury, a young and zealous divine, who had ridden in haste to pray by the bedside of the expiring minister. There was the nurse, no hired handmaiden of death, but one whose calm affection had endured thus long in secrecy, in solitude, amid the chill of age, and would not perish, even at the dying hour. Who, but Elizabeth! And there lay the hoary head of good Father Hooper upon the death pillow, with the black veil still swathed about his brow, and reaching down over his face, so that each more difficult gasp of his faint breath caused it to stir. All through life that piece of crape had hung between him and the world: it had separated him from cheerful brotherhood and woman's love, and kept him in that saddest of all prisons, his own heart; and still it lay upon his face, as if to deepen the gloom of his darksome chamber, and shade him from the sunshine of eternity.

For some time previous, his mind had been confused, wavering doubtfully between the past and the present, and hovering forward, as it were, at intervals, into the indistinctness of the world to come. There had been feverish turns, which tossed him from side to side, and wore away what little strength he had. But in his most convulsive struggles, and in the wildest vagaries of his intellect, when no other thought retained its sober influence, he still showed an awful solicitude lest the black veil should slip aside. Even if his bewildered soul could have

51) pang: a sudden sharp spasm of pain.

forgotten, there was a faithful woman at this pillow, who, with averted eyes, would have covered that aged face, which she had last beheld in the comeliness of manhood. At length the death-stricken old man lay quietly in the torpor of mental and bodily exhaustion, with an imperceptible pulse, and breath that grew fainter and fainter, except when a long, deep, and irregular inspiration seemed to prelude the flight of his spirit.

The minister of Westbury approached the bedside.

"Venerable Father Hooper," said he, "the moment of your release is at hand. Are you ready for the lifting of the veil that shuts in time from eternity?"

Father Hooper at first replied merely by a feeble motion of his head; then, apprehensive, perhaps, that his meaning might be doubted, he exerted himself to speak.

"Yea," said he, in faint accents, "my soul hath a patient weariness until that veil be lifted."

"And is it fitting," resumed the Reverend Mr. Clark, "that a man so given to prayer, of such a blameless example, holy in deed and thought, so far as mortal judgment may pronounce; is it fitting that a father in the church should leave a shadow on his memory, that may seem to blacken a life so pure? I pray you, my venerable brother, let not this thing be! Suffer us to be gladdened by your triumphant aspect as you go to your reward. Before the veil of eternity be lifted, let me cast aside this black veil from your face!"

And thus speaking, the Reverend Mr. Clark bent forward to reveal the mystery of so many years. But, exerting a sudden energy, that made all the beholders stand aghast, Father Hooper snatched both his hands from beneath the bedclothes, and pressed them strongly on the black veil, resolute to struggle, if the minister of Westbury would contend with a dying man.

"Never!" cried the veiled clergyman. "On earth, never!"

"Dark old man!" exclaimed the affrighted minister, "with what horrible crime upon your soul are you now passing to the judgment?"

Father Hooper's breath heaved; it rattled in his throat; but, with a mighty effort, grasping forward with his hands, he caught hold of life, and held it back till he should speak. He even raised himself in bed; and there he sat, shivering with the arms of death around him, while the black veil hung down, awful, at that last moment, in the gathered terrors of a life-time. And yet the faint, sad smile, so often there, now seemed to glimmer from its obscurity, and linger on Father Hooper's lips.

"Why do you tremble at me alone?" cried he, turning his veiled face round the circle of pale spectators. "Tremble also at each other! Have men avoided me, and women shown no pity, and children screamed and fled, only for my black veil? What, but the mystery which it obscurely typifies, has made this piece of crape so awful? When the friend shows his inmost heart to his friend; the lover to his best beloved; when man does not vainly shrink from the eye of his Creator, loathsomely treasuring up the secret of his sin; then deem me a monster, for the symbol beneath which I have lived, and die! I look around me, and, lo! on every visage a Black Veil!"

While his auditors shrank from one another, in mutual affright, Father Hooper fell back upon his pillow, a veiled corpse, with a faint smile lingering on the lips. Still veiled, they laid him in his coffin, and a veiled corpse they bore him to the grave. The grass of many years has sprung up and withered on that grave, the burial stone is moss-grown, and good Mr. Hooper's face is dust; but awful is still the thought that it mouldered beneath the Black Veil!

[1] Another clergyman in New England, Mr. Joseph Moody, of York, Maine, who died about eighty years since, made himself remarkable by the same eccentricity that is here related of the Reverend Mr. Hooper. In his case, however, the symbol had a different import.[52] In early life he had accidentally killed a beloved friend, and from that day till the hour of his own death, he hid his face from men.

---

52) import: = meaning.

Egotism; or, The Bosom Serpent

"Here he comes!" shouted the boys along the street. "Here comes the man with a snake in his bosom!"

This outcry, saluting Herkimer's ears as he was about to enter the iron gate of the Elliston mansion, made him pause. It was not without a shudder that he found himself on the point of meeting his former acquaintance, whom he had known in the glory of youth, and whom now after an interval of five years, he was to find the victim either of a diseased fancy or a horrible physical misfortune.

"A snake in his bosom!" repeated the young sculptor to himself. "It must be he. No second man on earth has such a bosom friend. And now, my poor Rosina, Heaven grant me wisdom to discharge my errand aright![1] Woman's faith must be strong indeed since thine[2] has not yet failed."

Thus musing, he took his stand at the entrance of the gate and waited until the personage so singularly announced[3] should make his appearance. After an instant or two he beheld the figure of a lean man, of unwholesome look, with glittering eyes and long black hair, who seemed to imitate the motion of a

1) aright: rightly.

2) thine: Rosina's. Hawthorne의 여성시각의 단면을 보임. 여성은 고난에 강하다고 봄.

3) so singularly announced: 매우 독특하게 소개된. 즉 "가슴에 뱀을 품은 남자"로.

snake; for, instead of walking straight forward with open front, he undulated[4] along the pavement in a curved line. It may be too fanciful to say that something, either in his moral or material aspect, suggested the idea that a miracle had been wrought by transforming a serpent into a man, but so imperfectly that the snaky nature was yet hidden, and scarcely hidden, under the mere outward guise of humanity. Herkimer remarked that his complexion had a greenish tinge over its sickly white, reminding him of a species of marble out of which he had once wrought a head of Envy,[5] with her snaky locks.

The wretched being approached the gate, but, instead of entering, stopped short[6] and fixed the glitter of his eye full upon the compassionate yet steady countenance of the sculptor.

"It gnaws me! It gnaws me!" he exclaimed.

And then there was an audible hiss, but whether it came from the apparent lunatic's own lips, or was the real hiss of a serpent, might admit of a discussion. At all events, it made Herkimer shudder to his heart's core.[7]

"Do you know me, George Herkimer?" asked the snake-possessed.

Herkimer did know him; but it demanded all the intimate

4) undulate: to move with a wavelike motion.

5) a head of Envy: 질투의 頭像. 조각작품. 여기서 독자는 화자가 조각가임을 알 수 있다.

6) short: abruptly.

7) to his heart's core: 철저하게, 마음속까지.

and practical acquaintance with the human face, acquired by modelling actual likenesses in clay,[8] to recognize the features of Roderick Elliston in the visage that now met the sculptor's gaze.[9] Yet it was he. It added nothing to the wonder to reflect that the once brilliant young man had undergone this odious and fearful change during the no more than five brief years of Herkimer's abode at Florence. The possibility of such a transformation being granted, it was as easy to conceive it effected in a moment as in an age. Inexpressibly shocked and startled, it was still the keenest pang when Herkimer remembered that the fate of his cousin Rosina, the ideal of gentle womanhood, was indissolubly interwoven with that of a being[10] whom Providence seemed to have unhumanized.

"Elliston! Roderick!" cried he, "I had heard of this; but my conception came far short[11] of the truth. What has befallen you? Why do I find you thus?"

"Oh, 'tis a mere nothing! A snake! A snake! The commonest thing in the world. A snake in the bosom—that's all," answered Roderick Elliston. "But how is your own breast?" continued he, looking the sculptor in the eye with the most acute and penetrating glance that it had ever been his fortune to encounter. "All pure and wholesome? No reptile there? By my faith and conscience, and by the devil within me, here is a wonder! A man without a serpent in his bosom!"

---

8) modelling actual likenesses in clay: 진흙으로 실제와 닮은꼴을 만듦.

9) it demanded~ gaze: 로데릭의 용모가 사람의 모습을 알아볼 수 없을 정도로 변했음을 말함.

10) a being: Roderick Elliston.

11) come (far) short (of): fail to meet expectations or standards.

"Be calm, Elliston," whispered George Herkimer, laying his hand upon the shoulder of the snake-possessed. "I have crossed the ocean to meet you. Listen! Let us be private. I bring a message from Rosina — from your wife!"

"It gnaws me! It gnaws me!" muttered Roderick.

With this exclamation, the most frequent in his mouth, the unfortunate man clutched both hands upon his breast as if an intolerable sting or torture impelled him to rend[12] it open and let out the living mischief, even should it be intertwined with his own life. He then freed himself from Herkimer's grasp by a subtle motion, and, gliding through the gate, took refuge in his antiquated family residence. The sculptor did not pursue him. He saw that no available intercourse could be expected at such a moment, and was desirous, before another meeting, to inquire closely into the nature of Roderick's disease and the circumstances that had reduced him to so lamentable a condition. He succeeded in obtaining the necessary information from an eminent medical gentleman.

Shortly after Elliston's separation from his wife — now nearly four years ago — his associates had observed a singular gloom spreading over his daily life, like those chill, gray mists that sometimes steal away the sunshine from a summer's morning. The symptoms caused them endless perplexity. They knew not whether ill health were robbing his spirits of elasticity, or whether a canker of the mind was gradually eating, as such cankers do, from his moral system into the physical frame, which is but the

12) rend: to tear apart or into pieces violently.

shadow of the former. They looked for the root of this trouble in his shattered schemes of domestic bliss, — wilfully shattered by himself, — but could not be satisfied of its existence there. Some thought that their once brilliant friend was in an incipient stage of insanity, of which his passionate impulses had perhaps been the forerunners; others prognosticated a general blight and gradual decline. From Roderick's own lips they could learn nothing. More than once, it is true, he had been heard to say, clutching his hands convulsively upon his breast, — "It gnaws me! It gnaws me!" — but, by different auditors, a great diversity of explanation was assigned to this ominous expression. What could it be that gnawed the breast of Roderick Elliston? Was it sorrow? Was it merely the tooth of physical disease? Or, in his reckless course, often verging upon profligacy, if not plunging into its depths, had he been guilty of some deed which made his bosom a prey to the deadlier fangs of remorse? There was plausible ground for each of these conjectures; but it must not be concealed that more than one elderly gentleman, the victim of good cheer and slothful habits, magisterially pronounced the secret of the whole matter to be Dyspepsia![13]

Meanwhile, Roderick seemed aware how generally he had become the subject of curiosity and conjecture, and, with a morbid repugnance to such notice, or to any notice whatsoever, estranged himself from all companionship. Not merely the eye of man was a horror to him; not merely the light of a friend's countenance; but even the blessed sunshine, likewise, which in its universal beneficence typifies the radiance of the Creator's face, expressing his love for all the creatures of his hand. The

13) Dyspepsia: indigestion.

dusky twilight was now too transparent for Roderick Elliston; the blackest midnight was his chosen hour to steal abroad;[14) and if ever he were seen, it was when the watchman's lantern gleamed upon his figure, gliding along the street, with his hands clutched upon his bosom, still muttering, "It gnaws me! It gnaws me!" What could it be that gnawed him?

After a time, it became known that Elliston was in the habit of resorting to all the noted quacks that infested the city, or whom money would tempt to journey thither from a distance. By one of these persons, in the exultation of a supposed cure, it was proclaimed far and wide, by dint of handbills and little pamphlets on dingy paper, that a distinguished gentleman, Roderick Elliston, Esq., had been relieved of a SNAKE in his stomach! So here was the monstrous secret, ejected from its lurking place into public view, in all its horrible deformity. The mystery was out; but not so the bosom serpent. He, if it were anything but a delusion, still lay coiled in his living den. The empiric's[15) cure had been a sham, the effect, it was supposed, of some stupefying drug which more nearly caused the death of the patient than of the odious reptile that possessed him. When Roderick Elliston regained entire sensibility, it was to find his misfortune the town talk—the more than nine days' wonder and horror—while, at his bosom, he felt the sickening motion of a thing alive, and the gnawing of that restless fang which seemed to gratify at once a physical appetite and a fiendish spite.

He summoned the old black servant, who had been bred up in

14) steal abroad: move away from one's home; covering a large area.

15) empiric: 경험주의자.

his father's house, and was a middle-aged man while Roderick lay in his cradle.

"Scipio!" he began; and then paused, with his arms folded over his heart. "What do people say of me, Scipio."

"Sir! my poor master! that you had a serpent in your bosom," answered the servant with hesitation.

"And what else?" asked Roderick, with a ghastly look at the man.

"Nothing else, dear master," replied Scipio, "only that the doctor gave you a powder, and that the snake leaped out upon the floor."

"No, no!" muttered Roderick to himself, as he shook his head, and pressed his hands with a more convulsive force upon his breast, "I feel him still. It gnaws me! It gnaws me!"

From this time the miserable sufferer ceased to shun the world, but rather solicited and forced himself upon the notice of acquaintances and strangers. It was partly the result of desperation on finding that the cavern of his own bosom had not proved deep and dark enough to hide the secret, even while it was so secure a fortress for the loathsome fiend that had crept into it. But still more, this craving for notoriety was a symptom of the intense morbidness which now pervaded his nature. All persons chronically diseased are egotists, whether the disease be of the mind or body; whether it be sin, sorrow, or merely the more tolerable calamity of some endless pain, or mischief among the cords of mortal life. Such individuals are made acutely conscious of a self, by the torture in which it dwells. Self, therefore, grows to be so prominent an object with them that they cannot but present it to the face of every casual passer-by. There is a pleasure — perhaps the greatest of which the sufferer is susceptible — in displaying the wasted or ulcerated limb, or the cancer in the breast; and the fouler the crime, with so much the more difficulty does the perpetrator prevent it from thrusting up its snake-like head to frighten the world; for it is that cancer, or that crime, which constitutes their respective individuality. Roderick Elliston, who, a little while before, had held himself so scornfully above the common lot of men, now paid full allegiance to this humiliating law. The snake in his bosom seemed the symbol of a monstrous egotism to which everything was referred, and which he pampered, night and day, with a continual and exclusive sacrifice of devil worship.

He soon exhibited what most people considered indubitable[16) tokens of insanity. In some of his moods, strange to say, he prided and gloried himself on being marked out from the ordinary experience of mankind, by the possession of a double nature, and a life within a life. He appeared to imagine that the snake was a divinity, — not celestial, it is true, but darkly infernal, — and that he thence derived an eminence and a sanctity, horrid, indeed, yet more desirable than whatever ambition aims at. Thus he drew his misery around him like a regal mantle, and looked down triumphantly upon those whose vitals nourished no deadly monster. Oftener, however, his human nature asserted its empire over him in the shape of a yearning

16) indubitable: unquestionable.

for fellowship. It grew to be his custom to spend the whole day in wandering about the streets, aimlessly, unless it might be called an aim to establish a species of brotherhood between himself and the world. With cankered ingenuity, he sought out his own disease in every breast. Whether insane or not, he showed so keen a perception of frailty, error, and vice, that many persons gave him credit for being possessed not merely with a serpent, but with an actual fiend, who imparted this evil faculty of recognizing whatever was ugliest in man's heart.

For instance, he met an individual, who, for thirty years, had cherished a hatred against his own brother. Roderick, amidst the throng of the street, laid his hand on this man's chest, and looking full into his forbidding face, "How is the snake to-day?" he inquired, with a mock expression of sympathy.

"The snake!" exclaimed the brother hater — "what do you mean?"

"The snake! The snake! Does it gnaw you?" persisted Roderick. "Did you take counsel with[17] him this morning when you should have been saying your prayers? Did he sting, when you thought of your brother's health, wealth, and good repute? Did he caper[18] for joy, when you remembered the profligacy[19] of his only son? And whether he stung, or whether he frolicked, did you feel his poison throughout your body and soul, converting everything to sourness and bitterness? That is the way of such

17) take counsel with: 의논하다, 협의하다.

18) caper: to leap;

19) profligacy: 방탕, 품행 불량.

serpents. I have learned the whole nature of them from my own!"

"Where is the police?" roared the object of Roderick's persecution, at the same time giving an instinctive clutch to his breast. "Why is this lunatic[20] allowed to go at large?"[21]

"Ha, ha!" chuckled Roderick, releasing his grasp of the man.—"His bosom serpent has stung him then!"

Often it pleased the unfortunate young man to vex people with a lighter satire, yet still characterized by somewhat of snake-like virulence.[22] One day he encountered an ambitious statesman, and gravely inquired after the welfare of his boa constrictor;[23] for of that species, Roderick affirmed, this gentleman's serpent must needs be,[24] since its appetite was enormous enough to devour the whole country and constitution. At another time, he stopped a close-fisted old fellow, of great wealth, but who skulked about the city in the guise of a scarecrow, with a patched blue surtout,[25] brown hat, and mouldy boots, scraping pence together, and picking up rusty nails. Pretending to look earnestly at this respectable person's stomach, Roderick assured him that his snake was a copper-head[26] and had been generated by the immense quantities of that base metal with which he

20) this lunatic: the bosom serpent.
21) at large: at liberty.
22) virulence: 독성.
23) boa constrictor: 먹이를 졸라 죽이는 왕뱀.
24) must needs be: 꼭 ~일 것이다.
25) surtout /surtu:/ 남자용 외투.
26) copper-head: 북미산 살무사의 일종.

daily defiled his fingers. Again, he assaulted a man of rubicund[27)] visage, and told him that few bosom serpents had more of the devil in them than those that breed in the vats[28)] of a distillery. The next whom Roderick honored with his attention was a distinguished clergyman, who happened just then to be engaged in a theological controversy, where human wrath was more perceptible than divine inspiration.

"You have swallowed a snake in a cup of sacramental[29)] wine," quoth[30)] he.

"Profane wretch!" exclaimed the divine[31)]; but, nevertheless, his hand stole to his breast.

He met a person of sickly sensibility, who, on some early disappointment, had retired from the world, and thereafter held no intercourse with his fellow-men, but brooded sullenly or passionately over the irrevocable past. This man's very heart, if Roderick might be believed, had been changed into a serpent, which would finally torment both him and itself to death. Observing a married couple, whose domestic troubles were matter of notoriety, he condoled with both on having mutually taken a house adder[32)] to their bosoms. To an envious author, who depreciated works which he could never equal, he said that his snake was the slimiest and filthiest of all the reptile tribe,

27) rubicund: inclined to a healthy rosiness.

28) vat: a large vessel, as a tub, cistern.

29) sacramental: 성찬식(의).

30) quoth: (古) =uttered, said.

31) the divine: 성직자.

32) adder: a venomous Old World snake.

but was fortunately without a sting. A man of impure life, and a brazen face, asking Roderick if there were any serpent in his breast, he told him that there was, and of the same species that once tortured Don Rodrigo, the Goth.[33)] He took a fair young girl by the hand, and gazing sadly into her eyes, warned her that she cherished a serpent of the deadliest kind within her gentle breast; and the world found the truth of those ominous words, when, a few months afterwards, the poor girl died of love and shame. Two ladies, rivals in fashionable life who tormented one another with a thousand little stings of womanish spite, were given to understand that each of their hearts was a nest of diminutive snakes, which did quite as much mischief as one great one.

But nothing seemed to please Roderick better than to lay hold of a person infected with jealousy, which he represented as an enormous green reptile, with an ice-cold length of body, and the sharpest sting of any snake save[34)] one.

"And what one is that?" asked a by-stander, overhearing him.

It was a dark-browed man who put the question; he had an evasive eye, which in the course of a dozen years had looked no mortal[35)] directly in the face. There was an ambiguity about this person's character,—a stain upon his reputation,—yet none could tell precisely of what nature, although the city gossips, male and female, whispered the most atrocious surmises. Until a recent period he had followed the sea, and was, in fact, the very

33) the Goth: a member of a Germanic people who invaded the Roman Empire during the early Christian era.

34) save: except.

35) mortal: human being.

shipmaster whom George Herkimer had encountered, under such singular circumstances, in the Grecian Archipelago.[36)]

"What bosom serpent has the sharpest sting?" repeated this man; but he put the question as if by a reluctant necessity, and grew pale while he was uttering it.

"Why need you ask?" replied Roderick, with a look of dark intelligence. "Look into your own breast. Hark![37)] my serpent bestirs[38)] himself! He acknowledges the presence of a master fiend!"

And then, as the by-standers afterwards affirmed, a hissing sound was heard, apparently in Roderick Elliston's breast. It was said, too, that an answering hiss came from the vitals[39)] of the shipmaster, as if a snake were actually lurking there and had been aroused by the call of its brother reptile. If there were in fact any such sound, it might have been caused by a malicious exercise of ventriloquism[40)] on the part of Roderick.

Thus making his own actual serpent — if a serpent there actually was in his bosom — the type of each man's fatal error, or hoarded sin, or unquiet conscience, and striking his sting so unremorsefully into the sorest spot, we may well imagine

---

36) Grecian Archipelago: Aegean Sea, separating Greece from Asia Minor. It is studded with a vast number of small islands.

37) hark: to listen attentively or closely.

38) bestir: to rouse.

39) vitals: bodily parts or organs considered as the source of life. 여기서는 심장이라고 보면 됨.

40) ventriloquism: [Latin, venter=belly; loqui=to speak]

that Roderick became the pest of the city. Nobody could elude him — none could withstand him. He grappled with the ugliest truth that he could lay his hand on, and compelled his adversary to do the same. Strange spectacle in human life where it is the instinctive effort of one and all to hide those sad realities, and leave them undisturbed beneath a heap of superficial topics which constitute the materials of intercourse between man and man! It was not to be tolerated that Roderick Elliston should break through the tacit compact by which the world has done its best to secure repose without relinquishing evil. The victims of his malicious remarks, it is true, had brothers[41)] enough to keep them in countenance[42)]; for, by Roderick's theory, every mortal bosom harbored either a brood of small serpents or one overgrown monster that had devoured all the rest. Still the city could not bear this new apostle. It was demanded by nearly all, and particularly by the most respectable inhabitants,[43)] that Roderick should no longer be permitted to violate the received rules of decorum by obtruding[44)] his own bosom serpent to the public gaze, and dragging those of decent people from their lurking places.

Accordingly, his relatives interfered and placed him in a private asylum for the insane. When the news was noised abroad,[45)] it was observed that many persons walked the streets

---

41) brothers: 비슷한 입장의 사람들.

42) keep them in countenance: 체면, 평정을 유지하게 하다.

43) the most respectable inhabitants: 가장 존경스러운 주민들도 로데릭에 대한 행동제재 처분을 요구하는 것은 그들 자신의 내면이 공공연히 드러나는 것 같아 불편하기 때문이다.

44) obtrude: to force upon others with undue insistence.

45) noised abroad: talked about widely.

with freer countenances and covered their breasts less carefully with their hands.[46)]

His confinement, however, although it contributed not a little[47)] to the peace of the town, operated unfavorably upon Roderick himself. In solitude his melancholy grew more black and sullen. He spent whole days — indeed, it was his sole occupation — in communing with the serpent. A conversation was sustained, in which, as it seemed, the hidden monster bore a part, though unintelligibly to the listeners, and inaudible except in a hiss. Singular as it may appear, the sufferer[48)] had now contracted a sort of affection for his tormentor,[49)] mingled, however, with the intensest loathing and horror. Nor were such discordant emotions[50)] incompatible. Each, on the contrary, imparted strength and poignancy to its opposite.[51)] Horrible love — horrible antipathy — embracing one another in his bosom, and both concentrating themselves upon a being that had crept into his vitals or been engendered there, and which was nourished with his food, and lived upon his life, and was as intimate with him as his own heart, and yet was the foulest of all created things! But not the less was it the true type of a morbid nature.

Sometimes, in his moments of rage and bitter hatred against the snake and himself, Roderick determined to be the death of

---

46) 그들의 내면을 지목하는 존재가 사라지니, (죄성을 지닌) 주민들이 가슴을 펴고 다닐 수가 있다고 변명하고 있다.

47) not a little: very, a lot.

48) the sufferer: 후퍼 목사

49) tormentor: 가슴 속의 뱀

50) such discordant emotions: 이런 어울리지 않는 감정들 — 한편으로는 뱀에 대한 긍휼, 다른 한편으로는 혐오감과 공포.

51) embracing one another: 서로가 상대방에게.

him, even at the expense of his own life. Once he attempted it by starvation; but, while the wretched man was on the point of famishing, the monster seemed to feed upon his heart, and to thrive and wax gamesome,[52] as if it were his sweetest and most congenial diet. Then he privily[53] took a dose of active poison, imagining that it would not fail to kill either himself or the devil that possessed him, or both together. Another mistake; for if Roderick had not yet been destroyed by his own poisoned heart nor the snake by gnawing it, they had little to fear from arsenic[54] or corrosive sublimate.[55] Indeed, the venomous pest appeared to operate as an antidote against all other poisons. The physicians tried to suffocate the fiend with tobacco smoke. He breathed it as freely as if it were his native atmosphere. Again, they drugged their patient[56] with opium and drenched him with intoxicating liquors, hoping that the snake might thus be reduced to stupor and perhaps be ejected from the stomach. They succeeded in rendering Roderick insensible; but, placing their hands upon his breast, they were inexpressibly horror stricken to feel the monster wriggling, twining, and darting to and fro within his narrow limits, evidently enlivened by the opium or alcohol, and incited to unusual feats of activity. Thenceforth they gave up all attempts at cure or palliation.[57] The doomed sufferer submitted to his fate, resumed his former loathsome affection for the bosom fiend, and spent whole miserable days before a looking-glass, with his mouth wide open, watching, in hope and horror,

---

52) gamesome: playful.

53) privily: secretly.

54) arsenic: 비소.

55) corrosive sublimate: mercuric chloride, 즉 염화 제2 수은.

56) their patient: Roderick.

57) palliation: 일시 억제, 완화.

to catch a glimpse of the snake's head far down within his throat. It is supposed that he succeeded; for the attendants once heard a frenzied shout, and, rushing into the room, found Roderick lifeless upon the floor.

He was kept but little longer under restraint. After minute investigation, the medical directors of the asylum decided that his mental disease did not amount to insanity, nor would warrant his confinement, especially as its influence upon his spirits was unfavorable, and might produce the evil which it was meant to remedy. His eccentricities were doubtless great; he had habitually violated many of the customs and prejudices of society; but the world was not, without surer ground, entitled to treat him as a madman. On this decision of such competent authority Roderick was released, and had returned to his native city the very day before his encounter with George Herkimer.

As soon as possible after learning these particulars the sculptor, together with a sad and tremulous companion, sought Elliston at his own house. It was a large, sombre edifice of wood, with pilasters and a balcony, and was divided from one of the principal streets by a terrace of three elevations, which was ascended by successive flights of stone steps. Some immense old elms almost concealed the front of the mansion. This spacious and once magnificent family residence was built by a grandee[58) of the race early in the past century, at which epoch, land being of small comparative value, the garden and other grounds had formed quite an extensive domain. Although a portion of the ancestral heritage had been alienated, there was still a shadowy

58) grandee: a nobleman of the highest rank in Portugal or Spain. 대공, 고관.

enclosure in the rear of the mansion where a student, or a dreamer, or a man of stricken heart might lie all day upon the grass, amid the solitude of murmuring boughs, and forget that a city had grown up around him.

Into this retirement the sculptor and his companion were ushered by Scipio, the old black servant, whose wrinkled visage grew almost sunny with intelligence and joy as he paid his humble greetings to one of the two visitors.

"Remain in the arbor," whispered the sculptor to the figure that leaned upon his arm. "You will know whether, and when, to make your appearance."

"God will teach me," was the reply. "May He support me too!"

Roderick was reclining on the margin of a fountain which gushed into the fleckered sunshine with the same clear sparkle and the same voice of airy quietude as when trees of primeval growth flung their shadows cross its bosom. How strange is the life of a fountain!—born at every moment, yet of an age coeval with the rocks, and far surpassing the venerable antiquity of a forest.

"You are come! I have expected you," said Elliston, when he became aware of the sculptor's presence.

His manner was very different from that of the preceding day—quiet, courteous, and, as Herkimer thought, watchful both over his guest and himself. This unnatural restraint was almost the only trait that betokened anything amiss. He had just thrown a book upon the grass, where it lay half opened, thus disclosing itself to be a natural history of the serpent tribe, illustrated by lifelike plates. Near it lay that bulky volume, the Ductor Dubitantium of Jeremy Taylor,[59] full of cases of conscience, and in which most men, possessed of a conscience, may find something applicable to their purpose.

"You see," observed Elliston, pointing to the book of serpents, while a smile gleamed upon his lips, "I am making an effort to become better acquainted with my bosom friend; but I find nothing satisfactory in this volume. If I mistake not, he will prove to be sui generis,[60] and akin to no other reptile in creation."

"Whence came this strange calamity?" inquired the sculptor.

"My sable friend Scipio has a story," replied Roderick, "of a snake that had lurked in this fountain — pure and innocent as it looks — ever since it was known to the first settlers. This insinuating personage once crept into the vitals of my great grandfather and dwelt there many years, tormenting the old gentleman beyond mortal endurance. In short it is a family peculiarity. But, to tell you the truth, I have no faith in this idea of the snake's being an heirloom.[61] He is my own snake, and no man's else."

"But what was his origin?" demanded Herkimer.

---

59) *Ductor Dubitantium*: Jeremy Taylor(1613-1667)의 저술인 이 책의 부제는 *The Rule of Conscience in all her generall measures serving as a great instrument for the determination of cases of conscience* 로 4권으로 되어있다. 1660년 런던에서 출간되었으며, 인간의 마음, 양심의 법칙, 선과 악의 판단 등이 주관심사다.

60) sui generis: [Latin] one of a kind, unique.

61) heirloom: a valued family possession handed down from generation to generation.

"Oh, there is poisonous stuff in any man's heart sufficient to generate a brood of serpents," said Elliston with a hollow laugh. "You should have heard my homilies[62] to the good town's-people. Positively, I deem myself fortunate in having bred but a single serpent. You, however, have none in your bosom, and therefore cannot sympathize with the rest of the world. It gnaws me! It gnaws me!"

With this exclamation Roderick lost his self-control and threw himself upon the grass, testifying his agony by intricate writhings, in which Herkimer could not but fancy a resemblance to the motions of a snake. Then, likewise, was heard that frightful hiss, which often ran through the sufferer's speech, and crept between the words and syllables without interrupting their succession.

"This is awful indeed!" exclaimed the sculptor — "an awful infliction, whether it be actual or imaginary. Tell me, Roderick Elliston, is there any remedy for this loathsome evil?"

"Yes, but an impossible one," muttered Roderick, as he lay wallowing with his face in the grass. "Could I for one moment forget myself, the serpent might not abide within me. It is my diseased self-contemplation that has engendered and nourished him."

"Then forget yourself, my husband," said a gentle voice above him; "forget yourself in the idea of another!"

Rosina had emerged from the arbor, and was bending over

62) homily: a sermon, esp. one meant to edify a congregation on a practical matter.

him with the shadow of his anguish reflected in her countenance, yet so mingled with hope and unselfish love that all anguish seemed but an earthly shadow and a dream. She touched Roderick with her hand. A tremor shivered through his frame. At that moment, if report be trustworthy, the sculptor beheld a waving motion through the grass, and heard a tinkling sound, as if something had plunged into the fountain. Be the truth as it might, it is certain that Roderick Elliston sat up like a man renewed, restored to his right mind, and rescued from the fiend which had so miserably overcome him in the battle-field of his own breast.

"Rosina!" cried he, in broken and passionate tones, but with nothing of the wild wail that had haunted his voice so long, "forgive! forgive!"

Her happy tears bedewed his face.

"The punishment has been severe," observed the sculptor. "Even Justice might now forgive; how much more a woman's tenderness! Roderick Elliston, whether the serpent was a physical reptile, or whether the morbidness of your nature suggested that symbol to your fancy, the moral of the story is not the less true and strong. A tremendous Egotism, manifesting itself in your case in the form of jealousy, is as fearful a fiend as ever stole into the human heart. Can a breast, where it has dwelt so long, be purified?"

"Oh yes," said Rosina with a heavenly smile. "The serpent was but a dark fantasy, and what it typified was as shadowy as itself. The past, dismal as it seems, shall fling no gloom upon the future. To give it its due importance we must think of it but as an anecdote in our Eternity."

The Birthmark

In the latter part of the last century there lived a man of science, an eminent proficient[1)] in every branch of natural philosophy, who not long before our story opens[2)] had made experience of a spiritual affinity more attractive than any chemical one.[3)] He had left his laboratory to the care of an assistant, cleared his fine countenance from the furnace smoke, washed the stain of acids from his fingers, and persuaded a beautiful woman to become his wife. In those days when the comparatively recent discovery of electricity and other kindred mysteries of Nature[4)] seemed to open paths into the region of miracle, it was not unusual for the love of science to rival the love of woman in its depth and absorbing energy. The higher intellect, the imagination, the spirit, and even the heart might all find their congenial aliment in pursuits which, as some of their ardent votaries believed, would ascend from one step of powerful intelligence to another, until the philosopher should lay his hand on the secret of creative force and perhaps make new worlds for himself. We know not whether Aylmer possessed this degree of faith in man's ultimate control over Nature. He had

1) proficient: 大家
2) not long before our story opens를 삽입구로 생각할 것. 즉 "who … had made로 연결.
3) a spiritual affinity more attractive than any chemical one: 과학적 관계보다 더 멋진 정신적 인척관계, 즉 여기서는 결혼을 의미한다.
4) electricity and other kindred mysteries of Nature: 전기나 기타 유사한 자연의 비밀(의 발견)으로 인해 기적의 영역이 감소하고 있음을 말하고 있음.

devoted himself, however, too unreservedly to scientific studies ever to be weaned from them by any second passion.[5)] His love for his young wife might prove the stronger of the two; but it could only be[6)] by intertwining itself with his love of science, and uniting the strength of the latter to his own.

Such a union accordingly took place, and was attended with truly remarkable consequences and a deeply impressive moral. One day, very soon after their marriage, Aylmer sat gazing at his wife with a trouble in his countenance that grew stronger until he spoke.

"Georgiana," said he, "has it never occurred to you that the mark upon your cheek might be removed?"

"No, indeed," said she, smiling; but perceiving the seriousness of his manner, she blushed deeply. "To tell you the truth it has been so often called a charm that I was simple enough to imagine it might be so."

"Ah, upon another face perhaps it might," replied her husband; "but never on yours. No, dearest Georgiana, you came so nearly perfect from the hand of Nature that this slightest possible defect, which we hesitate whether to term a defect or a beauty, shocks me,[7)] as being the visible mark of earthly imperfection."

"Shocks you, my husband!" cried Georgiana, deeply hurt; at

5) 과학탐구에 푹 빠져서 어떤 제 2의 열정으로도 그것으로부터 떼어놓을 수 없음을 말함.

6) be (the stronger of the two).

7) shocks me의 주어는 this slightest possible defect.

first reddening with momentary anger, but then bursting into tears. "Then why did you take me from my mother's side? You cannot love what shocks you!"

To explain this conversation it must be mentioned that in the centre of Georgiana's left cheek there was a singular mark, deeply interwoven, as it were, with the texture and substance of her face. In the usual state of her complexion — a healthy though delicate bloom — the mark wore a tint of deeper crimson, which imperfectly defined its shape amid the surrounding rosiness. When she blushed it gradually became more indistinct, and finally vanished amid the triumphant rush of blood that bathed the whole cheek with its brilliant glow. But if any shifting motion caused her to turn pale there was the mark again, a crimson stain upon the snow, in what Aylmer sometimes deemed an almost fearful distinctness. Its shape bore not a little similarity to the human hand, though of the smallest pygmy size. Georgiana's lovers were wont to say that some fairy at her birth hour had laid her tiny hand upon the infant's cheek, and left this impress there in token of the magic endowments that were to give her such sway over all hearts. Many a desperate swain[8) would have risked life for the privilege of pressing his lips to the mysterious hand. It must not be concealed, however, that the impression wrought by this fairy sign manual varied exceedingly, according to the difference of temperament in the beholders. Some fastidious persons — but they were exclusively of her own sex — affirmed that the bloody hand, as they chose to call it, quite destroyed the effect of Georgiana's beauty, and rendered her countenance even hideous. But it would be as reasonable to

8) a swain: a male suitor.

say that one of those small blue stains which sometimes occur in the purest statuary marble would convert the Eve of Powers to a monster. Masculine observers, if the birthmark did not heighten their admiration, contented themselves with wishing it away, that the world might possess one living specimen of ideal loveliness without the semblance of a flaw. After his marriage, — for he thought little or nothing of the matter before, — Aylmer discovered that this was the case with himself.

Had she been less beautiful, — if Envy's self could have found aught else to sneer at, — he might have felt his affection heightened by the prettiness of this mimic hand, now vaguely portrayed, now lost, now stealing forth again and glimmering to and fro with every pulse of emotion that throbbed within her heart;[9)] but seeing her otherwise so perfect, he found this one defect grow more and more intolerable with every moment of their united lives. It was the fatal flaw of humanity which Nature, in one shape or another, stamps ineffaceably on all her productions, either to imply that they are temporary and finite, or that their perfection must be wrought by toil and pain. The crimson hand expressed the ineludible[10)] gripe in which mortality clutches the highest and purest of earthly mould,[11)] degrading them[12)] into kindred with the lowest, and even with the very brutes, like whom their visible frames return to dust. In this manner, selecting it as the symbol of his wife's liability to sin, sorrow, decay, and death, Aylmer's sombre imagination was not

---

9) now vaguely portrayed, now lost, now stealing forth again ~ : 조지아나의 감정 기복에 따라 희미하다가, 사라졌다가, 또 슬그머니 나타나는 현상을 그리고 있음.

10) ineludible: not eludible; inescapable.

11) the highest and purest of earthly mould: 至高, 至純 즉 지상최고의 미인들.

12) them: 지상최고의 미인들.

long in rendering the birthmark a frightful object, causing him more trouble and horror than ever Georgiana's beauty, whether of soul or sense, had given him delight.

At all the seasons which should have been their happiest, he invariably and without intending it, nay, in spite of a purpose to the contrary, reverted to this one disastrous topic. Trifling as it at first appeared, it so connected itself with innumerable trains of thought and modes of feeling that it became the central point of all. With the morning twilight Aylmer opened his eyes upon his wife's face and recognized the symbol of imperfection; and when they sat together at the evening hearth his eyes wandered stealthily to her cheek, and beheld, flickering with the blaze of the wood fire, the spectral hand that wrote mortality where he would fain[13)] have worshipped. Georgiana soon learned to shudder at his gaze. It needed but a glance with the peculiar expression that his face often wore to change the roses of her cheek into a deathlike paleness, amid which the crimson hand was brought strongly out, like a bass-relief of ruby on the whitest marble.

Late one night when the lights were growing dim, so as hardly to[14)] betray the stain on the poor wife's cheek, she herself, for the first time, voluntarily took up the subject.

"Do you remember, my dear Aylmer," said she, with a feeble attempt at a smile, "have you any recollection of a dream last night about this odious hand?"

13) fain: preferably, happily.

14) so as hardly to: so as to의 부정.

"None! none whatever!" replied Aylmer, starting; but then he added, in a dry, cold tone, affected for the sake of concealing the real depth of his emotion, "I might well dream of it; for before I fell asleep it had taken a pretty firm hold of my fancy."

"And you did dream of it?" continued Georgiana, hastily; for she dreaded lest a gush of tears should interrupt what she had to say. "A terrible dream! I wonder that you can forget it. Is it possible to forget this one expression?—'It is in her heart now; we must have it out!' Reflect, my husband; for by all means I would have you recall that dream."

The mind is in a sad state when Sleep, the all-involving, cannot confine her spectres within the dim region of her sway, but suffers them to break forth, affrighting this actual life with secrets that perchance belong to a deeper one. Aylmer now remembered his dream. He had fancied himself with his servant Aminadab, attempting an operation for the removal of the birthmark; but the deeper went the knife, the deeper sank the hand, until at length its tiny grasp appeared to have caught hold of Georgiana's heart; whence, however, her husband was inexorably resolved to cut or wrench it away.

When the dream had shaped itself perfectly in his memory, Aylmer sat in his wife's presence with a guilty feeling. Truth often finds its way to the mind close[15] muffled in robes of sleep, and then speaks with uncompromising directness of matters in regard to which we practise an unconscious self-deception during our waking moments.[16] Until now he had not been aware of the

15) close: closely

16) 깨어있을 때는 무의식적으로 자신을 속이듯 하던 것도 수면상태에서는 가차 없이

tyrannizing influence acquired by one idea over his mind, and of the lengths which he might find in his heart to go for the sake of giving himself peace.

"Aylmer," resumed Georgiana, solemnly, "I know not what may be the cost to both of us to rid me of this fatal birthmark. Perhaps its removal may cause cureless deformity; or it may be the stain goes[17)] as deep as life itself. Again: do we know that there is a possibility, on any terms, of unclasping the firm gripe of this little hand which was laid upon me before I came into the world?"

"Dearest Georgiana, I have spent much thought upon the subject," hastily interrupted Aylmer. "I am convinced of the perfect practicability of its removal."

"If there be the remotest possibility of it," continued Georgiana, "let the attempt be made at whatever risk. Danger is nothing to me; for life, while this hateful mark makes me the object of your horror and disgust,—life is a burden which I would fling down with joy. Either remove this dreadful hand, or take my wretched life! You have deep science. All the world bears witness of it. You have achieved great wonders. Cannot you remove this little, little mark, which I cover with the tips of two small fingers? Is this beyond your power, for the sake of your own peace, and to save your poor wife from madness?"

"Noblest, dearest, tenderest wife," cried Aylmer, rapturously,

---

직접적으로 진실을 드러낸다는 것이 저자의 생각이다.

17) the stain goes: the stain [that] goes로 생각할 것.

"doubt not my power. I have already given this matter the deepest thought—thought which might almost have enlightened me to create a being less perfect than yourself. Georgiana, you have led me deeper than ever into the heart of science. I feel myself fully competent to render this dear cheek as faultless as its fellow;[18] and then, most beloved,[19] what will be my triumph when I shall have corrected what Nature left imperfect in her fairest work! Even Pygmalion, when his sculptured woman assumed life,[20] felt not greater ecstasy than mine will be."

"It is resolved, then," said Georgiana, faintly smiling. "And, Aylmer, spare me not, though you should find the birthmark take refuge in my heart at last."

Her husband tenderly kissed her cheek—her right cheek—not that which bore the impress of the crimson hand.

The next day Aylmer apprised his wife of a plan that he had formed whereby he might have opportunity for the intense thought and constant watchfulness which the proposed operation would require; while Georgiana, likewise, would enjoy the perfect repose essential to its success. They were to seclude themselves in the extensive apartments occupied by Aylmer as a laboratory, and where, during his toilsome youth, he had made discoveries in the elemental powers of Nature that had roused the admiration of all the learned societies in Europe. Seated

18) its fellow: the other cheek.

19) most beloved: my most beloved.

20) George Bernard Shaw의 동명 작품으로 더욱 유명해진 Pygmalion 신화를 비유하고 있음. Pygmalion이 조각한 여인상이 생명을 지니게 되어 가진 기쁨보다 Georgiana의 완벽해진 아름다움에서 오는 자신의 기쁨이 더 크리라는 것.

calmly in this laboratory, the pale philosopher[21] had investigated the secrets of the highest cloud region and of the profoundest mines; he had satisfied himself of the causes that kindled and kept alive the fires of the volcano; and had explained the mystery of fountains, and how it is that they gush forth, some so bright and pure, and others with such rich medicinal virtues, from the dark bosom of the earth. Here, too, at an earlier period, he had studied the wonders of the human frame, and attempted to fathom the very process by which Nature assimilates all her precious influences from earth and air, and from the spiritual world, to create and foster man, her masterpiece. The latter pursuit, however, Aylmer had long laid aside in unwilling recognition of the truth — against which all seekers sooner or later stumble — that our great creative Mother, while she amuses us with apparently working in the broadest sunshine, is yet severely careful to keep her own secrets, and, in spite of her pretended openness, shows us nothing but results. She permits us, indeed, to mar, but seldom to mend, and, like a jealous patentee, on no account to make.[22] Now, however, Aylmer resumed these half-forgotten investigations; not, of course, with such hopes or wishes as first[23] suggested them[24]; but because they involved much physiological truth and lay in the path of his proposed scheme for the treatment of Georgiana.

As he led her over the threshold of the laboratory, Georgiana

21) the pale philosopher: 즉 Aylmer. "pale"은 Aylmer의 intellect가 heart를 압도하여 heart가 질식되고 있음을 보여준다.

22) to mar, to mend, to make 등 두음의 효과를 유의할 것. make(창조)는 절대로 인간에게 허락되지 않았다.

23) first(investigations)로 볼 것. 초기의 연구들.

24) them: hopes or wishes.

was cold and tremulous. Aylmer looked cheerfully into her face, with intent to reassure her, but was so startled with the intense glow of the birthmark upon the whiteness of her cheek that he could not restrain a strong convulsive shudder. His wife fainted.

"Aminadab! Aminadab!" shouted Aylmer, stamping violently on the floor.

Forthwith there issued from an inner apartment a man of low stature, but bulky frame, with shaggy hair hanging about his visage, which was grimed with the vapors of the furnace. This personage had been Aylmer's underworker during his whole scientific career, and was admirably fitted for that office by his great mechanical readiness, and the skill with which, while incapable of comprehending a single principle, he executed all the details of his master's experiments. With his vast strength, his shaggy hair, his smoky aspect, and the indescribable earthiness that incrusted him, he seemed to represent man's physical nature; while Aylmer's slender figure, and pale, intellectual face, were no less apt a type of the spiritual element.[25)]

"Throw open the door of the boudoir, Aminadab," said Aylmer, "and burn a pastil.[26)]"

"Yes, master," answered Aminadab, looking intently at the lifeless form of Georgiana; and then he muttered to himself, "If she were my wife, I'd never part with that birthmark."

When Georgiana recovered consciousness she found herself

---

25) 여기서 연구조수 Aminadab는 육체를, Aylmer는 정신을 나타낸다고 본다.

26) pastil(le): an aromatic tablet burned to fumigate or deodorize the air.

breathing an atmosphere of penetrating fragrance, the gentle potency of which had recalled her from her deathlike faintness. The scene around her looked like enchantment. Aylmer had converted those smoky, dingy, sombre rooms, where he had spent his brightest years in recondite pursuits, into a series of beautiful apartments not unfit to be the secluded abode of a lovely woman. The walls were hung with gorgeous curtains, which imparted the combination of grandeur and grace that no other species of adornment can achieve; and as they fell from the ceiling to the floor, their rich and ponderous folds, concealing all angles and straight lines, appeared to shut in the scene from infinite space. For aught Georgiana knew, it might be a pavilion among the clouds. And Aylmer, excluding the sunshine, which would have interfered with his chemical processes, had supplied its place with perfumed lamps, emitting flames of various hue, but all uniting in a soft, impurpled[27)] radiance. He now knelt by his wife's side, watching her earnestly, but without alarm; for he was confident in his science, and felt that he could draw a magic circle round her within which no evil might intrude.

"Where am I? Ah, I remember," said Georgiana, faintly; and she placed her hand over her cheek to hide the terrible mark from her husband's eyes.

"Fear not, dearest!" exclaimed he. "Do not shrink from me! Believe me, Georgiana, I even rejoice in this single imperfection, since it will be such a rapture to remove it."

"Oh, spare me!" sadly replied his wife. "Pray do not look at it

---

27) Impurple: To color or tinge with purple; to make red or reddish; to purple.

again. I never can forget that convulsive shudder."

In order to soothe Georgiana, and, as it were, to release her mind from the burden of actual things, Aylmer now put in practice some of the light and playful secrets which science had taught him among its profounder lore. Airy figures, absolutely bodiless ideas, and forms of unsubstantial beauty came and danced before her, imprinting their momentary footsteps on beams of light. Though she had some indistinct idea of the method of these optical phenomena, still the illusion was almost perfect enough to warrant the belief that her husband possessed sway over the spiritual world. Then again, when she felt a wish to look forth from her seclusion, immediately, as if her thoughts were answered, the procession of external existence flitted across a screen. The scenery and the figures of actual life were perfectly represented, but with that bewitching, yet indescribable difference which always makes a picture, an image, or a shadow so much more attractive than the original. When wearied of this, Aylmer bade her cast her eyes upon a vessel containing a quantity of earth. She did so, with little interest at first; but was soon startled to perceive the germ of a plant shooting upward from the soil. Then came the slender stalk; the leaves gradually unfolded themselves; and amid them was a perfect and lovely flower.

"It is magical!" cried Georgiana. "I dare not touch it."

"Nay, pluck it," answered Aylmer,—"pluck it, and inhale its brief perfume while you may. The flower will wither in a few moments and leave nothing save its brown seed vessels; but thence may be perpetuated a race as ephemeral as itself."

But Georgiana had no sooner touched the flower than the whole plant suffered a blight, its leaves turning coal-black as if by the agency of fire.

"There was too powerful a stimulus," said Aylmer, thoughtfully.

To make up for this abortive experiment, he proposed to take her portrait by a scientific process of his own invention. It was to be effected by rays of light striking upon a polished plate of metal. Georgiana assented; but, on looking at the result, was affrighted to find the features of the portrait blurred and indefinable; while the minute figure of a hand appeared where the cheek should have been. Aylmer snatched the metallic plate and threw it into a jar of corrosive acid.

Soon, however, he forgot these mortifying failures. In the intervals of study and chemical experiment he came to her flushed and exhausted, but seemed invigorated by her presence, and spoke in glowing language of the resources of his art. He gave a history of the long dynasty of the alchemists, who spent so many ages in quest of the universal solvent by which the golden principle might be elicited from all things vile and base. Aylmer appeared to believe that, by the plainest scientific logic, it was altogether within the limits of possibility to discover this long-sought medium; "but," he added, "a philosopher who should go deep enough to acquire the power would attain too lofty a wisdom to stoop to the exercise of it." Not less singular were his opinions in regard to the elixir vitae.28) He more than intimated

28) elixir: a substance believed to cure all illse; lixir vitae: elixir of life, a hypothetical

that it was at his option to concoct a liquid that should prolong life for years, perhaps interminably; but that it would produce a discord in Nature which all the world, and chiefly the quaffer[29] of the immortal nostrum[30]would find cause to curse.

"Aylmer, are you in earnest?" asked Georgiana, looking at him with amazement and fear. "It is terrible to possess such power, or even to dream of possessing it."

"Oh, do not tremble, my love," said her husband. "I would not wrong either you or myself by working such inharmonious effects upon our lives; but I would have you consider how trifling, in comparison, is the skill requisite[31] to remove this little hand."

At the mention of the birthmark, Georgiana, as usual, shrank as if a redhot iron had touched her cheek.

Again Aylmer applied himself to his labors. She could hear his voice in the distant furnace room giving directions to Aminadab, whose harsh, uncouth, misshapen tones were audible in response, more like the grunt or growl of a brute than human speech. After hours of absence, Aylmer reappeared and proposed that she should now examine his cabinet of chemical products and natural treasures of the earth. Among the former he showed her a small vial, in which, he remarked, was contained a gentle yet most powerful fragrance, capable of impregnating all the breezes that blow across a kingdom. They were of inestimable value, the

---

substance believed to maintain life indefinitely.

29) to quaff: to drink heartily.

30) nostrum: a medicine, esp. a quack remedy.

31) requisite: required.

contents of that little vial; and, as he said so, he threw some of the perfume into the air and filled the room with piercing and invigorating delight.

"And what is this?" asked Georgiana, pointing to a small crystal globe containing a gold-colored liquid. "It is so beautiful to the eye that I could imagine it the elixir of life."

"In one sense it is," replied Aylmer; "or, rather, the elixir of immortality. It is the most precious poison that ever was concocted in this world. By its aid I could apportion[32)] the lifetime of any mortal at whom you might point your finger. The strength of the dose would determine whether he were to linger out years, or drop dead in the midst of a breath. No king on his guarded throne could keep his life if I, in my private station, should deem that the welfare of millions justified me in depriving him of it."

"Why do you keep such a terrific drug?" inquired Georgiana in horror.

"Do not mistrust me, dearest," said her husband, smiling; "its virtuous potency is yet greater than its harmful one. But see! here is a powerful cosmetic. With a few drops of this in a vase of water, freckles may be washed away as easily as the hands are cleansed. A stronger infusion would take the blood out of the cheek, and leave the rosiest beauty a pale ghost."

"Is it with this lotion that you intend to bathe my cheek?"

---

32) apportion: to divide or distribute according to a plan.

asked Georgiana, anxiously.

"Oh, no," hastily replied her husband; "this is merely superficial. Your case demands a remedy that shall go deeper."

In his interviews with Georgiana, Aylmer generally made minute inquiries as to her sensations and whether the confinement of the rooms and the temperature of the atmosphere agreed with her. These questions had such a particular drift that Georgiana began to conjecture that she was already subjected to certain physical influences, either breathed in with the fragrant air or taken with her food. She fancied likewise, but it might be altogether fancy, that there was a stirring up of her system—a strange, indefinite sensation creeping through her veins, and tingling, half painfully, half pleasurably, at her heart. Still, whenever she dared to look into the mirror, there she beheld herself pale as a white rose and with the crimson birthmark stamped upon her cheek. Not even Aylmer now hated it so much as she.

To dispel the tedium of the hours which her husband found it necessary to devote to the processes of combination and analysis, Georgiana turned over the volumes of his scientific library. In many dark old tomes she met with chapters full of romance and poetry. They were the works of philosophers of the middle ages, such as Albertus Magnus,[33] Cornelius Agrippa,[34] Paracelsus,[35]

---

33) Albertus Magnus (1206?-1280): 방대한 지식과 천재성으로 "Albert the Great"로 알려진 과학자, 철학자, 신학자.

34) Heinrich Cornelius Agrippa (1486-1535). 독일의 철학자, 신학자.

35) Paracelsus (1493?-1541): 독일계 스위스의 의사, 연금술사. 의학에 유용한 화학의 역할을 밝힘.

and the famous friar who created the prophetic Brazen Head.[36)] All these antique naturalists stood in advance of their centuries, yet were imbued with some of their credulity, and therefore were believed, and perhaps imagined themselves to have acquired from the investigation of Nature a power above Nature, and from physics a sway over the spiritual world. Hardly less curious and imaginative were the early volumes of the Transactions of the Royal Society,[37)] in which the members, knowing little of the limits of natural possibility, were continually recording wonders or proposing methods whereby wonders might be wrought.

But to Georgiana the most engrossing volume was a large folio from her husband's own hand, in which he had recorded every experiment of his scientific career, its original aim, the methods adopted for its development, and its final success or failure, with the circumstances to which either event was attributable. The book, in truth, was both the history and emblem of his ardent, ambitious, imaginative, yet practical and laborious life. He handled physical details as if there were nothing beyond them; yet spiritualized them all, and redeemed himself from materialism by his strong and eager aspiration towards the infinite. In his grasp the veriest clod of earth assumed a soul. Georgiana, as she read, reverenced Aylmer and loved him more profoundly than ever, but with a less entire dependence on his

36) the prophetic Brazen Head: 무슨 질문이든지 답하는 능력을 가진 머리. Albert the Great와 동시대인인 Roger Bacon(1214/1220-1292) 프란체스코회 수도사가 만들었다고 전해짐.

37) Transactions of the Royal Society: Sir Francis Bacon의 원리를 구현하기 위해 1660년에 설립된 The Royal Society의 회보. 1665년 3월 창간호 발간. 초기 회보에 뉴톤이 17개의 논문을 게재하였으며, Charles Darwin 등을 비롯한 많은 과학자들의 연구 결과가 발표되었다.

judgment than heretofore. Much as he had accomplished, she could not but observe that his most splendid successes were almost invariably failures, if compared with the ideal at which he aimed. His brightest diamonds were the merest pebbles, and felt to be so by himself, in comparison with the inestimable gems which lay hidden beyond his reach. The volume, rich with achievements that had won renown for its author, was yet as melancholy a record as ever mortal hand had penned. It was the sad confession and continual exemplification of the shortcomings of the composite man, the spirit burdened with clay and working in matter, and of the despair that assails[38)] the higher nature at finding itself so miserably thwarted by the earthly part. Perhaps every man of genius in whatever sphere might recognize the image of his own experience in Aylmer's journal.

So deeply did these reflections affect Georgiana that she laid her face upon the open volume and burst into tears. In this situation she was found by her husband.

"It is dangerous to read in a sorcerer's books," said he with a smile, though his countenance was uneasy and displeased. "Georgiana, there are pages in that volume which I can scarcely glance over and keep my senses. Take heed lest it prove as detrimental to you."

"It has made me worship you more than ever," said she.

"Ah, wait for this one success," rejoined he, "then worship me if you will. I shall deem myself hardly unworthy of it. But

---

38) assail: to attack with or as if with violent blows.

come, I have sought you for the luxury of your voice. Sing to me, dearest."

So she poured out the liquid music of her voice to quench the thirst of his spirit. He then took his leave with a boyish exuberance of gayety, assuring her that her seclusion would endure but a little longer, and that the result was already certain. Scarcely had he departed when Georgiana felt irresistibly impelled to follow him. She had forgotten to inform Aylmer of a symptom which for two or three hours past had begun to excite her attention. It was a sensation in the fatal birthmark, not painful, but which induced a restlessness throughout her system. Hastening after her husband, she intruded for the first time into the laboratory.

The first thing that struck her eye was the furnace, that hot and feverish worker, with the intense glow of its fire, which by the quantities of soot clustered above it seemed to have been burning for ages. There was a distilling apparatus in full operation. Around the room were retorts,[39)] tubes, cylinders, crucibles, and other apparatus of chemical research. An electrical machine stood ready for immediate use. The atmosphere felt oppressively close, and was tainted with gaseous odors which had been tormented forth by the processes of science. The severe and homely simplicity of the apartment, with its naked walls and brick pavement, looked strange, accustomed as Georgiana had become[40)] to the fantastic elegance of her boudoir. But what

39) retort: 증류기. a closed laboratory vessel with an outlet tube, used for distillation, sublimation, or decomposition by heat.

40) accustomed as Georgiana had become: 도치된 문장. = as Georgiana had become accustomed (to).

chiefly, indeed almost solely, drew her attention, was the aspect of Aylmer himself.

He was pale as death, anxious and absorbed, and hung over the furnace as if it depended upon his utmost watchfulness whether the liquid which it was distilling should be the draught of immortal happiness or misery. How different from the sanguine and joyous mien that he had assumed for Georgiana's encouragement!

"Carefully now, Aminadab; carefully, thou human machine; carefully, thou man of clay!" muttered Aylmer, more to himself than his assistant. "Now, if there be a thought too much or too little, it is all over."

"Ho! ho!" mumbled Aminadab. "Look, master! look!"

Aylmer raised his eyes hastily, and at first reddened, then grew paler than ever, on beholding Georgiana. He rushed towards her and seized her arm with a gripe that left the print of his fingers upon it.

"Why do you come hither? Have you no trust in your husband?" cried he, impetuously. "Would you throw the blight of that fatal birthmark over my labors? It is not well done. Go, prying woman, go!"

"Nay, Aylmer," said Georgiana with the firmness of which she possessed no stinted[41] endowment, "it is not you that have a

41) stinted: limited.

right to complain. You mistrust your wife; you have concealed the anxiety with which you watch the development of this experiment. Think not so unworthily of me, my husband. Tell me all the risk we run, and fear not that I shall shrink; for my share in it is far less than your own."

"No, no, Georgiana!" said Aylmer, impatiently; "it must not be."

"I submit," replied she calmly. "And, Aylmer, I shall quaff whatever draught you bring me; but it will be on the same principle that would induce me to take a dose of poison if offered by your hand."

"My noble wife," said Aylmer, deeply moved, "I knew not the height and depth of your nature until now. Nothing shall be concealed. Know, then, that this crimson hand, superficial as it seems, has clutched its grasp into your being with a strength of which I had no previous conception. I have already administered agents powerful enough to do aught except to change your entire physical system. Only one thing remains to be tried. If that fail us we are ruined."

"Why did you hesitate to tell me this?" asked she.

"Because, Georgiana," said Aylmer, in a low voice, "there is danger."

"Danger? There is but one danger—that this horrible stigma shall be left upon my cheek!" cried Georgiana. "Remove it, remove it, whatever be the cost, or we shall both go mad!"

"Heaven knows your words are too true," said Aylmer, sadly. "And now, dearest, return to your boudoir. In a little while all will be tested."

He conducted her back and took leave of her with a solemn tenderness which spoke far more than his words how much was now at stake. After his departure Georgiana became rapt in musings. She considered the character of Aylmer, and did it completer justice than at any previous moment. Her heart exulted, while it trembled, at his honorable love — so pure and lofty that it would accept nothing less than perfection nor miserably make itself contented with an earthlier nature than he had dreamed of. She felt how much more precious was such a sentiment than that meaner kind which would have borne with the imperfection for her sake, and have been guilty of treason to holy love by degrading its perfect idea to the level of the actual; and with her whole spirit she prayed that, for a single moment, she might satisfy his highest and deepest conception. Longer than one moment she well knew it could not be; for his spirit was ever on the march, ever ascending, and each instant required something that was beyond the scope of the instant before.

The sound of her husband's footsteps aroused her. He bore a crystal goblet containing a liquor colorless as water, but bright enough to be the draught of immortality. Aylmer was pale; but it seemed rather the consequence of a highly-wrought state of mind and tension of spirit than of fear or doubt.

"The concoction of the draught has been perfect," said he, in answer to Georgiana's look. "Unless all my science have deceived me, it cannot fail."

"Save on your account, my dearest Aylmer," observed his wife, "I might wish to put off this birthmark of mortality by relinquishing mortality itself in preference to any other mode. Life is but a sad possession to those who have attained precisely the degree of moral advancement at which I stand. Were I weaker and blinder it might be happiness. Were I stronger, it might be endured hopefully. But, being what I find myself, methinks[42] I am of all mortals the most fit to die."

"You are fit for heaven without tasting death!" replied her husband "But why do we speak of dying? The draught cannot fail. Behold its effect upon this plant."

On the window seat there stood a geranium diseased with yellow blotches, which had overspread all its leaves. Aylmer poured a small quantity of the liquid upon the soil in which it grew. In a little time, when the roots of the plant had taken up the moisture, the unsightly blotches began to be extinguished in a living verdure.

"There needed no proof," said Georgiana, quietly. "Give me the goblet I joyfully stake all upon your word."

"Drink, then, thou lofty creature!" exclaimed Aylmer, with fervid admiration. "There is no taint of imperfection on thy spirit. Thy sensible frame, too, shall soon be all perfect."

She quaffed the liquid and returned the goblet to his hand.

42) methinks: (고어) =it seems to me.

"It is grateful," said she with a placid smile. "Methinks it is like water from a heavenly fountain; for it contains I know not what of unobtrusive fragrance and deliciousness. It allays[43)] a feverish thirst that had parched me for many days. Now, dearest, let me sleep. My earthly senses are closing over my spirit like the leaves around the heart of a rose at sunset."

She spoke the last words with a gentle reluctance, as if it required almost more energy than she could command to pronounce the faint and lingering syllables. Scarcely had they loitered through her lips ere she was lost in slumber. Aylmer sat by her side, watching her aspect with the emotions proper to a man the whole value of whose existence was involved in the process now to be tested. Mingled with this mood, however, was the philosophic investigation characteristic of the man of science. Not the minutest symptom escaped him. A heightened flush of the cheek, a slight irregularity of breath, a quiver of the eyelid, a hardly perceptible tremor through the frame, — such were the details which, as the moments passed, he wrote down in his folio volume. Intense thought had set its stamp upon every previous page of that volume, but the thoughts of years were all concentrated upon the last.

While thus employed, he failed not to gaze often at the fatal hand, and not without a shudder. Yet once, by a strange and unaccountable impulse he pressed it with his lips. His spirit recoiled, however, in the very act, and Georgiana, out of the midst of her deep sleep, moved uneasily and murmured as if in remonstrance. Again Aylmer resumed his watch. Nor was

43) allay: to relieve or lessen.

it without avail. The crimson hand, which at first had been strongly visible upon the marble paleness of Georgiana's cheek, now grew more faintly outlined. She remained not less pale than ever; but the birthmark with every breath that came and went, lost somewhat of its former distinctness. Its presence had been awful; its departure was more awful still. Watch the stain of the rainbow fading out the sky, and you will know how that mysterious symbol passed away.

"By Heaven! it is well-nigh gone!" said Aylmer to himself, in almost irrepressible ecstasy. "I can scarcely trace it now. Success! success! And now it is like the faintest rose color. The lightest flush of blood across her cheek would overcome it. But she is so pale!"

He drew aside the window curtain and suffered the light of natural day to fall into the room and rest upon her cheek. At the same time he heard a gross, hoarse chuckle, which he had long known as his servant Aminadab's expression of delight.

"Ah, clod! ah, earthly mass!" cried Aylmer, laughing in a sort of frenzy, "you have served me well! Matter and spirit — earth and heaven — have both done their part in this! Laugh, thing of the senses! You have earned the right to laugh."

These exclamations broke Georgiana's sleep. She slowly unclosed her eyes and gazed into the mirror which her husband had arranged for that purpose. A faint smile flitted over her lips when she recognized how barely perceptible was now that crimson hand which had once blazed forth with such disastrous brilliancy as to scare away all their happiness. But then her eyes sought Aylmer's face with a trouble and anxiety that he could by no means account for.[44)]

"My poor Aylmer!" murmured she.

"Poor? Nay, richest, happiest, most favored!" exclaimed he. "My peerless bride, it is successful! You are perfect!"

"My poor Aylmer," she repeated, with a more than human tenderness, "you have aimed loftily; you have done nobly. Do not repent that with so high and pure a feeling, you have rejected the best the earth could offer. Aylmer, dearest Aylmer, I am dying!"

Alas! it was too true! The fatal hand had grappled with the mystery of life, and was the bond by which an angelic spirit kept itself in union with a mortal frame. As the last crimson tint of the birthmark — that sole token of human imperfection — faded from her cheek, the parting breath of the now perfect woman passed into the atmosphere, and her soul, lingering a moment near her husband, took its heavenward flight. Then a hoarse, chuckling laugh was heard again! Thus ever does the gross fatality of earth exult in its invariable triumph over the immortal essence which, in this dim sphere of half development, demands the completeness of a higher state. Yet, had Aylmer reached a profounder wisdom, he need not thus have flung away the happiness which would have woven his mortal life of the selfsame texture with the celestial. The momentary circumstance

44) with a trouble and anxiety that he could by no means account for: 깨어난 조지아나의 얼굴에 가득한 근심과 걱정을 에일머는 알 길이 없다.

was too strong for him; he failed to look beyond the shadowy scope of time, and, living once for all in eternity, to find the perfect future in the present.

The Artist of the Beautiful

AN elderly man, with his pretty daughter on his arm, was passing along the street, and emerged from the gloom of the cloudy evening into the light that fell across the pavement from the window of a small shop. It was a projecting window;[1] and on the inside were suspended a variety of watches, pinchbeck,[2] silver, and one or two of gold, all with their faces turned from the streets, as if churlishly[3] disinclined to inform the wayfarers what o'clock[4] it was. Seated within the shop, sidelong to the window with his pale face bent earnestly over some delicate piece of mechanism on which was thrown the concentrated lustre of a shade lamp, appeared a young man.

"What can Owen Warland be about?" muttered old Peter Hovenden himself a retired watchmaker, and the former master of this same young man whose occupation he was now wondering at. "What can the fellow be about? These six months past I have never come by his shop without seeing him just as steadily at work as now. It would be a flight beyond his usual foolery[5] to

---

1) a projecting window: 밖으로 내민 창. 퇴창(退窓): a window projecting from the outer wall of a building and forming a recess within. a bay window.

2) pinchbeck: 발명가인 Christopher Pinchbeck(1670?-1732)의 이름을 딴 아연과 동의 합금.

3) churlishly: 심술쟁이(churl)같이, 야비하게.

4) o'clock: time.

5) foolery: 어리석은 짓.

seek for the perpetual motion; and yet I know enough of my old business to be certain that what he is now so busy with[6] is no part of the machinery of a watch."

"Perhaps, father," said Annie, without showing much interest in the question, "Owen is inventing a new kind of timekeeper. I am sure he has ingenuity enough."

"Poh, child![7] He has not the sort of ingenuity to invent anything better than a Dutch toy," answered her father, who had formerly been put to much vexation[8] by Owen Warland's irregular genius. "A plague on[9] such ingenuity! All the effect that ever I knew of it[10] was to spoil the accuracy of some of the best watches in my shop. He would turn the sun out of its orbit and derange the whole course of time, if, as I said before, his ingenuity could grasp anything bigger than a child's toy!"

"Hush, father! He hears you!" whispered Annie, pressing the old man's arm. "His ears are as delicate as his feelings; and you know how easily disturbed they are. Do let us move on."

So Peter Hovenden and his daughter Annie plodded on without further conversation, until in a by-street of the town they found themselves passing the open door of a blacksmith's shop. Within was seen the forge,[11] now blazing up and illuminating

---

6) what he is now so busy with: 저 친구가 골똘하고 있는 것(이).

7) Poh, child!: 츳, 애야.

8) had formerly been put to much vexation: 전에 속 깨나 썩었던.

9) A plague on ~ : 제기랄! 빌어먹을!

10) it: Warland's ingenuity.

11) Within was seen the forge: 도치된 문장. 안쪽에 대장간이 보였다.

the high and dusky roof, and now confining its lustre to a narrow precinct of the coal-strewn floor, according as the breath of the bellows was puffed forth or again inhaled into its vast leathern lungs. In the intervals of brightness it was easy to distinguish objects in remote corners of the shop and the horseshoes that hung upon the wall; in the momentary gloom the fire seemed to be glimmering amidst the vagueness of unenclosed space. Moving about in this red glare and alternate dusk was the figure of the blacksmith,[12] well worthy to be viewed in so picturesque an aspect of light and shade, where the bright blaze struggled with the black night, as if each would have snatched his comely strength from the other. Anon[13] he drew a white-hot bar of iron from the coals, laid it on the anvil, uplifted his arm of might,[14] and was soon enveloped in the myriads of sparks which the strokes of his hammer scattered into the surrounding gloom.

"Now, that is a pleasant sight," said the old watchmaker. "I know what it is to work in gold; but give me the worker in iron after all is said and done.[15] He spends his labor upon a reality. What say you, daughter Annie?"

"Pray don't speak so loud, father," whispered Annie, "Robert Danforth will hear you."

"And what if he should hear me?" said Peter Hovenden. "I say again, it is a good and a wholesome thing to depend upon main strength and reality, and to earn one's bread with the bare

12) the figure of the blacksmith가 주어.
13) anon: (古) soon.
14) of might: mighty, strong.
15) after all is said and done: 결국.

and brawny arm of a blacksmith. A watchmaker gets his brain puzzled by his wheels within a wheel, or loses his health or the nicety of his eyesight, as was my case, and finds himself at middle age, or a little after, past labor[16)] at his own trade and fit for nothing else, yet too poor to live at his ease. So I say once again, give me main strength for my money. And then, how it takes the nonsense out of a man! Did you ever hear of a blacksmith being such a fool as Owen Warland yonder?"

"Well said, uncle Hovenden!" shouted Robert Danforth from the forge, in a full, deep, merry voice, that made the roof reecho. "And what says Miss Annie to that doctrine? She, I suppose, will think it a genteeler business to tinker up a lady's watch than to forge a horseshoe or make a gridiron."

Annie drew her father onward without giving him time for reply.

But we must return to Owen Warland's shop, and spend more meditation upon his history and character than either Peter Hovenden, or probably his daughter Annie, or Owen's old school-fellow, Robert Danforth, would have thought due[17)] to so slight a subject. From the time that his little fingers could grasp a penknife, Owen had been remarkable for a delicate ingenuity, which sometimes produced pretty shapes in wood, principally figures of flowers and birds, and sometimes seemed to aim at the hidden mysteries of mechanism. But it was always for purposes of grace, and never with any mockery of the useful. He did not,

---

16) finds himself … past labor: 중년 혹은 그 즈음에 일할 수 없음을 알게 됨.

17) due:=fitting, appropriate.

like the crowd of school-boy artisans, construct little windmills on the angle of a barn or watermills across the neighboring brook. Those who discovered such peculiarity in the boy as to think it worth their while to observe him closely, sometimes saw reason to suppose that he was attempting to imitate the beautiful movements of Nature as exemplified in the flight of birds or the activity of little animals. It seemed, in fact, a new development of the love of the beautiful, such as might have made him a poet, a painter, or a sculptor, and which was as completely refined from all utilitarian coarseness as it could have been in either of the fine arts. He looked with singular distaste at the stiff and regular processes of ordinary machinery. Being once carried to see a steam-engine, in the expectation that his intuitive comprehension of mechanical principles would be gratified, he turned pale and grew sick, as if something monstrous and unnatural had been presented to him. This horror was partly owing to the size and terrible energy of the iron laborer; for the character of Owen's mind was microscopic, and tended naturally to the minute, in accordance with his diminutive frame and the marvellous smallness and delicate power of his fingers. Not that his sense of beauty was thereby diminished into a sense of prettiness. The beautiful idea has no relation to size, and may be as perfectly developed in a space too minute for any but[18] microscopic investigation as within the ample verge that is measured by the arc of the rainbow. But, at all events, this characteristic minuteness in his objects and accomplishments made the world even more incapable than it might otherwise have been of appreciating Owen Warland's genius. The boy's relatives saw nothing better to be done — as perhaps there was

---

18) any but: only.

not — than to bind him apprentice to a watchmaker, hoping that his strange ingenuity might thus be regulated and put to utilitarian purposes.

Peter Hovenden's opinion of his apprentice has already been expressed. He could make nothing of the lad. Owen's apprehension of the professional mysteries, it is true, was inconceivably quick; but he altogether forgot or despised the grand object of a watchmaker's business, and cared no more for the measurement of time than if it had been merged into eternity. So long, however, as he remained under his old master's care, Owen's lack of sturdiness made it possible, by strict injunctions and sharp oversight, to restrain his creative eccentricity within bounds; but when his apprenticeship was served out, and he had taken the little shop which Peter Hovenden's failing eyesight compelled him to relinquish, then did people recognize[19)] how unfit a person was Owen Warland to lead old blind Father Time along his daily course. One of his most rational projects was to connect a musical operation with the machinery of his watches, so that all the harsh dissonances of life might be rendered tuneful, and each flitting moment fall into the abyss of the past in golden drops of harmony. If a family clock was intrusted to him for repair, — one of those tall, ancient clocks that have grown nearly allied to human nature by measuring out the lifetime of many generations, — he would take upon himself[20)] to arrange a dance or funeral procession of figures across its venerable face, representing twelve mirthful or melancholy hours. Several freaks[21)] of this kind quite destroyed

19) then did people recognize: 그제서야 사람들은 인식하였다.

20) take upon himself: take responsibility, often without consulting other people.

21) freak: 변덕, 장난.

the young watchmaker's credit with that steady and matter-of-fact class of people who hold the opinion that time is not to be trifled with, whether considered as the medium of advancement and prosperity in this world or preparation for the next. His custom[22) rapidly diminished — a misfortune, however, that was probably reckoned among his better accidents by Owen Warland,[23) who was becoming more and more absorbed in a secret occupation which drew all his science and manual dexterity into itself, and likewise gave full employment to the characteristic tendencies of his genius. This pursuit had already consumed many months.

After the old watchmaker and his pretty daughter had gazed at him out of the obscurity of the street, Owen Warland was seized with a fluttering of the nerves, which made his hand tremble too violently to proceed with such delicate labor as he was now engaged upon.

"It was Annie herself!" murmured he. "I should have known it, by this throbbing of my heart, before I heard her father's voice. Ah, how it throbs! I shall scarcely be able to work again on this exquisite mechanism to-night. Annie! dearest Annie! thou shouldst give firmness to my heart and hand, and not shake them thus; for if I strive to put the very spirit of beauty into form and give it motion, it is for thy sake alone. O throbbing heart, be quiet! If my labor be thus thwarted, there will come vague and unsatisfied dreams which will leave me spiritless to-morrow."

As he was endeavoring to settle himself again to his task,

22) custom: 단골손님.

23) 불행한 일이지만, 아마도 오웬은 그게 잘 된 일이라고 생각한다.

the shop door opened and gave admittance to no other than the stalwart figure which Peter Hovenden had paused to admire, as seen amid the light and shadow of the blacksmith's shop. Robert Danforth had brought a little anvil of his own manufacture, and peculiarly constructed, which the young artist had recently bespoken.[24)] Owen examined the article and pronounced it fashioned according to his wish.

"Why, yes," said Robert Danforth, his strong voice filling the shop as with the sound of a bass viol, "I consider myself equal to anything in the way of my own trade; though I should have made but a poor figure at yours[25)] with such a fist as this," added he, laughing, as he laid his vast hand beside the delicate one of Owen. "But what then? I put more main strength into one blow of my sledge hammer than all that you have expended since you were a 'prentice. Is not that the truth?"

"Very probably," answered the low and slender voice of Owen. "Strength is an earthly monster. I make no pretensions to it. My force, whatever there may be of it, is altogether spiritual."

"Well, but, Owen, what are you about?" asked his old school-fellow, still in such a hearty volume of tone that it made the artist shrink, especially as the question related to a subject so sacred as the absorbing dream of his imagination. "Folks do say that you are trying to discover the perpetual motion."

"The perpetual motion? Nonsense!" replied Owen Warland,

24) bespoken: bespeak (주문하다), bespoke, bespoken.

25) yours: your trade.

with a movement of disgust; for he was full of little petulances. "It can never be discovered. It is a dream that may delude men whose brains are mystified with matter, but not me. Besides, if such a discovery were possible, it would not be worth my while to make it only to have the secret turned to such purposes as are now effected by steam and water power. I am not ambitious to be honored with the paternity of a new kind of cotton machine."

"That would be droll enough!" cried the blacksmith, breaking out into such an uproar of laughter that Owen himself and the bell glasses on his work-board quivered in unison. "No, no, Owen! No child of yours will have iron joints and sinews. Well, I won't hinder you any more. Good night, Owen, and success, and if you need any assistance, so far as a downright blow of hammer upon anvil will answer the purpose, I'm your man."

And with another laugh the man of main strength left the shop.

"How strange it is," whispered Owen Warland to himself, leaning his head upon his hand, "that all my musings, my purposes, my passion for the beautiful, my consciousness of power to create it, — a finer, more ethereal power, of which this earthly giant[26] can have no conception, — all, all, look so vain and idle whenever my path is crossed by Robert Danforth! He would drive me mad were I[27] to meet him often. His hard, brute force darkens and confuses the spiritual element within me; but I, too, will be strong in my own way. I will not yield to him."

---

26) this earthly giant: Robert Danforth.

27) were I: if I were (to meet).

He took from beneath a glass a piece of minute machinery, which he set in the condensed light of his lamp, and, looking intently at it through a magnifying glass, proceeded to operate with a delicate instrument of steel. In an instant, however, he fell back in his chair and clasped his hands, with a look of horror on his face that made its small features as impressive as those of a giant would have been.

"Heaven! What have I done?" exclaimed he. "The vapor, the influence of that brute force,[28)]—it has bewildered me and obscured my perception. I have made the very stroke—the fatal stroke—that I have dreaded from the first. It is all over—the toil of months, the object of my life. I am ruined!"

And there he sat, in strange despair, until his lamp flickered in the socket and left the Artist of the Beautiful in darkness.

Thus it is that ideas, which grow up within the imagination and appear so lovely to it[29)] and of a value beyond whatever men call valuable, are exposed to be shattered and annihilated by contact with the practical. It is requisite for the ideal artist to possess a force of character that seems hardly compatible with its delicacy; he must keep his faith in himself while the incredulous world assails him with its utter disbelief; he must stand up against mankind and be his own sole disciple, both as respects[30)] his genius and the objects to which it is directed.

For a time Owen Warland succumbed to this severe but inevi-

---

28) that brute force: 즉 Robert Danforth의 영향.

29) it: the imagination

30) as respects: as regards, with regard to, as to.

table test. He spent a few sluggish weeks with his head so continually resting in his hands that the towns-people had scarcely an opportunity to see his countenance. When at last it was again uplifted to the light of day, a cold, dull, nameless change was perceptible upon it. In the opinion of Peter Hovenden, however, and that order[31)] of sagacious understandings who think that life should be regulated, like clockwork, with leaden weights, the alteration was entirely for the better. Owen now, indeed, applied himself to business with dogged[32)] industry. It was marvellous to witness the obtuse gravity with which he would inspect the wheels of a great old silver watch thereby delighting the owner, in whose fob[33)] it had been worn till he deemed it a portion of his own life, and was accordingly jealous of its treatment. In consequence of the good report thus acquired, Owen Warland was invited by the proper authorities to regulate the clock in the church steeple. He succeeded so admirably in this matter of public interest that the merchants gruffly acknowledged his merits on 'Change; the nurse whispered his praises as she gave the potion in the sick-chamber; the lover blessed him at the hour of appointed interview; and the town in general thanked Owen for the punctuality of dinner time. In a word, the heavy weight upon his spirits kept everything in order, not merely within his own system, but wheresoever the iron accents of the church clock were audible. It was a circumstance, though minute, yet characteristic of his present state, that, when employed to engrave names or initials on silver spoons, he now wrote the requisite letters in the plainest possible style, omitting

31) that order: 그 계급, 사람들.

32) dogged: stubbornly unyielding; obstinate.

33) fob: 바지 앞 쪽의 시계 넣는 작은 주머니.

a variety of fanciful flourishes that had heretofore distinguished his work in this kind.

One day, during the era of this happy transformation, old Peter Hovenden came to visit his former apprentice.

"Well, Owen," said he, "I am glad to hear such good accounts of you from all quarters, and especially from the town clock yonder, which speaks in your commendation every hour of the twenty-four. Only get rid altogether of your nonsensical trash about the beautiful, which I nor nobody else, nor yourself to boot,[34] could ever understand,—only free yourself of that, and your success in life is as sure as daylight. Why, if you go on in this way, I should even venture to let you doctor[35] this precious old watch of mine; though, except my daughter Annie, I have nothing else so valuable in the world."

"I should hardly dare touch it, sir," replied Owen, in a depressed tone; for he was weighed down[36] by his old master's presence.

"In time," said the latter,—"In time, you will be capable of it."

The old watchmaker, with the freedom naturally consequent on his former authority, went on inspecting the work which Owen had in hand at the moment, together with other matters

34) to boot: in addition, besides.

35) doctor: to repair.

36) weigh down: be oppressive, be disheartening to.

that were in progress. The artist, meanwhile, could scarcely lift his head. There was nothing so antipodal[37) to his nature as this man's cold, unimaginative sagacity, by contact with which everything was converted into a dream except the densest matter of the physical world. Owen groaned in spirit and prayed fervently to be delivered from him.

"But what is this?" cried Peter Hovenden abruptly, taking up a dusty bell glass, beneath which appeared a mechanical something, as delicate and minute as the system of a butterfly's anatomy. "What have we here? Owen! Owen! there is witchcraft in these little chains, and wheels, and paddles. See! with one pinch of my finger and thumb I am going to deliver you from all future peril."

"For Heaven's sake," screamed Owen Warland, springing up with wonderful energy, "as you would not drive me mad, do not touch it! The slightest pressure of your finger would ruin me forever."

"Aha, young man! And is it so?" said the old watchmaker, looking at him with just enough penetration to torture Owen's soul with the bitterness of worldly criticism. "Well, take your own course; but I warn you again that in this small piece of mechanism lives your evil spirit. Shall I exorcise him?"

"You are my evil spirit," answered Owen, much excited, — "you and the hard, coarse world! The leaden thoughts and the despondency that you fling upon me are my clogs,[38) else I

37) antipodal: diametrically opposed.

38) clog: An obstacle, hindrance.

should long ago have achieved the task that I was created for."

Peter Hovenden shook his head, with the mixture of contempt and indignation which mankind, of whom he was partly a representative, deem themselves entitled to feel towards all simpletons who seek other prizes than the dusty one along the highway. He then took his leave, with an uplifted finger and a sneer upon his face that haunted the artist's dreams for many a night afterwards. At the time of his old master's visit, Owen was probably on the point of taking up the relinquished task; but, by this sinister event, he was thrown back into the state whence he had been slowly emerging.

But the innate tendency of his soul had only been accumulating fresh vigor during its apparent sluggishness. As the summer advanced he almost totally relinquished his business, and permitted Father Time, so far as the old gentleman[39] was represented by the clocks and watches under his[40] control, to stray at random through human life, making infinite confusion among the train of bewildered hours. He wasted the sunshine, as people said, in wandering through the woods and fields and along the banks of streams. There, like a child, he found amusement in chasing butterflies or watching the motions of water insects. There was something truly mysterious in the intentness with which he contemplated these living playthings as they sported on the breeze or examined the structure of an imperial insect whom he had imprisoned. The chase of butterflies was an apt emblem of the ideal pursuit in which he had spent

39) the old gentleman: Father Time.

40) his: Owen's.

so many golden hours; but would the beautiful idea ever be yielded to his hand like the butterfly that symbolized it? Sweet, doubtless, were these days, and congenial to the artist's soul. They were full of bright conceptions, which gleamed through his intellectual world as the butterflies gleamed through the outward atmosphere, and were real to him, for the instant, without the toil, and perplexity, and many disappointments of attempting to make them visible to the sensual eye. Alas that the artist, whether in poetry, or whatever other material, may not content himself with the inward enjoyment of the beautiful, but must chase the flitting mystery beyond the verge of his ethereal domain, and crush its frail being in seizing it with a material grasp. Owen Warland felt the impulse to give external reality to his ideas as irresistibly as any of the poets or painters who have arrayed the world in a dimmer and fainter beauty, imperfectly copied from the richness of their visions.

The night was now his time for the slow progress of re-creating the one idea to which all his intellectual activity referred itself. Always at the approach of dusk he stole into the town, locked himself within his shop, and wrought with patient delicacy of touch for many hours. Sometimes he was startled by the rap of the watchman, who, when all the world should be asleep, had caught the gleam of lamplight through the crevices of Owen Warland's shutters. Daylight, to the morbid sensibility of his mind, seemed to have an intrusiveness that interfered with his pursuits. On cloudy and inclement days, therefore, he sat with his head upon his hands, muffling, as it were, his sensitive brain in a mist of indefinite musings, for it was a relief to escape from the sharp distinctness with which he was compelled to shape out his thoughts during his nightly toil.

From one of these fits of torpor[41] he was aroused by the entrance of Annie Hovenden, who came into the shop with the freedom of a customer, and also with something of the familiarity of a childish friend. She had worn a hole through her silver thimble,[42] and wanted Owen to repair it.

"But I don't know whether you will condescend to such a task," said she, laughing, "now that you are so taken up with the notion of putting spirit into machinery."

"Where did you get that idea, Annie?" said Owen, starting in surprise.

"Oh, out of my own head," answered she, "and from something that I heard you say, long ago, when you were but a boy and I a little child. But come, will you mend this poor thimble of mine?"

"Anything for your sake, Annie," said Owen Warland, — "anything, even were it to work at Robert Danforth's forge."

"And that would be a pretty sight!" retorted Annie, glancing with imperceptible slightness at the artist's small and slender frame. "Well; here is the thimble."

"But that is a strange idea of yours," said Owen, "about the spiritualization of matter."

41) torpor: mental or physical inactivity or insensibility.

42) thimble: a small metal, ceramic, or plastic cup worn to protect the finger that pushes the sewing needle.

And then the thought stole into his mind that this young girl possessed the gift to comprehend him better than all the world besides. And what a help and strength would it be to him in his lonely toil if he could gain the sympathy of the only being whom he loved! To persons whose pursuits are insulated from the common business of life — who are either in advance of mankind or apart from it — there often comes a sensation of moral cold that makes the spirit shiver as if it had reached the frozen solitudes around the pole. What the prophet, the poet, the reformer, the criminal, or any other man with human yearnings, but separated from the multitude by a peculiar lot, might feel, poor Owen felt.[43)]

"Annie," cried he, growing pale as death at the thought, "how gladly would I tell you the secret of my pursuit! You, methinks, would estimate it rightly. You, I know, would hear it with a reverence that I must not expect from the harsh, material world."

"Would I not? to be sure I would!" replied Annie Hovenden, lightly laughing. "Come; explain to me quickly what is the meaning of this little whirligig, so delicately wrought that it might be a plaything for Queen Mab.[44)] See! I will put it in motion."

"Hold!" exclaimed Owen, "hold!"

Annie had but given the slightest possible touch, with the

43) 전체 문장을 "Poor Owen felt what … might feel."로 재배치하여 생각할 것.

44) Queen Mab: [애란.영국 민요] 퀸 맵. A mischievous, tantalizing fairy who governs and produces people's dreams.

point of a needle, to the same minute portion of complicated machinery which has been more than once mentioned, when the artist seized her by the wrist with a force that made her scream aloud. She was affrighted at the convulsion of intense rage and anguish that writhed across his features. The next instant he let his head sink upon his hands.

"Go, Annie," murmured he; "I have deceived myself, and must suffer for it. I yearned for sympathy, and thought, and fancied, and dreamed that you might give it me; but you lack the talisman, Annie, that should admit you into my secrets. That touch has undone the toil of months and the thought of a lifetime! It was not your fault, Annie; but you have ruined me!"

Poor Owen Warland! He had indeed erred, yet pardonably; for if any human spirit could have sufficiently reverenced the processes so sacred in his eyes, it must have been a woman's. Even Annie Hovenden, possibly might not have disappointed him had she been enlightened by the deep intelligence of love.

The artist spent the ensuing winter in a way that satisfied any persons who had hitherto retained a hopeful opinion of him that he was, in truth, irrevocably doomed to unutility[45] as regarded the world, and to an evil destiny on his own part. The decease of a relative had put him in possession of a small inheritance. Thus freed from the necessity of toil, and having lost the steadfast influence of a great purpose,—great, at least, to him,—he abandoned himself to habits from which it might have been supposed[46] the mere

45) unutility: inutility, having no practical use, uselessness.

46) "it might have been supposed"를 삽입절로 볼 것.

delicacy of his organization would have availed to secure him.[47] But when the ethereal portion of a man of genius is obscured[48] the earthly part assumes an influence the more uncontrollable,[49] because the character is now thrown off the balance to which Providence had so nicely adjusted it, and which, in coarser natures, is adjusted by some other method. Owen Warland made proof of whatever show of bliss may be found in riot. He looked at the world through the golden medium of wine, and contemplated the visions that bubble up so gayly around the brim of the glass, and that people the air with shapes of pleasant madness, which so soon grow ghostly and forlorn. Even when this dismal and inevitable change had taken place, the young man might still have continued to quaff the cup of enchantments, though its vapor did but shroud life in gloom and fill the gloom with spectres that mocked at him. There was a certain irksomeness of spirit,[50] which, being real, and the deepest sensation of which the artist was now conscious, was more intolerable than any fantastic miseries and horrors that the abuse of wine could summon up. In the latter case he could remember, even out of the midst of his trouble, that all was but a delusion; in the former, the heavy anguish was his actual life.

From this perilous state he was redeemed by an incident which more than one person witnessed, but of which the shrewdest could not explain or conjecture the operation on Owen Warland's mind. It was very simple. On a warm afternoon of

47) (버릇으로부터) 그를 지키는데 도움이 되었을 ~
48) obscured: ,를 넣어서 생각할 것.
49) the more uncontrollable: 바로 앞의 an influence를 수식함.
50) a certain irksomeness of spirit: 영혼의 지루함. 오웬은 이 지루함을 사실적으로, 깊이 의식하고 있으며, 이 때문에 자기 삶의 현장에서 고뇌에 빠져 있다.

spring, as the artist sat among his riotous companions with a glass of wine before him, a splendid butterfly flew in at the open window and fluttered about his head.

"Ah," exclaimed Owen, who had drank freely, "are you alive again, child of the sun and playmate of the summer breeze, after your dismal winter's nap? Then it is time for me to be at work!"

And, leaving his unemptied glass upon the table, he departed and was never known to sip another drop of wine.

And now, again, he resumed his wanderings in the woods and fields. It might be fancied that the bright butterfly, which had come so spirit-like into the window as Owen sat with the rude revellers, was indeed a spirit commissioned to recall him to the pure, ideal life that had so etheralized him among men. It might be fancied that he went forth to seek this spirit in its sunny haunts; for still, as in the summer time gone by, he was seen to steal gently up wherever a butterfly had alighted, and lose himself in contemplation of it. When it took flight his eyes followed the winged vision, as if its airy track would show the path to heaven. But what could be the purpose of the unseasonable toil, which was again resumed, as the watchman knew by the lines of lamplight through the crevices of Owen Warland's shutters?[51)] The towns-people had one comprehensive explanation of all these singularities. Owen Warland had gone mad! How universally efficacious—how satisfactory, too, and soothing to the injured sensibility of narrowness and dulness—is

51) 셔터가 닫힌 틈으로 새어나오는 불빛을 보면 오웬이 다시 때아닌 수고에 몰입하고 있음을 알 수 있다.

this easy method of accounting for whatever lies beyond the world's most ordinary scope! From St. Paul's days[52] down to our poor little Artist of the Beautiful, the same talisman had been applied to the elucidation of all mysteries in the words or deeds of men who spoke or acted too wisely or too well. In Owen Warland's case the judgment of his towns-people may have been correct. Perhaps he was mad. The lack of sympathy—that contrast between himself and his neighbors which took away the restraint of example—was enough to make him so. Or possibly he had caught just so much of ethereal radiance as served to bewilder him, in an earthly sense, by its intermixture with the common daylight.

One evening, when the artist had returned from a customary ramble and had just thrown the lustre of his lamp on the delicate piece of work so often interrupted, but still taken up again, as if his fate were embodied in its mechanism, he was surprised by the entrance of old Peter Hovenden. Owen never met this man without a shrinking of the heart. Of all the world he was most terrible, by reason of a keen understanding which saw so distinctly what it did see, and disbelieved so uncompromisingly in what it could not see. On this occasion the old watchmaker had merely a gracious word or two to say.

"Owen, my lad," said he, "we must see you at my house to-morrow night."

The artist began to mutter some excuse.

---

52) From St. Paul's days: 기독교 초대교회 시절, 즉 1세기부터.

"Oh, but it must be so," quoth Peter Hovenden, "for the sake of the days when you were one of the household. What, my boy! don't you know that my daughter Annie is engaged to Robert Danforth? We are making an entertainment, in our humble way, to celebrate the event."

That little monosyllable was all he uttered; its tone seemed cold and unconcerned to an ear like Peter Hovenden's; and yet there was in it the stifled outcry of the poor artist's heart, which he compressed within him like a man holding down an evil spirit. One slight outbreak. however, imperceptible to the old watchmaker, he allowed himself. Raising the instrument with which he was about to begin his work, he let it fall upon the little system of machinery that had, anew, cost him months of thought and toil. It was shattered by the stroke!

Owen Warland's story would have been no tolerable representation of the troubled life of those who strive to create the beautiful, if, amid all other thwarting influences, love had not interposed to steal the cunning from his hand. Outwardly he had been no ardent or enterprising lover; the career of his passion had confined its tumults and vicissitudes so entirely within the artist's imagination that Annie herself had scarcely more than a woman's intuitive perception of it; but, in Owen's view, it covered the whole field of his life. Forgetful of the time when she had shown herself incapable of any deep response, he had persisted in connecting all his dreams of artistical success with Annie's image; she was the visible shape in which the spiritual power that he worshipped, and on whose altar he hoped to lay a not unworthy offering, was made manifest to him. Of course he had deceived himself; there were no such attributes in Annie

Hovenden as his imagination had endowed her with. She, in the aspect which she wore to his inward vision, was as much a creature of his own as the mysterious piece of mechanism would be were it ever realized.[53)] Had he become convinced of his mistake through the medium of successful love, — had he won Annie to his bosom, and there beheld her fade from angel into ordinary woman, — the disappointment might have driven him back, with concentrated energy, upon his sole remaining object. On the other hand, had he found Annie what he fancied, his lot would have been so rich in beauty that out of its mere redundancy he might have wrought the beautiful into many a worthier type than he had toiled for; but the guise in which his sorrow came to him, the sense that the angel of his life[54)] had been snatched away and given to a rude man of earth and iron, who could neither need nor appreciate her ministrations, — this was the very perversity of fate that makes human existence appear too absurd and contradictory to be the scene of one other hope or one other fear. There was nothing left for Owen Warland but to sit down like a man that had been stunned.

He went through a fit of illness. After his recovery his small and slender frame assumed an obtuser garniture of flesh than it had ever before worn. His thin cheeks became round; his delicate little hand, so spiritually fashioned to achieve fairy task-work, grew plumper than the hand of a thriving infant. His aspect had a childishness such as might have induced a stranger to pat him on the head — pausing, however, in the act, to wonder what manner of child was here. It was as if the spirit had gone

---

53) were it ever realized: if it were ever realized.

54) the angel of his life: Annie.

out of him, leaving the body to flourish in a sort of vegetable existence. Not that Owen Warland was idiotic. He could talk, and not irrationally. Somewhat of a babbler, indeed, did people begin to think him; for he was apt to discourse at wearisome length of marvels of mechanism that he had read about in books, but which he had learned to consider as absolutely fabulous. Among them he enumerated the Man of Brass,[55)] constructed by Albertus Magnus,[56)] and the Brazen Head of Friar Bacon;[57)] and, coming down to later times, the automata of a little coach and horses, which it was pretended had been manufactured for the Dauphin of France;[58)] together with an insect that buzzed about the ear like a living fly, and yet was but a contrivance of minute steel springs. There was a story, too, of a duck that waddled, and quacked, and ate; though, had any honest citizen purchased it for dinner, he would have found himself cheated with the mere mechanical apparition of a duck.

"But all these accounts," said Owen Warland, "I am now satisfied are mere impositions."

Then, in a mysterious way, he would confess that he once thought differently. In his idle and dreamy days he had considered it possible, in a certain sense, to spiritualize machinery, and to combine with the new species of life and

---

55) the Man of Brass: 독일의 스콜라 철학자인 Albertus Magnus가 삼십 년 걸려 완성시킨 황동인간.

56) Albertus Magnus: 알베르투스 마그누스(1193?-1280). Thomas Aquinus의 스승.

57) the Brazen Head of Friar Bacon: 프란체스코회 로저 베이콘(Roger Bacon: 1214-1292) 수도사(별명: Doctor Mirabilis)가 만들었다고 전해지는 만능의 머리.

58) the Dauphin of France: 프랑스의 왕세자. "dauphin"은 "dolphin"을 뜻하는 불어로 프랑스 왕가의 紋章에 그려져 있다.

motion thus produced a beauty[59)] that should attain to the ideal which Nature has proposed to herself in all her creatures, but has never taken[60)] pains to realize. He seemed, however, to retain no very distinct perception either of the process of achieving this object or of the design itself.

"I have thrown it all aside now," he would say. "It was a dream such as young men are always mystifying themselves with. Now that I have acquired a little common sense, it makes me laugh to think of it."

Poor, poor and fallen Owen Warland! These were the symptoms that he had ceased to be an inhabitant of the better sphere that lies unseen around us. He had lost his faith in the invisible, and now prided himself, as such unfortunates invariably do, in the wisdom which rejected much that even his eye could see, and trusted confidently in nothing but what his hand could touch. This is the calamity of men whose spiritual part dies out of them and leaves the grosser understanding to assimilate them more and more to the things of which alone it can take cognizance;[61)] but in Owen Warland the spirit was not dead nor passed away; it only slept.

How it awoke again is not recorded. Perhaps the torpid slumber was broken by a convulsive pain. Perhaps, as in a former instance, the butterfly came and hovered about his head and reinspired him, — as indeed this creature of the sunshine

59) a beauty: 앞의 동사 combine의 목적어.

60) has never taken: Nature를 주어로 하며, has proposed와 병행하는 문구.

61) take cognizance: recognize.

had always a mysterious mission for the artist,—reinspired him with the former purpose of his life. Whether it were pain or happiness that thrilled through his veins, his first impulse was to thank Heaven for rendering him again the being of thought, imagination, and keenest sensibility that he had long ceased to be.

"Now for my task," said he. "Never did I feel such strength for it as now."

Yet, strong as he felt himself, he was incited to toil the more diligently by an anxiety lest death should[62)] surprise him in the midst of his labors. This anxiety, perhaps, is common to all men who set their hearts upon anything so high, in their own view of it, that life becomes of importance only as conditional to its accomplishment. So long as we love life for itself, we seldom dread the losing it. When we desire life for the attainment of an object, we recognize the frailty of its texture. But, side by side with this sense of insecurity, there is a vital faith in our invulnerability to the shaft of death while engaged in any task that seems assigned by Providence as our proper thing to do, and which the world would have cause to mourn for should we leave[63)] it unaccomplished. Can the philosopher, big with the inspiration of an idea that is to reform mankind, believe that he is to be beckoned from this sensible existence at the very instant when he is mustering his breath to speak the word of light? Should he perish so, the weary ages may pass away—the world's, whose life sand may fall, drop by drop—before another intellect is prepared to develop the truth that might have been

62) lest ~ should: ~ 하지나 않을까.

63) should we leave: if we should leave . . .

uttered then. But history affords many an example where the most precious spirit, at any particular epoch manifested in human shape, has gone hence untimely, without space allowed him, so far as mortal judgment could discern, to perform his mission on the earth. The prophet dies, and the man of torpid heart and sluggish brain lives on. The poet leaves his song half sung, or finishes it, beyond the scope of mortal ears, in a celestial choir. The painter — as Allston[64)] did — leaves half his conception on the canvas to sadden us with its imperfect beauty, and goes to picture forth the whole, if it be no irreverence to say so, in the hues of heaven. But rather such incomplete designs of this life will be perfected nowhere. This so frequent abortion of man's dearest projects must be taken as a proof that the deeds of earth, however etherealized by piety or genius, are without value, except as exercises and manifestations of the spirit. In heaven, all ordinary thought is higher and more melodious than Milton's song. Then, would he add another verse to any strain that he had left unfinished here?

But to return to Owen Warland. It was his fortune, good or ill, to achieve the purpose of his life. Pass we over[65)] a long space of intense thought, yearning effort, minute toil, and wasting anxiety, succeeded by an instant of solitary triumph: let all this be imagined; and then behold the artist, on a winter evening, seeking admittance to Robert Danforth's fireside circle. There he found the man of iron, with his massive substance thoroughly

64) Washington Allston (1779-1843): 낭만주의 화가로 풍경, 역사, 문학을 소재로 극적인 공포나 고요한 신비를 일으키는 화법을 사용. 오랜 기간동안 붓을 중단했던 대작 Belshazzar's Feast는 B.C. 6세기 바빌론 왕에게 왕국의 몰락을 경고하는 다니엘 선지자의 모습을 묘사한 작품으로 미완으로 남음.

65) Pass we over: We pass over의 동사 강조 형태.

warmed and attempered by domestic influences. And there was Annie, too, now transformed into a matron, with much of her husband's plain and sturdy nature, but imbued, as Owen Warland still believed, with a finer grace, that might enable her to be the interpreter between strength and beauty. It happened, likewise, that old Peter Hovenden was a guest this evening at his daughter's fireside, and it was his well-remembered expression of keen, cold criticism that first encountered the artist's glance.

"My old friend Owen!" cried Robert Danforth, starting up, and compressing the artist's delicate fingers within a hand that was accustomed to gripe bars of iron. "This is kind and neighborly to come to us at last. I was afraid your perpetual motion had bewitched you out of the remembrance of old times."

"We are glad to see you," said Annie, while a blush reddened her matronly cheek. "It was not like a friend to stay from us so long."

"Well, Owen," inquired the old watchmaker, as his first greeting, "how comes on the beautiful? Have you created it at last?"

The artist did not immediately reply, being startled by the apparition of a young child of strength that was tumbling about on the carpet,—a little personage who had come mysteriously out of the infinite, but with something so sturdy and real in his composition that he seemed moulded out of the densest substance which earth could supply. This hopeful infant crawled towards the new-comer, and setting himself on end,[66] as Robert

66) on end: upright.

Danforth expressed the posture, stared at Owen with a look of such sagacious observation that the mother could not help exchanging a proud glance with her husband. But the artist was disturbed by the child's look, as imagining a resemblance between it and Peter Hovenden's habitual expression. He could have fancied that the old watchmaker was compressed into this baby shape, and looking out of those baby eyes, and repeating, as he now did, the malicious question:—

"The beautiful, Owen! How comes on the beautiful? Have you succeeded in creating the beautiful?"

"I have succeeded," replied the artist, with a momentary light of triumph in his eyes and a smile of sunshine, yet steeped in such depth of thought that it was almost sadness. "Yes, my friends, it is the truth. I have succeeded."

"Indeed!" cried Annie, a look of maiden mirthfulness peeping out of her face again. "And is it lawful, now, to inquire what the secret is?"

"Surely; it is to disclose it that I have come," answered Owen Warland. "You shall know, and see, and touch, and possess the secret! For, Annie,—if by that name I may still address the friend of my boyish years,—Annie, it is for your bridal gift that I have wrought this spiritualized mechanism, this harmony of motion, this mystery of beauty. It comes late, indeed; but it is as we go onward in life, when objects begin to lose their freshness of hue and our souls[67] their delicacy of perception, that the spirit

---

67) (begin to lose)가 생략됨. 즉 our souls begin to lose their delicacy of perception이 全文.

of beauty is most needed. If, — forgive me, Annie, — if you know how — to value this gift, it can never come too late."

He produced, as he spoke, what seemed a jewel box. It was carved richly out of ebony by his own hand, and inlaid with a fanciful tracery of pearl, representing a boy in pursuit of a butterfly, which, elsewhere, had become a winged spirit, and was flying heavenward; while the boy, or youth, had found such efficacy in his strong desire that he ascended from earth to cloud, and from cloud to celestial atmosphere, to win the beautiful. This case of ebony[68)] the artist opened, and bade Annie place her fingers on its edge. She did so, but almost screamed as a butterfly fluttered forth, and, alighting on her finger's tip, sat waving the ample magnificence of its purple and gold-speckled wings, as if in prelude to a flight. It is impossible to express by words the glory, the splendor, the delicate gorgeousness which were softened into the beauty of this object. Nature's ideal butterfly was here realized in all its perfection; not in the pattern of such faded insects as flit[69)] among earthly flowers, but of those which hover across the meads[70)] of paradise for child-angels and the spirits of departed infants to disport themselves with. The rich down[71)] was visible upon its wings; the lustre of its eyes seemed instinct with spirit. The firelight glimmered around this wonder — the candles gleamed upon it; but it glistened apparently by its own radiance, and illuminated the finger and out-stretched hand on which it rested with a white gleam like that of precious stones. In its perfect beauty, the consideration of

68) This case of ebony: 뒤에 나오는 동사 opened의 목적어. 주어는 the artist.
69) flit: to move about rapidly and nimbly.
70) mead: a meadow.
71) down: fine, soft, fluffy feathers.

size was entirely lost. Had its wings overreached the firmament, the mind could not have been more filled or satisfied.

"Beautiful! beautiful!" exclaimed Annie. "Is it alive? Is it alive?"

"Alive? To be sure it is," answered her husband. "Do you suppose any mortal has skill enough to make a butterfly, or would put himself to the trouble of making one, when any child may catch a score of them in a summer's afternoon? Alive? Certainly! But this pretty box is undoubtedly of our friend Owen's manufacture; and really it does him credit."

At this moment the butterfly waved its wings anew, with a motion so absolutely lifelike that Annie was startled, and even awestricken; for, in spite of her husband's opinion, she could not satisfy herself whether it was indeed a living creature or a piece of wondrous mechanism.

"Is it alive?" she repeated, more earnestly than before.

"Judge for yourself," said Owen Warland, who stood gazing in her face with fixed attention.

The butterfly now flung itself upon the air, fluttered round Annie's head, and soared into a distant region of the parlor, still making itself perceptible to sight by the starry gleam in which the motion of its wings enveloped it. The infant on the floor followed its course with his sagacious little eyes. After flying about the room, it returned in a spiral curve and settled again on Annie's finger.

"But is it alive?" exclaimed she again; and the finger on which the gorgeous mystery had alighted was so tremulous that the butterfly was forced to balance himself with his wings. "Tell me if it be alive, or whether you created it."

"Wherefore ask who created it, so it be beautiful?" replied Owen Warland.

"Alive? Yes, Annie; it may well be said to possess life, for it has absorbed my own being into itself; and in the secret of that butterfly, and in its beauty, — which is not merely outward, but deep as its whole system, — is represented the intellect, the imagination, the sensibility, the soul of an Artist of the Beautiful![72] Yes; I created it. But" — and here his countenance somewhat changed — "this butterfly is not now to me what it was when I beheld it afar off in the daydreams of my youth."

"Be it what it may, it is a pretty plaything," said the blacksmith, grinning with childlike delight. "I wonder whether it would condescend to alight on such a great clumsy finger as mine? Hold it hither, Annie."

By the artist's direction, Annie touched her finger's tip to that of her husband; and, after a momentary delay, the butterfly fluttered from one to the other. It preluded a second flight by a similar, yet not precisely the same, waving of wings as in the first experiment; then, ascending from the blacksmith's stalwart finger, it rose in a gradually enlarging curve to the ceiling,

---

72) "the intellect, the imagination, the sensibility, the soul of an Artist of the Beautiful!"~ "is represented" ~ "in its beauty." 긴 주어로 인해 도치된 문장.

made one wide sweep around the room, and returned with an undulating movement to the point whence it had started.

"Well, that does beat[73] all nature!" cried Robert Danforth, bestowing the heartiest praise that he could find expression for; and, indeed, had he paused there,[74] a man of finer words and nicer perception could not easily have said more. "That goes beyond me, I confess. But what then? There is more real use in one downright blow of my sledge hammer than in the whole five years' labor that our friend Owen has wasted on this butterfly."

Here the child clapped his hands and made a great babble of indistinct utterance, apparently demanding that the butterfly should be given him for a plaything.

Owen Warland, meanwhile, glanced sidelong at Annie, to discover whether she sympathized in her husband's estimate of the comparative value of the beautiful and the practical. There was, amid all her kindness towards himself, amid all the wonder and admiration with which she contemplated the marvellous work of his hands and incarnation of his idea, a secret scorn — too secret, perhaps, for her own consciousness, and perceptible only to such intuitive discernment as that of the artist. But Owen, in the latter stages of his pursuit, had risen out of the region in which such a discovery might have been torture. He knew that the world, and Annie as the representative of the world, whatever praise might be bestowed, could never say[75]

73) beat: defeat, surpass.

74) had he paused: if he had paused.

75) could never say의 주어는 the world and Annie.

the fitting word nor feel the fitting sentiment which should be the perfect recompense of an artist who, symbolizing a lofty moral by a material trifle, — converting what was earthly to spiritual gold, — had won the beautiful into his handiwork. Not at this latest moment was he to learn that the reward of all high performance must be sought within itself, or sought in vain. There was, however, a view of the matter which Annie and her husband, and even Peter Hovenden, might fully have understood, and which would have satisfied them that the toil of years had here been worthily bestowed. Owen Warland might have told them that this butterfly, this plaything, this bridal gift of a poor watchmaker to a blacksmith's wife, was, in truth, a gem of art that a monarch would have purchased with honors and abundant wealth, and have treasured it among the jewels of his kingdom as the most unique and wondrous of them all. But the artist smiled and kept the secret to himself .

"Father," said Annie, thinking that a word of praise from the old watchmaker might gratify his former apprentice, "do come and admire this pretty butterfly."

"Let us see," said Peter Hovenden, rising from his chair, with a sneer upon his face that always made people doubt, as he himself did, in everything but a material existence. "Here is my finger for it to alight upon. I shall understand it better when once I have touched it."

But, to the increased astonishment of Annie, when the tip of her father's finger was pressed against that of her husband, on which the butterfly still rested, the insect drooped its wings and seemed on the point of falling to the floor. Even the bright spots of gold upon its wings and body, unless her eyes deceived her, grew dim, and the glowing purple took a dusky hue, and the starry lustre that gleamed around the blacksmith's hand became faint and vanished.

"It is dying! it is dying!" cried Annie, in alarm.

"It has been delicately wrought," said the artist, calmly. "As I told you, it has imbibed a spiritual essence — call it magnetism, or what you will. In an atmosphere of doubt and mockery its exquisite susceptibility suffers torture, as does the soul of him who instilled his own life into it. It has already lost its beauty; in a few moments more its mechanism would be irreparably injured."

"Take away your hand, father!" entreated Annie, turning pale. "Here is my child; let it rest on his innocent hand. There, perhaps, its life will revive and its colors grow brighter than ever."

Her father, with an acrid smile, withdrew his finger. The butterfly then appeared to recover the power of voluntary motion, while its hues assumed much of their original lustre, and the gleam of starlight, which was its most ethereal attribute, again formed a halo round about it. At first, when transferred from Robert Danforth's hand to the small finger of the child, this radiance grew so powerful that it positively threw the little fellow's shadow back against the wall. He, meanwhile, extended his plump hand as he had seen his father and mother do, and watched the waving of the insect's wings with infantine delight. Nevertheless, there was a certain odd expression of sagacity that made Owen Warland feel as if here were old Pete Hovenden, partially, and but partially, redeemed from his hard scepticism into childish faith.

"How wise the little monkey[76] looks!" whispered Robert Danforth to his wife.

"I never saw such a look on a child's face," answered Annie, admiring her own infant, and with good reason, far more than the artistic butterfly. "The darling knows more of the mystery than we do."

As if the butterfly, like the artist, were conscious of something not entirely congenial in the child's nature, it alternately sparkled and grew dim. At length it arose from the small hand of the infant with an airy motion that seemed to bear it upward without an effort, as if the ethereal instincts with which its master's spirit had endowed it impelled this fair vision involuntarily to a higher sphere. Had there been no obstruction, it might have soared into the sky and grown immortal. But its lustre gleamed upon the ceiling; the exquisite texture of its wings brushed against that earthly medium; and a sparkle or two, as of stardust, floated downward and lay glimmering on the carpet. Then the butterfly came fluttering down, and, instead of returning to the infant, was apparently attracted towards the artist's hand.

"Not so! not so!" murmured Owen Warland, as if his handiwork could have understood him. "Thou has gone forth out of thy master's heart. There is no return for thee."

---

76) the little monkey: 아들의 이름.

With a wavering movement, and emitting a tremulous radiance, the butterfly struggled, as it were, towards the infant, and was about to alight upon his finger; but while it still hovered in the air, the little child of strength, with his grandsire's sharp and shrewd expression in his face, made a snatch at the marvellous insect and compressed it in his hand. Annie screamed. Old Peter Hovenden burst into a cold and scornful laugh. The blacksmith, by main force, unclosed the infant's hand, and found within the palm a small heap of glittering fragments, whence the mystery of beauty had fled forever. And as for Owen Warland, he looked placidly at what seemed the ruin of his life's labor, and which was yet no ruin. He had caught a far other butterfly than this. When the artist rose high enough to achieve the beautiful, the symbol by which he made it perceptible to mortal senses became of little value in his eyes while his spirit possessed itself in the enjoyment of the reality.

Rappaccini's Daughter

We do not remember to have seen any translated specimens of the productions of M. de l'Aubepine[1] — a fact the less to be wondered at, as his very name is unknown to many of his own countrymen as well as to the student of foreign literature. As a writer, he seems to occupy an unfortunate position between the Transcendentalists[2] (who, under one name or another, have their share in all the current literature of the world) and the great body of pen-and-ink men who address the intellect and sympathies of the multitude. If not too refined, at all events too remote, too shadowy, and unsubstantial in his modes of development to suit the taste of the latter class, and yet too popular to satisfy the spiritual or metaphysical requisitions of the former, he must necessarily find himself without an audience, except here and there an individual or possibly an isolated clique. His writings, to do them justice, are not altogether destitute of fancy and

1) M. de l'Aubepine: A character in Nathaniel Hawthorne's "Rappaccini's Daughter" and is essentially Hawthorne writing about himself under the guise of a French name, which when translated literally means "of the hawthorn." If you look at the title of the works attributed to the Frenchman, you would further notice that all of his writings are just French translations of Hawthorne's own writings. (from wiki. answers.com).

2) Transcendentalists: 19세기 중엽 미국의 뉴잉글런드 지방에서 피어난 초월주의 운동. 매서추세츠 주의 콩코드(Concord)를 중심으로 에머슨(Ralph Waldo Emerson), 소로(Henry David Thoreau), 풀러(Margaret Fuller) 등이 주축이 되어 펼친 일종의 낭만주의 문학사조. 이성보다는 감성, 지식보다는 직관을 중시하였다. 호손은 인간의 神聖과 무한한 가능성을 믿는 초월주의자들과는 거리를 두고 있었다.

originality; they might have won him greater reputation but for an inveterate love of allegory, which is apt to invest his plots and characters with the aspect of scenery and people in the clouds, and to steal away the human warmth out of his conceptions. His fictions are sometimes historical, sometimes of the present day, and sometimes, so far as can be discovered, have little or no reference either to time or space. In any case, he generally contents himself with a very slight embroidery of outward manners, — the faintest possible counterfeit of real life, — and endeavors to create an interest by some less obvious peculiarity of the subject. Occasionally a breath of Nature, a raindrop of pathos and tenderness, or a gleam of humor, will find its way into the midst of his fantastic imagery, and make us feel as if, after all, we were yet within the limits of our native earth. We will only add to this very cursory notice that M. de l'Aubepine's productions, if the reader chance to take them in precisely the proper point of view, may amuse a leisure hour as well as those of a brighter man; if otherwise, they can hardly fail to look excessively like nonsense.

Our author is voluminous; he continues to write and publish with as much praiseworthy and indefatigable prolixity as if his efforts were crowned with the brilliant success that so justly attends those of Eugène Sue.[3] His first appearance was by a collection of stories in a long series of volumes entitled "Contes deux fois racontees."[4] The titles of some of his more recent works (we quote from memory) are as follows: "Le Voyage Celeste a Chemin de Fer,"[5] 3 tom., 1838; "Le nouveau Pere

3) Eugène Sue (1804-1857): 프랑스의 소설가. 파리에 그의 이름을 딴 거리가 있다.

4) "Contes deux fois racontees": *Twice-told Tales*.

5) "Le Voyage Celeste a Chemin de Fer": "The Celestial Railroad."

Adam et la nouvelle Mere Eve," 2 tom., 1839; "Roderic; ou le Serpent a l'estomac,"[6)7)] 2 tom., 1840; "Le Culte du Feu," a folio volume of ponderous research into the religion and ritual of the old Persian Ghebers, published in 1841; "La Soiree du Chateau en Espagne," 1 tom., 8vo, 1842; and "L'Artiste du Beau; ou le Papillon Mecanique," 5 tom., 4to, 1843. Our somewhat wearisome perusal of this startling catalogue of volumes has left behind it a certain personal affection and sympathy, though by no means admiration, for M. de l'Aubepine; and we would fain do the little in our power towards introducing him favorably to the American public. The ensuing tale is a translation of his "Beatrice; ou la Belle Empoisonneuse,"[8)] recently published in "La Revue Anti-Aristocratique." This journal, edited by the Comte de Bearhaven, has for some years past led the defence of liberal principles and popular rights with a faithfulness and ability worthy of all praise.

Rappaccini's Daughter

A young man, named Giovanni Guasconti, came, very long ago, from the more southern region of Italy, to pursue his studies at the University of Padua.[9)] Giovanni, who had but a scanty supply of gold ducats in his pocket, took lodgings in a high and gloomy chamber of an old edifice which looked not unworthy to have been the palace of a Paduan noble, and which, in fact,

---

6) "Roderic; ou le Serpent a l'estomac": "Roderick; or the Serpent in the Stomach"

7) "L'Artiste du Beau; ou le Papillon Mecanique": "The Artist of the Beautiful; or the Mechanical Butterfly"

8) "Beatrice; ou la Belle Empoisonneuse": "Beatrice; or the Poisonous Beauty"

9) the University of Padua: 1222년에 설립된 이탈리아에서 두 번째로 역사가 깊은 대학. 특히 1545년에 대학에서 설립한 식물원은 세계적으로 유명하다.

exhibited over its entrance the armorial bearings of a family long since extinct. The young stranger, who was not unstudied in the great poem of his country, recollected that one of the ancestors of this family, and perhaps an occupant of this very mansion, had been pictured by Dante as a partaker of the immortal agonies of his Inferno. These reminiscences and associations, together with the tendency to heartbreak natural to a young man for the first time out of his native sphere, caused Giovanni to sigh heavily as he looked around the desolate and ill-furnished apartment.

"Holy Virgin, signor!" cried old Dame Lisabetta, who, won by the youth's remarkable beauty of person, was kindly endeavoring to give the chamber a habitable air, "what a sigh was that to come out of a young man's heart! Do you find this old mansion gloomy? For the love of Heaven, then, put your head out of the window, and you will see as bright sunshine as you have left in Naples."

Guasconti mechanically did as the old woman advised, but could not quite agree with her that the Paduan sunshine was as cheerful as that of southern Italy. Such as it was, however, it fell upon a garden beneath the window and expended its fostering influences on a variety of plants, which seemed to have been cultivated with exceeding care.

"Does this garden belong to the house?" asked Giovanni.

"Heaven forbid, signor, unless it were fruitful of better pot herbs than any that grow there now," answered old Lisabetta. "No; that garden is cultivated by the own hands of Signor Giacomo Rappaccini, the famous doctor, who, I warrant him, has been heard of as far as Naples. It is said that he distils these plants into medicines that are as potent as a charm. Oftentimes you may see the signor doctor[10] at work, and perchance[11] the signora, his daughter, too, gathering the strange flowers that grow in the garden."

The old woman had now done what she could for the aspect[12] of the chamber; and, commending[13] the young man to the protection of the saints,[14] took her departure[15]

Giovanni still found no better occupation[16] than to look down into the garden beneath his window. From its appearance, he judged it to be one of those botanic gardens which were of earlier date in Padua than elsewhere in Italy or in the world. Or, not improbably, it might once have been the pleasure-place of an opulent[17] family; for there was the ruin of a marble fountain in the centre, sculptured with rare art, but so wofully shattered that it was impossible to trace the original design from the chaos of remaining fragments. The water, however, continued to gush and sparkle into the sunbeams as cheerfully as ever. A little gurgling sound ascended to the young man's window, and made him feel as if the fountain were an immortal spirit that sung its song unceasingly and without heeding the vicissitudes[18] around it, while one century imbodied[19] it in marble and another[20]

10) the signor doctor: 의사 선생님.
11) perchance: perhaps.
12) aspect: appearance.
13) commend: entrust.
14) to the protection of the saints: 신의 가호를 빌고.
15) took her departure: she left.
16) occupation: an activity to pass time.
17) opulent: affluent; very wealthy.
18) vicissitudes: changes.
19) imbodied: embodied.
20) another: another century.

scattered the perishable garniture[21] on the soil. All about[22] the pool into which the water subsided grew various plants, that seemed to require a plentiful supply of moisture for the nourishment of gigantic leaves, and in some instances, flowers gorgeously magnificent. There was one shrub in particular, set in a marble vase in the midst of the pool, that bore a profusion[23] of purple blossoms, each of which had the lustre and richness of a gem; and the whole together made a show so resplendent that it seemed enough to illuminate the garden, even had there been[24] no sunshine. Every portion of the soil was peopled with plants and herbs, which, if less beautiful, still bore tokens of assiduous[25] care, as if all had their individual virtues, known to the scientific mind[26] that fostered[27] them. Some were placed in urns, rich with old carving, and others in common garden pots; some crept serpent-like along the ground or climbed on high, using whatever means of ascent was offered them. One plant had wreathed itself round a statue of Vertumnus,[28] which was thus quite veiled and shrouded in a drapery of hanging foliage, so happily arranged that it might have served a sculptor for a study.

While Giovanni stood at the window he heard a rustling behind a screen of leaves, and became aware that a person was at work in the garden. His figure soon emerged into view, and showed itself to be that of no common laborer, but a tall,

---

21) garniture: embellishment; ornamentation.
22) about: around.
23) profusion: abundance.
24) even had there been: even if there had been.
25) assiduous: diligent.
26) the scientific mind: Dr Rappaccini를 가리킴.
27) foster: to bring up; nurture.
28) Vertumnus: [로마신화] 베르툼누스. 4계절을 관장하는 신. 정원과 과수의 신.

emaciated,[29] sallow,[30] and sickly-looking man, dressed in a scholar's garb of black. He was beyond the middle term of life, with gray hair, a thin, gray beard, and a face singularly marked with intellect and cultivation, but which could never, even in his more youthful days, have expressed much warmth of heart.

Nothing could exceed the intentness with which this scientific gardener examined every shrub which grew in his path: it seemed as if he was looking into their inmost nature, making observations in regard to their creative essence, and discovering why one leaf grew in this shape and another in that, and wherefore such and such flowers differed among themselves in hue and perfume. Nevertheless, in spite of this deep intelligence on his part, there was no approach to intimacy between himself and these vegetable existences. On the contrary, he avoided their actual touch or the direct inhaling of their odors with a caution that impressed Giovanni most disagreeably; for the man's demeanor was that of one walking among malignant influences, such as savage beasts, or deadly snakes, or evil spirits, which, should he allow them one moment of license, would wreak upon[31] him some terrible fatality. It was strangely frightful to the young man's imagination to see this air of insecurity in a person cultivating a garden, that most simple and innocent of human toils,[32] and which[33] had been alike the joy and labor of the unfallen parents of the race. Was this garden, then, the Eden of

29) emaciated: 야윈, 쇠약한.

30) sallow: low in hue or complexion.

31) wreak(up)on: to cause damage or destruction to someone or something.

32) that most simple and innocent of human toils: cultivating a garden을 다시 설명하고 있다.

33) which: 역시 cultivating a garden을 가리킴.

the present world? And this man, with such a perception of harm in what his own hands caused to grow,—was he the Adam?

The distrustful gardener, while plucking away the dead leaves or pruning the too luxuriant growth of the shrubs, defended his hands with a pair of thick gloves. Nor were these his only armor. When, in his walk through the garden, he came to the magnificent plant that hung its purple gems beside the marble fountain, he placed a kind of mask over his mouth and nostrils, as if all this beauty did but conceal a deadlier malice; but, finding his task still too dangerous, he drew back, removed the mask, and called loudly, but in the infirm[34) voice of a person affected with inward disease, "Beatrice! Beatrice!"

"Here am I, my father. What would you?"[35) cried a rich and youthful voice from the window of the opposite house—a voice as rich as a tropical sunset, and which made Giovanni, though he knew not why, think of deep hues of purple or crimson and of perfumes heavily delectable.[36) "Are you in the garden?"

"Yes, Beatrice," answered the gardener, "and I need your help."

Soon there emerged from under a sculptured portal the figure of a young girl, arrayed with as much richness of taste as the most splendid of the flowers, beautiful as the day, and with a bloom so deep and vivid that one shade more would have been

---

34) infirm: physically weak, esp. from old age; feeble.

35) What would you?: What would you like me to do?의 생략형이라 할 수 있다.

36) delectable: greatly pleasing: delicious.

too much. She looked redundant[37)] with life, health, and energy; all of which attributes were bound down and compressed, as it were and girdled tensely, in their luxuriance, by her virgin zone. Yet Giovanni's fancy must have grown morbid while he looked down into the garden; for the impression which the fair stranger made upon him was as if here were another flower, the human sister of those vegetable ones, as beautiful as they, more beautiful than the richest of them, but still to be touched only with a glove, nor to be approached without a mask. As Beatrice came down the garden path, it was observable that she handled and inhaled the odor of several of the plants which her father had most sedulously[38)] avoided.

"Here, Beatrice," said the latter, "see how many needful offices[39)] require to be done to our chief treasure. Yet, shattered[40)] as I am, my life might pay the penalty of approaching it so closely as circumstances demand. Henceforth, I fear, this plant must be consigned[41)] to your sole charge."

"And gladly will I undertake it," cried again the rich tones of the young lady, as she bent towards the magnificent plant and opened her arms as if to embrace it. "Yes, my sister, my splendour, it shall be Beatrice's task to nurse and serve thee; and thou shalt reward her with thy kisses and perfumed breath, which to her is as the breath of life."

---

37) redundant: exceeding what is required or natural.

38) sedulously: diligently: painstakingly.

39) office: 직무, 소임, 임무.

40) shattered: weakened.

41) consign: to turn over to another's charge or control.

Then, with all the tenderness in her manner that was so strikingly expressed in her words, she busied herself with such attentions as the plant seemed to require; and Giovanni, at his lofty window, rubbed his eyes and almost doubted whether it were a girl tending her favorite flower, or one sister performing the duties of affection to another. The scene soon terminated. Whether Dr. Rappaccini had finished his labors in the garden, or that his watchful eye had caught the stranger's face, he now took his daughter's arm and retired. Night was already closing in; oppressive exhalations seemed to proceed from the plants and steal upward past the open window; and Giovanni, closing the lattice, went to his couch and dreamed of a rich flower and beautiful girl. Flower and maiden were different, and yet the same, and fraught with[42)] some strange peril in either shape.

But there is an influence in the light of morning that tends to rectify whatever errors of fancy, or even of judgment, we may have incurred during the sun's decline, or among the shadows of the night, or in the less wholesome glow of moonshine. Giovanni's first movement, on starting from sleep, was to throw open the window and gaze down into the garden which his dreams had made so fertile of mysteries. He was surprised and a little ashamed to find how real and matter-of-fact an affair it proved to be, in the first rays of the sun which gilded the dew-drops that hung upon leaf and blossom, and, while giving a brighter beauty to each rare flower, brought everything within the limits of ordinary experience. The young man rejoiced that, in the heart of the barren city, he had the privilege of overlooking this spot of lovely and luxuriant vegetation. It would

42) fraught with: filled or charged with.

serve, he said to himself, as a symbolic language to keep him in communion with Nature. Neither the sickly and thoughtworn[43] Dr. Giacomo Rappaccini, it is true, nor his brilliant daughter, were now visible; so that Giovanni could not determine how much of the singularity which he attributed to both was due to their own qualities and how much to his wonder-working fancy; but he was inclined to take a most rational view of the whole matter.

In the course of the day he paid his respects to Signor Pietro Baglioni, professor of medicine in the university, a physician of eminent repute[44] to whom Giovanni had brought a letter of introduction. The professor was an elderly personage, apparently of genial nature, and habits that might almost be called jovial. He kept the young man to dinner, and made himself very agreeable by the freedom and liveliness of his conversation, especially when warmed by a flask or two of Tuscan wine. Giovanni, conceiving that men of science, inhabitants of the same city, must needs be on familiar terms with one another, took an opportunity to mention the name of Dr. Rappaccini. But the professor did not respond with so much cordiality as he had anticipated.

"Ill would it become[45] a teacher of the divine art of medicine," said Professor Pietro Baglioni, in answer to a question of Giovanni, "to withhold due and well-considered praise of a physician so eminently skilled as Rappaccini; but, on the other

---

43) thoughtworn: 知的 작업에 절은.

44) repute: reputation.

45) Ill would it become: It would become (=look) ill (=cruel) [for] a teacher [to]로 이해할 것.

hand, I should answer it but scantily to my conscience were I to permit a worthy youth like yourself, Signor Giovanni, the son of an ancient friend, to imbibe erroneous ideas respecting[46] a man who might hereafter chance to hold your life and death in his hands. The truth is, our worshipful Dr. Rappaccini has as much science as any member of the faculty — with perhaps one single exception — in Padua, or all Italy; but there are certain grave objections to his professional character."

"And what are they?" asked the young man.

"Has my friend Giovanni any disease of body or heart, that he is so inquisitive about physicians?" said the professor, with a smile. "But as for Rappaccini, it is said of him — and I, who know the man well, can answer for its truth — that he cares infinitely more for science than for mankind. His patients are interesting to him only as subjects for some new experiment. He would sacrifice human life, his own among the rest, or whatever else was dearest to him, for the sake of adding so much as a grain of mustard seed to the great heap of his accumulated knowledge."

"Methinks[47] he is an awful man indeed," remarked Guasconti, mentally recalling the cold and purely intellectual aspect of Rappaccini. "And yet, worshipful professor, is it not a noble spirit? Are there many men capable of so spiritual a love of science?"

---

46) respecting: about.

47) Methinks: (古) It seems to me.

"God forbid," answered the professor, somewhat testily; "at least, unless they take sounder views of the healing art than those adopted by Rappaccini. It is his theory that all medicinal virtues are comprised within those substances which we term vegetable poisons. These he cultivates with his own hands, and is said even to have produced new varieties of poison, more horribly deleterious[48] than Nature, without the assistance of this learned person, would ever have plagued the world withal.[49] That the signor doctor does less mischief than might be expected with such dangerous substances is undeniable. Now and then, it must be owned, he has effected, or seemed to effect, a marvellous cure; but, to tell you my private mind, Signor Giovanni, he should receive little credit for such instances of success,—they being probably the work of chance, —but should be held strictly accountable[50] for his failures, which may justly be considered his own work."

The youth might have taken Baglioni's opinions with many grains of allowance[51] had he known that there was a professional warfare of long continuance between him and Dr. Rappaccini, in which the latter was generally thought to have gained the advantage. If the reader be inclined to judge for himself, we refer him to certain black-letter tracts[52] on both sides, preserved in the medical department of the University of Padua.

---

48) deleterious: harmful.

49) withal: despite that.

50) accountable: answerable.

51) with many grains of allowance: 새겨(들었을 것).

52) black-letter tracts: 관련 사람들에게 자신의 주장을 알리는 팸플릿으로, 각 글자의 첫 머리와 끝에 장식적 돌출부가 있는 진한 활자체를 사용.

"I know not, most learned professor," returned Giovanni, after musing on what had been said of Rappaccini's exclusive zeal for science, — "I know not how dearly this physician may love his art; but surely there is one object more dear to him. He has a daughter."

"Aha!" cried the professor, with a laugh. "So now our friend Giovanni's secret is out. You have heard of this daughter, whom all the young men in Padua are wild about, though not half a dozen have ever had the good hap[53)] to see her face. I know little of the Signora Beatrice save that Rappaccini is said to have instructed her deeply in his science, and that, young and beautiful as fame reports her, she is already qualified to fill a professor's chair. Perchance her father destines her for mine! Other absurd rumors there be, not worth talking about or listening to. So now, Signor Giovanni, drink off your glass of lachryma.[54)]"

Guasconti returned to his lodgings somewhat heated with the wine he had quaffed, and which caused his brain to swim with strange fantasies in reference to Dr. Rappaccini and the beautiful Beatrice. On his way, happening to pass by a florist's, he bought a fresh bouquet of flowers.

Ascending to his chamber, he seated himself near the window, but within the shadow thrown by the depth of the wall, so that he could look down into the garden with little risk of being discovered. All beneath his eye was a solitude. The strange plants were basking in the sunshine, and now and then nodding

---

53) hap: fortune: chance.

54) lachryma: Lachryma Christi. 이탈리아의 포도주

gently to one another, as if in acknowledgment of sympathy and kindred. In the midst, by the shattered fountain, grew the magnificent shrub, with its purple gems clustering all over it; they glowed in the air, and gleamed back again out of the depths of the pool, which thus seemed to overflow with colored radiance from the rich reflection that was steeped in it. At first, as we have said, the garden was a solitude. Soon, however, — as Giovanni had half hoped, half feared, would be the case, — a figure appeared beneath the antique sculptured portal, and came down between the rows of plants, inhaling their various perfumes as if she were one of those beings of old classic fable that lived upon sweet odors. On again beholding Beatrice, the young man was even startled to perceive how much her beauty exceeded his recollection of it; so brilliant, so vivid, was its character, that she glowed amid the sunlight, and, as Giovanni whispered to himself, positively illuminated the more shadowy intervals of the garden path. Her face being now more revealed than on the former occasion, he was struck by its expression of simplicity and sweetness, — qualities that had not entered into his idea of her character, and which made him ask anew what manner of mortal she might be. Nor did he fail again to observe, or imagine, an analogy between the beautiful girl and the gorgeous shrub that hung its gemlike flowers over the fountain, — a resemblance which Beatrice seemed to have indulged a fantastic humor in heightening, both by the arrangement of her dress and the selection of its hues.

Approaching the shrub, she threw open her arms, as with a passionate ardor, and drew its branches into an intimate embrace — so intimate that her features were hidden in its leafy bosom and her glistening ringlets all intermingled with the flowers.

"Give me thy breath, my sister," exclaimed Beatrice; "for I am faint with common air. And give me this flower of thine, which I separate with gentlest fingers from the stem and place it close beside my heart."

With these words the beautiful daughter of Rappaccini plucked one of the richest blossoms of the shrub, and was about to fasten it in her bosom. But now, unless Giovanni's draughts of wine had bewildered his senses, a singular incident occurred. A small orange-colored reptile, of the lizard or chameleon species, chanced to be creeping along the path, just at the feet of Beatrice. It appeared to Giovanni, — but, at the distance from which he gazed, he could scarcely have seen anything so minute, — it appeared to him, however, that a drop or two of moisture from the broken stem of the flower descended upon the lizard's head. For an instant the reptile contorted itself violently, and then lay motionless in the sunshine. Beatrice observed this remarkable phenomenon and crossed herself, sadly, but without surprise; nor did she therefore hesitate to arrange the fatal flower in her bosom. There it blushed, and almost glimmered with the dazzling effect of a precious stone, adding to her dress and aspect the one appropriate charm which nothing else in the world could have supplied. But Giovanni, out of the shadow of his window, bent forward and shrank back, and murmured and trembled.

"Am I awake? Have I my senses?" said he to himself. "What is this being? Beautiful shall I call her, or inexpressibly terrible?"

Beatrice now strayed carelessly through the garden, approaching closer beneath Giovanni's window, so that he was compelled to thrust his head quite out of its concealment in order to gratify the intense and painful curiosity which she excited. At this moment there came a beautiful insect over the garden wall; it had, perhaps, wandered through the city, and found no flowers or verdure among those antique haunts of men until the heavy perfumes of Dr. Rappaccini's shrubs had lured it from afar. Without alighting on the flowers, this winged brightness seemed to be attracted by Beatrice, and lingered in the air and fluttered about her head. Now, here it could not be but that Giovanni Guasconti's eyes deceived him. Be that as it might, he fancied that, while Beatrice was gazing at the insect with childish delight, it grew faint and fell at her feet; its bright wings shivered; it was dead — from no cause that he could discern, unless it were the atmosphere of her breath. Again Beatrice crossed herself and sighed heavily as she bent over the dead insect.

An impulsive movement of Giovanni drew her eyes to the window. There she beheld the beautiful head of the young man — rather a Grecian than an Italian head,[55)] with fair, regular features, and a glistening of gold among his ringlets — gazing down upon her like a being that hovered in mid air. Scarcely knowing what he did, Giovanni threw down the bouquet which he had hitherto held in his hand.

"Signora," said he, "there are pure and healthful flowers. Wear them for the sake of Giovanni Guasconti."

---

55) 일반적으로 이탈리아인은 "다비드 像"같이 섬세하고 매끄러운 흰 피부에 잘 생긴 모습인데 반하여, 그리스 인은 큰 눈에, 콧대가 이마로부터 쭉 뻗어 내리고 대체로 억세고 거친 인상이다. 머리칼은 대개 검거나 짙은 밤색, 피부는 보통 올리브색 혹은 옅은 갈색이다. 그리스인에 가까운 조바니의 인상은 다소 거칠고 가부장적인 듯하다.

"Thanks, signor," replied Beatrice, with her rich voice, that came forth as it were like a gush of music, and with a mirthful expression half childish and half woman-like. "I accept your gift, and would fain[56] recompense it with this precious purple flower; but if I toss it into the air it will not reach you. So Signor Guasconti must even content himself with my thanks."

She lifted the bouquet from the ground, and then, as if inwardly ashamed at having stepped aside from her maidenly reserve to respond to a stranger's greeting, passed swiftly homeward through the garden. But few as the moments were, it seemed to Giovanni, when she was on the point of vanishing beneath the sculptured portal, that his beautiful bouquet was already beginning to wither in her grasp. It was an idle thought; there could be no possibility of distinguishing a faded flower from a fresh one at so great a distance.

For many days after this incident the young man avoided the window that looked into Dr. Rappaccini's garden, as if something ugly and monstrous would have blasted his eyesight had he been betrayed into a glance. He felt conscious of having put himself, to a certain extent, within the influence of an unintelligible power by the communication which he had opened with Beatrice. The wisest course would have been, if his heart were in any real danger, to quit his lodgings and Padua itself at once; the next wiser, to have accustomed himself, as far as possible, to the familiar and daylight view of Beatrice — thus bringing her rigidly and systematically within the limits of ordinary experience. Least of all, while avoiding her sight, ought

56) fain: gladly; happily.

Giovanni to have remained so near this extraordinary being that the proximity and possibility even of intercourse should give a kind of substance and reality to the wild vagaries which his imagination ran riot continually in producing. Guasconti had not a deep heart — or, at all events, its depths were not sounded now; but he had a quick fancy, and an ardent southern temperament, which rose every instant to a higher fever pitch. Whether or no Beatrice possessed those terrible attributes, that fatal breath, the affinity with those so beautiful and deadly flowers which were indicated by what Giovanni had witnessed, she had at least instilled a fierce and subtle poison into his system. It was not love, although her rich beauty was a madness to him; nor horror, even while he fancied her spirit to be imbued with the same baneful essence that seemed to pervade her physical frame; but a wild offspring of both love and horror that had each parent in it, and burned like one and shivered like the other. Giovanni knew not what to dread; still less did he know what to hope; yet hope and dread kept a continual warfare in his breast, alternately vanquishing one another and starting up afresh to renew the contest. Blessed are all simple emotions, be they dark or bright! It is the lurid intermixture of the two that produces the illuminating blaze of the infernal regions.

Sometimes he endeavored to assuage the fever of his spirit by a rapid walk through the streets of Padua or beyond its gates: his footsteps kept time with the throbbings of his brain, so that the walk was apt to accelerate itself to a race. One day he found himself arrested; his arm was seized by a portly personage, who had turned back on recognizing the young man and expended much breath in overtaking him.

"Signor Giovanni! Stay, my young friend!" cried he. "Have you forgotten me? That might well be the case if I were as much altered as yourself."

It was Baglioni, whom Giovanni had avoided ever since their first meeting, from a doubt that the professor's sagacity would look too deeply into his secrets. Endeavoring to recover himself, he stared forth wildly from his inner world into the outer one and spoke like a man in a dream.

"Yes; I am Giovanni Guasconti. You are Professor Pietro Baglioni. Now let me pass!"

"Not yet, not yet, Signor Giovanni Guasconti," said the professor, smiling, but at the same time scrutinizing the youth with an earnest glance. "What! did I grow up side by side with your father? and shall his son pass me like a stranger in these old streets of Padua? Stand still, Signor Giovanni; for we must have a word or two before we part."

"Speedily, then, most worshipful professor, speedily," said Giovanni, with feverish impatience. "Does not your worship see that I am in haste?"

Now, while he was speaking there came a man in black along the street, stooping and moving feebly like a person in inferior health. His face was all overspread with a most sickly and sallow hue, but yet so pervaded with an expression of piercing and active intellect that an observer might easily have overlooked the merely physical attributes and have seen only this wonderful energy. As he passed, this person exchanged a cold and distant salutation with Baglioni, but fixed his eyes upon Giovanni with an intentness that seemed to bring out whatever was within him worthy of notice. Nevertheless, there was a peculiar quietness in the look, as if taking merely a speculative, not a human interest, in the young man.

"It is Dr. Rappaccini!" whispered the professor when the stranger had passed. "Has he ever seen your face before?"

"Not that I know," answered Giovanni, starting at the name.

"He HAS seen you! he must have seen you!" said Baglioni, hastily. "For some purpose or other, this man of science is making a study of you. I know that look of his! It is the same that coldly illuminates his face as he bends over a bird, a mouse, or a butterfly, which, in pursuance of some experiment, he has killed by the perfume of a flower; a look as deep as Nature itself, but without Nature's warmth of love. Signor Giovanni, I will stake my life upon it, you are the subject of one of Rappaccini's experiments!"

"Will you make a fool of me?" cried Giovanni, passionately. "THAT, signor professor, were an untoward experiment."[57)]

"Patience! patience!" replied the imperturbable professor. "I tell thee, my poor Giovanni, that Rappaccini has a scientific interest in thee. Thou hast fallen into fearful hands! And the Signora Beatrice,—what part does she act in this mystery?"

---

57) untoward: not favorable; improper. 가상치도 않다는 화자의 의지를 드러내기 위하여 "were"를 씀.

But Guasconti, finding Baglioni's pertinacity intolerable, here broke away, and was gone before the professor could again seize his arm. He looked after the young man intently and shook his head.

"This must not be," said Baglioni to himself. "The youth is the son of my old friend, and shall not come to any harm from which the arcana[58)] of medical science can preserve him. Besides, it is too insufferable an impertinence in Rappaccini, thus to snatch the lad out of my own hands, as I may say, and make use of him for his infernal[59)] experiments. This daughter of his! It shall be looked to. Perchance, most learned Rappaccini, I may foil you where you little dream of it!"

Meanwhile Giovanni had pursued a circuitous route, and at length found himself at the door of his lodgings. As he crossed the threshold he was met by old Lisabetta, who smirked[60)] and smiled, and was evidently desirous to attract his attention; vainly, however, as the ebullition[61)] of his feelings had momentarily subsided into a cold and dull vacuity. He turned his eyes full upon the withered face that was puckering itself into a smile, but seemed to behold it not. The old dame, therefore, laid her grasp upon his cloak.

"Signor! signor!" whispered she, still with a smile over the whole breadth of her visage, so that it looked not unlike a grotesque carving in wood, darkened by centuries. "Listen,

58) arcana: arcanum (=a profound secret, mystery)의 복수형.

59) infernal: fiendish, devilish, abominable.

60) smirk: to smile in a self-conscious, knowing way.

61) ebullition: a sudden, violent outpouring, as of emotion.

signor! There is a private entrance into the garden!"

"What do you say?" exclaimed Giovanni, turning quickly about, as if an inanimate thing should start into feverish life. "A private entrance into Dr. Rappaccini's garden?"

"Hush! hush! not so loud!" whispered Lisabetta, putting her hand over his mouth. "Yes; into the worshipful doctor's garden, where you may see all his fine shrubbery. Many a young man in Padua would give gold to be admitted among those flowers."

Giovanni put a piece of gold into her hand.

"Show me the way," said he.

A surmise, probably excited by his conversation with Baglioni, crossed his mind, that this interposition of old Lisabetta might perchance be connected with the intrigue, whatever were its nature, in which the professor seemed to suppose that Dr. Rappaccini was involving him. But such a suspicion, though it disturbed Giovanni, was inadequate to restrain him. The instant that he was aware of the possibility of approaching Beatrice, it seemed an absolute necessity of his existence to do so. It mattered not whether she were angel or demon; he was irrevocably within her sphere, and must obey the law that whirled him onward, in ever-lessening circles, towards a result which he did not attempt to foreshadow; and yet, strange to say, there came across him a sudden doubt whether this intense interest on his part were not delusory; whether it were really of so deep and positive a nature as to justify him in now thrusting himself into an incalculable position; whether it were not merely the fantasy of a young man's brain, only slightly or not at all connected with his heart.

He paused, hesitated, turned half about, but again went on. His withered guide led him along several obscure passages, and finally undid a door, through which, as it was opened, there came the sight and sound of rustling leaves, with the broken sunshine glimmering among them. Giovanni stepped forth, and, forcing himself through the entanglement of a shrub that wreathed its tendrils over the hidden entrance, stood beneath his own window in the open area of Dr. Rappaccini's garden.

How often is it the case that, when impossibilities have come to pass and dreams have condensed their misty substance into tangible realities, we find ourselves calm, and even coldly self-possessed, amid circumstances which it would have been a delirium of joy or agony to anticipate! Fate delights to thwart us thus. Passion will choose his own time to rush upon the scene, and lingers sluggishly behind when an appropriate adjustment of events would seem to summon his appearance. So was it now with Giovanni. Day after day his pulses had throbbed with feverish blood at the improbable idea of an interview with Beatrice, and of standing with her, face to face, in this very garden, basking in the Oriental[62)] sunshine of her beauty, and snatching from her full gaze the mystery which he deemed the riddle of his own existence. But now there was a singular and untimely equanimity within his breast. He threw a glance around the garden to discover if Beatrice or her father were present, and, perceiving that he was alone, began a critical observation of the plants.

---

62) Oriental: lustrous and valuable.

The aspect of one and all of them dissatisfied him; their gorgeousness seemed fierce, passionate, and even unnatural. There was hardly an individual shrub which a wanderer, straying by himself through a forest, would not have been startled to find growing wild, as if an unearthly face had glared at him out of the thicket. Several also would have shocked a delicate instinct by an appearance of artificialness indicating that there had been such commixture, and, as it were, adultery, of various vegetable species, that the production was no longer of God's making, but the monstrous offspring of man's depraved fancy, glowing with only an evil mockery of beauty. They were probably the result of experiment, which in one or two cases had succeeded in mingling plants individually lovely into a compound possessing the questionable and ominous character that distinguished the whole growth of the garden. In fine, Giovanni recognized but two or three plants in the collection, and those of a kind that he well knew to be poisonous. While busy with these contemplations he heard the rustling of a silken garment, and, turning, beheld Beatrice emerging from beneath the sculptured portal.

Giovanni had not considered with himself what should be his deportment; whether he should apologize for his intrusion into the garden, or assume that he was there with the privity[63] at least, if not by the desire, of Dr. Rappaccini or his daughter; but Beatrice's manner placed him at his ease, though leaving him still in doubt by what agency he had gained admittance. She came lightly along the path and met him near the broken fountain. There was surprise in her face, but brightened by a simple and kind expression of pleasure.

63) privity: knowing of something private or secret shared between individuals.

"You are a connoisseur in flowers, signor," said Beatrice, with a smile, alluding to the bouquet which he had flung her from the window. "It is no marvel, therefore, if the sight of my father's rare collection has tempted you to take a nearer view. If he were here, he could tell you many strange and interesting facts as to the nature and habits of these shrubs; for he has spent a lifetime in such studies, and this garden is his world."

"And yourself, lady," observed Giovanni, "if fame says true,—you likewise are deeply skilled in the virtues indicated by these rich blossoms and these spicy perfumes. Would you deign[64)] to be my instructress, I should prove an apter scholar than if taught by Signor Rappaccini himself."

"Are there such idle rumors?" asked Beatrice, with the music of a pleasant laugh. "Do people say that I am skilled in my father's science of plants? What a jest is there! No; though I have grown up among these flowers, I know no more of them than their hues and perfume; and sometimes methinks I would fain rid myself of even that small knowledge. There are many flowers here, and those not the least brilliant, that shock and offend me when they meet my eye. But pray, signor, do not believe these stories about my science. Believe nothing of me save what you see with your own eyes."

"And must I believe all that I have seen with my own eyes?" asked Giovanni, pointedly, while the recollection of former scenes made him shrink. "No, signora; you demand too little of me. Bid me believe nothing save what comes from your own lips."

---

64) deign: condescend.

It would appear that Beatrice understood him. There came a deep flush to her cheek; but she looked full into Giovanni's eyes, and responded to his gaze of uneasy suspicion with a queenlike haughtiness.

"I do so bid you, signor," she replied. "Forget whatever you may have fancied in regard to me. If true to the outward senses, still it may be false in its essence; but the words of Beatrice Rappaccini's lips are true from the depths of the heart outward. Those you may believe."

A fervor glowed in her whole aspect and beamed upon Giovanni's consciousness like the light of truth itself; but while she spoke there was a fragrance in the atmosphere around her, rich and delightful, though evanescent, yet which the young man, from an indefinable reluctance, scarcely dared to draw into his lungs. It might be the odor of the flowers. Could it be Beatrice's breath which thus embalmed her words with a strange richness, as if by steeping them in her heart? A faintness passed like a shadow over Giovanni and flitted away; he seemed to gaze through the beautiful girl's eyes into her transparent soul, and felt no more doubt or fear.

The tinge of passion that had colored Beatrice's manner vanished; she became gay, and appeared to derive a pure delight from her communion with the youth not unlike what the maiden of a lonely island[65)] might have felt conversing with a voyager from the civilized world. Evidently her experience of life had been confined within the limits of that garden. She talked now

65) lonely island: 베아트리스의 고립을 잘 나타내는 표현.

about matters as simple as the daylight or summer clouds, and now asked questions in reference to the city, or Giovanni's distant home, his friends, his mother, and his sisters — questions indicating such seclusion, and such lack of familiarity with modes and forms, that Giovanni responded as if to an infant. Her spirit gushed out before him like a fresh rill that was just catching its first glimpse of the sunlight and wondering at the reflections of earth and sky which were flung into its bosom. There came thoughts, too, from a deep source, and fantasies of a gemlike brilliancy, as if diamonds and rubies sparkled upward among the bubbles of the fountain. Ever and anon there gleamed across the young man's mind a sense of wonder that he should be walking side by side with the being who had so wrought upon his imagination, whom he had idealized in such hues of terror, in whom he had positively witnessed such manifestations of dreadful attributes, — that he should be conversing with Beatrice like a brother, and should find her so human and so maidenlike. But such reflections were only momentary; the effect of her character was too real not to make itself familiar at once.

In this free intercourse they had strayed through the garden, and now, after many turns among its avenues, were come to the shattered fountain, beside which grew the magnificent shrub, with its treasury of glowing blossoms. A fragrance was diffused from it which Giovanni recognized as identical with that which he had attributed to Beatrice's breath, but incomparably more powerful. As her eyes fell upon it, Giovanni beheld her press her hand to her bosom as if her heart were throbbing suddenly and painfully.

"For the first time in my life," murmured she, addressing the shrub, "I had forgotten thee."

"I remember, signora," said Giovanni, "that you once promised to reward me with one of these living gems for the bouquet which I had the happy boldness to fling to your feet. Permit me now to pluck it as a memorial of this interview."

He made a step towards the shrub with extended hand; but Beatrice darted forward, uttering a shriek that went through his heart like a dagger. She caught his hand and drew it back with the whole force of her slender figure. Giovanni felt her touch thrilling through his fibres.

"Touch it not!" exclaimed she, in a voice of agony. "Not for thy life! It is fatal!"

Then, hiding her face, she fled from him and vanished beneath the sculptured portal. As Giovanni followed her with his eyes, he beheld the emaciated figure and pale intelligence of Dr. Rappaccini, who had been watching the scene, he knew not how long, within the shadow of the entrance.

No sooner was Guasconti alone in his chamber than the image of Beatrice came back to his passionate musings, invested with all the witchery that had been gathering around it ever since his first glimpse of her, and now likewise imbued with a tender warmth of girlish womanhood. She was human; her nature was endowed with all gentle and feminine qualities; she was worthiest to be worshipped; she was capable, surely, on her part, of the height and heroism of love. Those tokens which he had hitherto considered as proofs of a frightful peculiarity in her physical and moral system were now either forgotten, or, by the subtle sophistry of passion transmitted into a golden crown of enchantment, rendering Beatrice the more admirable by so much as she was the more unique. Whatever had looked ugly was now beautiful; or, if incapable of such a change, it stole away and hid itself among those shapeless half ideas which throng the dim region beyond the daylight of our perfect consciousness. Thus did he spend the night, nor fell asleep until the dawn had begun to awake the slumbering flowers in Dr. Rappaccini's garden, whither Giovanni's dreams doubtless led him. Up rose the sun in his due season, and, flinging his beams upon the young man's eyelids, awoke him to a sense of pain. When thoroughly aroused, he became sensible of a burning and tingling agony in his hand — in his right hand — the very hand which Beatrice had grasped in her own when he was on the point of plucking one of the gemlike flowers. On the back of that hand there was now a purple print like that of four small fingers, and the likeness of a slender thumb upon his wrist.

Oh, how stubbornly does love, — or even that cunning semblance of love which flourishes in the imagination, but strikes no depth of root into the heart, — how stubbornly does it hold its faith until the moment comes when it is doomed to vanish into thin mist! Giovanni wrapped a handkerchief about his hand and wondered what evil thing had stung him, and soon forgot his pain in a reverie of Beatrice.

After the first interview, a second was in the inevitable course of what we call fate. A third; a fourth; and a meeting with Beatrice in the garden was no longer an incident in Giovanni's daily life, but the whole space in which he might be said to live; for the anticipation and memory of that ecstatic hour made up the remainder. Nor was it otherwise with the daughter of Rappaccini. She watched for the youth's appearance, and flew to his side with confidence as unreserved as if they had been playmates from early infancy — as if they were such playmates still. If, by any unwonted chance, he failed to come at the appointed moment, she stood beneath the window and sent up the rich sweetness of her tones to float around him in his chamber and echo and reverberate throughout his heart: "Giovanni! Giovanni! Why tarriest thou?[66] Come down!" And down he hastened into that Eden of poisonous flowers.

But, with all this intimate familiarity, there was still a reserve in Beatrice's demeanor, so rigidly and invariably sustained that the idea of infringing it scarcely occurred to his imagination. By all appreciable signs, they loved; they had looked love with eyes that conveyed the holy secret from the depths of one soul into the depths of the other, as if it were too sacred to be whispered by the way; they had even spoken love in those gushes of passion when their spirits darted forth in articulated breath like tongues of long-hidden flame; and yet there had been no seal of lips, no clasp of hands, nor any slightest caress such as love claims and hallows. He had never touched one of the gleaming ringlets of her hair; her garment — so marked was the physical barrier between them — had never been waved against him by a breeze. On the few occasions when Giovanni had seemed tempted to overstep the limit, Beatrice grew so sad, so stern, and withal wore such a look of desolate separation, shuddering at itself, that not a spoken word was requisite to repel him. At

66) Why tarriest thou?; Why are you keeping late?

such times he was startled at the horrible suspicions that rose, monster-like, out of the caverns of his heart and stared him in the face; his love grew thin and faint as the morning mist, his doubts alone had substance. But, when Beatrice's face brightened again after the momentary shadow, she was transformed at once from the mysterious, questionable being whom he had watched with so much awe and horror; she was now the beautiful and unsophisticated girl whom he felt that his spirit knew with a certainty beyond all other knowledge.

A considerable time had now passed since Giovanni's last meeting with Baglioni. One morning, however, he was disagreeably surprised by a visit from the professor, whom he had scarcely thought of for whole weeks, and would willingly have forgotten still longer. Given up as he had long been to a pervading excitement, he could tolerate no companions except upon condition of their perfect sympathy with his present state of feeling. Such sympathy was not to be expected from Professor Baglioni.

The visitor chatted carelessly for a few moments about the gossip of the city and the university, and then took up another topic.

"I have been reading an old classic author lately," said he, "and met with a story that strangely interested me. Possibly you may remember it. It is of an Indian prince, who sent a beautiful woman as a present to Alexander the Great. She was as lovely as the dawn and gorgeous as the sunset; but what especially distinguished her was a certain rich perfume in her breath—richer than a garden of Persian roses. Alexander, as was natural to a youthful conqueror, fell in love at first sight with this magnificent stranger; but a certain sage physician, happening to be present, discovered a terrible secret in regard to her."

"And what was that?" asked Giovanni, turning his eyes downward to avoid those of the professor

"That this lovely woman," continued Baglioni, with emphasis, "had been nourished with poisons from her birth upward, until her whole nature was so imbued with them that she herself had become the deadliest poison in existence. Poison was her element of life. With that rich perfume of her breath she blasted the very air. Her love would have been poison — her embrace death. Is not this a marvellous tale?"

"A childish fable," answered Giovanni, nervously starting from his chair. "I marvel how your worship[67)] finds time to read such nonsense among your graver[68)] studies."

"By the by," said the professor, looking uneasily about him, "what singular fragrance is this in your apartment? Is it the perfume of your gloves? It is faint, but delicious; and yet, after all, by no means agreeable. Were I to breathe it long, methinks it would make me ill. It is like the breath of a flower; but I see no flowers in the chamber."

"Nor are there any," replied Giovanni, who had turned pale as

---

67) your worship: 특히 영국에서 名士를 칭하거나 부를 때 붙이는 존칭. '선생님께서'로 새기면 될 듯.

68) graver: serious.

the professor spoke; "nor, I think, is there any fragrance except in your worship's imagination. Odors, being a sort of element combined of the sensual and the spiritual, are apt to deceive us in this manner. The recollection of a perfume, the bare idea of it, may easily be mistaken for a present reality."

"Ay; but my sober imagination does not often play such tricks," said Baglioni; "and, were I to fancy any kind of odor, it would be that of some vile apothecary[69] drug, wherewith my fingers are likely enough to be imbued. Our worshipful friend Rappaccini, as I have heard, tinctures his medicaments with odors richer than those of Araby.[70] Doubtless, likewise, the fair and learned Signora Beatrice would minister to her patients with draughts as sweet as a maiden's breath; but woe to[71] him that sips them!"

Giovanni's face evinced many contending emotions. The tone in which the professor alluded to the pure and lovely daughter of Rappaccini was a torture to his soul; and yet the intimation of a view of her character opposite to his own, gave instantaneous distinctness to a thousand dim suspicions, which now grinned at him like so many demons. But he strove hard to quell them and to respond to Baglioni with a true lover's perfect faith.

"Signor professor," said he, "you were my father's friend; perchance, too, it is your purpose to act a friendly part towards his son. I would fain feel nothing towards you save respect and deference; but I pray you to observe, signor, that there is one

---

69) apothecary: pharmacist.

70) Araby: smells of Arabia.

71) woe to ~: 비탄이 있을지어다. 슬프도다.

subject on which we must not speak. You know not the Signora Beatrice. You cannot, therefore, estimate the wrong — the blasphemy, I may even say — that is offered to her character by a light or injurious word."

"Giovanni! my poor Giovanni!" answered the professor, with a calm expression of pity, "I know this wretched girl far better than yourself. You shall hear the truth in respect to the poisoner Rappaccini and his poisonous daughter; yes, poisonous as she is beautiful. Listen; for, even should you do violence to my gray hairs, it shall not silence me. That old fable of the Indian woman[72] has become a truth by the deep and deadly science of Rappaccini and in the person of the lovely Beatrice."

Giovanni groaned and hid his face.

"Her father," continued Baglioni, "was not restrained by natural affection from offering up his child in this horrible manner as the victim of his insane zeal for science; for, let us do him justice, he is as true a man of science as ever distilled his own heart in an alembic.[73] What, then, will be your fate? Beyond a doubt you are selected as the material of some new experiment. Perhaps the result is to be death; perhaps a fate more awful still. Rappaccini, with what he calls the interest of science

---

72) That old fable of the Indian woman: 생명을 구해 준 인디언 여인의 은혜를 원수로 갚은 뱀의 이야기를 연관시켜 말하는 듯: "Once upon a time, a woman was picking up firewood. She came upon a poisonous snake frozen in the snow. She took the snake home and nursed it back to health. One day the snake bit her on the cheek. As she lay dying, she asked the snake, "Why have you done this to me?" And the snake answered, "Look, bitch, you knew I was a snake." (from *Natural Born Killers*, 1994. www.imdb.com)

73) alembic: 증류기.

before his eyes, will hesitate at nothing."

"It is a dream," muttered Giovanni to himself; "surely it is a dream."

"But," resumed the professor, "be of good cheer,[74] son of my friend. It is not yet too late for the rescue. Possibly we may even succeed in bringing back this miserable child[75] within the limits of ordinary nature, from which her father's madness has estranged her. Behold this little silver vase! It was wrought by the hands of the renowned Benvenuto Cellini,[76] and is well worthy to be a love gift to the fairest dame in Italy. But its contents are invaluable. One little sip of this antidote would have rendered the most virulent[77] poisons of the Borgias[78] innocuous.[79] Doubt not that it will be as efficacious against those of Rappaccini. Bestow the vase, and the precious liquid within it, on your Beatrice, and hopefully await the result."

Baglioni laid a small, exquisitely wrought silver vial on the table and withdrew, leaving what he had said to produce its effect upon the young man's mind.

"We will thwart Rappaccini yet," thought he, chuckling to himself, as he descended the stairs; "but, let us confess the truth

74) be of good cheer: 기운을 내라, 정신 차려.

75) this miserable child: Beatrice.

76) Benvenuto Cellini (15001571): 이탈리아의 조각가.

77) virulent: extremely poisonous.

78) the Borgias: 교황을 두 명—Pope Calixtus III, his nephew Pope Alexander IV—이나 배출한 15-16세기 이탈리아의 악명 높은 가문으로 탐욕과 권력, 욕정과 살인에 연루되어있다.

79) innocuous: harmless.

of him, he is a wonderful man — a wonderful man indeed; a vile empiric, however, in his practice, and therefore not to be tolerated by those who respect the good old rules of the medical profession."

Throughout Giovanni's whole acquaintance with Beatrice, he had occasionally, as we have said, been haunted by dark surmises as to her character; yet so thoroughly had she made herself felt by him as a simple, natural, most affectionate, and guileless creature, that the image now held up by Professor Baglioni looked as strange and incredible as if it were not in accordance with his own original conception. True, there were ugly recollections connected with his first glimpses of the beautiful girl; he could not quite forget the bouquet that withered in her grasp, and the insect that perished amid the sunny air, by no ostensible agency save the fragrance of her breath. These incidents, however, dissolving in the pure light of her character, had no longer the efficacy of facts, but were acknowledged as mistaken fantasies, by whatever testimony of the senses they might appear to be substantiated. There is something truer and more real than what we can see with the eyes and touch with the finger. On such better evidence had Giovanni founded his confidence in Beatrice, though rather by the necessary force of her high attributes than by any deep and generous faith on his part. But now his spirit was incapable of sustaining itself at the height to which the early enthusiasm of passion had exalted it; he fell down, grovelling among earthly doubts, and defiled therewith the pure whiteness of Beatrice's image. Not that he gave her up; he did but distrust. He resolved to institute[80)] some

80) institute: to organize, establish and set in operation.

decisive test that should satisfy him, once for all, whether there were those dreadful peculiarities in her physical nature which could not be supposed to exist without some corresponding monstrosity of soul. His eyes, gazing down afar, might have deceived him as to the lizard, the insect, and the flowers; but if he could witness, at the distance of a few paces, the sudden blight of one fresh and healthful flower in Beatrice's hand, there would be room for no further question. With this idea he hastened to the florist's and purchased a bouquet that was still gemmed with the morning dew-drops.

It was now the customary hour of his daily interview with Beatrice. Before descending into the garden, Giovanni failed not to look at his figure in the mirror,—a vanity to be expected in a beautiful young man, yet, as displaying itself at that troubled and feverish moment, the token of a certain shallowness of feeling and insincerity of character. He did gaze, however, and said to himself that his features had never before possessed so rich a grace, nor his eyes such vivacity, nor his cheeks so warm a hue of superabundant life.

"At least," thought he, "her poison has not yet insinuated itself into my system. I am no flower to perish in her grasp."

With that thought he turned his eyes on the bouquet, which he had never once laid aside from his hand. A thrill of indefinable horror shot through his frame on perceiving that those dewy flowers were already beginning to droop; they wore the aspect of things that had been fresh and lovely yesterday. Giovanni grew white as marble, and stood motionless before the mirror, staring at his own reflection there as at the likeness of something frightful. He remembered Baglioni's remark about the fragrance that seemed to pervade the chamber. It must have been the poison in his breath! Then he shuddered — shuddered at himself. Recovering from his stupor, he began to watch with curious eye a spider that was busily at work hanging its web from the antique cornice of the apartment, crossing and recrossing the artful system of interwoven lines — as vigorous and active a spider as ever dangled from an old ceiling. Giovanni bent towards the insect, and emitted a deep, long breath. The spider suddenly ceased its toil; the web vibrated with a tremor originating in the body of the small artisan.[81)] Again Giovanni sent forth a breath, deeper, longer, and imbued with a venomous feeling out of his heart: he knew not whether he were wicked, or only desperate. The spider made a convulsive gripe with his limbs and hung dead across the window.

"Accursed! accursed!" muttered Giovanni, addressing himself. "Hast thou grown so poisonous that this deadly insect perishes by thy breath?"

At that moment a rich, sweet voice came floating up from the garden

"Giovanni! Giovanni! It is past the hour! Why tarriest thou? Come down!"

"Yes," muttered Giovanni again. "She is the only being whom my breath may not slay! Would that it might!"

81) artisan: craftsman. 여기서는 거미.

He rushed down, and in an instant was standing before the bright and loving eyes of Beatrice. A moment ago his wrath and despair had been so fierce that he could have desired nothing so much as to wither her by a glance; but with her actual presence there came influences which had too real an existence to be at once shaken off: recollections of the delicate and benign power of her feminine nature, which had so often enveloped him in a religious calm; recollections of many a holy and passionate outgush of her heart, when the pure fountain had been unsealed from its depths and made visible in its transparency to his mental eye; recollections which, had Giovanni known how to estimate them, would have assured him that all this ugly mystery was but an earthly illusion, and that, whatever mist of evil might seem to have gathered over her, the real Beatrice was a heavenly angel. Incapable as he was of such high faith, still her presence had not utterly lost its magic. Giovanni's rage was quelled into an aspect of sullen insensibility. Beatrice, with a quick spiritual sense, immediately felt that there was a gulf of blackness between them which neither he nor she could pass. They walked on together, sad and silent, and came thus to the marble fountain and to its pool of water on the ground, in the midst of which grew the shrub that bore gem-like blossoms. Giovanni was affrighted at the eager enjoyment—the appetite, as it were—with which he found himself inhaling the fragrance of the flowers.

"Beatrice," asked he, abruptly, "whence came this shrub?"

"My father created it," answered she, with simplicity.

"Created it! created it!" repeated Giovanni. "What mean you, Beatrice?"

"He is a man fearfully acquainted with the secrets of Nature," replied Beatrice; "and, at the hour when I first drew breath, this plant sprang from the soil, the offspring of his science, of his intellect, while I was but his earthly child. Approach it not!" continued she, observing with terror that Giovanni was drawing nearer to the shrub. "It has qualities that you little dream of. But I, dearest Giovanni, — I grew up and blossomed with the plant and was nourished with its breath. It was my sister, and I loved it with a human affection; for, alas! — hast thou not suspected it? — there was an awful doom."

Here Giovanni frowned so darkly upon her that Beatrice paused and trembled. But her faith in his tenderness reassured her, and made her blush that she had doubted for an instant.

"There was an awful doom," she continued, "the effect of my father's fatal love of science, which estranged me from all society of my kind. Until Heaven sent thee, dearest Giovanni, oh, how lonely was thy poor Beatrice!"

"Was it a hard doom?" asked Giovanni, fixing his eyes upon her.

"Only of late[82] have I known how hard it was," answered she, tenderly. "Oh, yes; but my heart was torpid, and therefore quiet."

Giovanni's rage broke forth from his sullen gloom like a lightning flash out of a dark cloud.

82) of late: recently.

"Accursed[83] one!" cried he, with venomous scorn and anger. "And, finding thy solitude wearisome, thou hast severed me likewise from all the warmth of life and enticed me into thy region of unspeakable horror!"

"Giovanni!" exclaimed Beatrice, turning her large bright eyes upon his face. The force of his words had not found its way into her mind; she was merely thunderstruck.

"Yes, poisonous thing!" repeated Giovanni, beside himself with passion. "Thou hast done it! Thou hast blasted me! Thou hast filled my veins with poison! Thou hast made me as hateful, as ugly, as loathsome and deadly a creature as thyself—a world's wonder of hideous monstrosity! Now, if our breath be happily as fatal to ourselves as to all others, let us join our lips in one kiss of unutterable hatred, and so die!"

"What has befallen me?" murmured Beatrice, with a low moan out of her heart. "Holy Virgin, pity me, a poor heart-broken child!"

"Thou,—dost thou pray?" cried Giovanni, still with the same fiendish scorn. "Thy very prayers, as they come from thy lips, taint the atmosphere with death. Yes, yes; let us pray! Let us to church and dip our fingers in the holy water at the portal! They that come after us will perish as by a pestilence! Let us sign crosses in the air! It will be scattering curses abroad in the likeness of holy symbols!"

---

83) accursed: under a curse; doomed.

"Giovanni," said Beatrice, calmly, for her grief was beyond passion, "why dost thou join thyself with me thus in those terrible words? I, it is true, am the horrible thing thou namest me. But thou, — what hast thou to do, save with one other shudder at my hideous misery to go forth out of the garden and mingle with thy race, and forget there ever crawled on earth such a monster as poor Beatrice?"

"Dost thou pretend ignorance?" asked Giovanni, scowling upon her. "Behold! this power have I gained from the pure daughter of Rappaccini.

There was a swarm of summer insects flitting through the air in search of the food promised by the flower odors of the fatal garden. They circled round Giovanni's head, and were evidently attracted towards him by the same influence which had drawn them for an instant within the sphere of several of the shrubs. He sent forth a breath among them, and smiled bitterly at Beatrice as at least a score of the insects fell dead upon the ground.

"I see it! I see it!" shrieked Beatrice. "It is my father's fatal science! No, no, Giovanni; it was not I! Never! never! I dreamed only to love thee and be with thee a little time, and so to let thee pass away, leaving but thine image in mine heart; for, Giovanni, believe it, though my body be nourished with poison, my spirit is God's creature, and craves love as its daily food. But my father, — he has united us in this fearful sympathy. Yes; spurn me, tread upon me, kill me! Oh, what is death after such words as thine? But it was not I. Not for a world of bliss would I have done it."

Giovanni's passion had exhausted itself in its outburst from his lips. There now came across him a sense, mournful, and not without tenderness, of the intimate and peculiar relationship between Beatrice and himself. They stood, as it were, in an utter solitude, which would be made none the less solitary by the densest throng of human life. Ought not, then, the desert of humanity around them to press this insulated pair closer together? If they should be cruel to one another, who was there to be kind to them? Besides, thought Giovanni, might there not still be a hope of his returning within the limits of ordinary nature, and leading Beatrice, the redeemed Beatrice, by the hand? O, weak, and selfish, and unworthy spirit, that could dream of an earthly union and earthly happiness as possible, after such deep love had been so bitterly wronged as was Beatrice's love by Giovanni's blighting words! No, no; there could be no such hope. She must pass heavily, with that broken heart, across the borders of Time — she must bathe her hurts in some fount of paradise, and forget her grief in the light of immortality, and THERE be well.

But Giovanni did not know it.

"Dear Beatrice," said he, approaching her, while she shrank away as always at his approach, but now with a different impulse, "dearest Beatrice, our fate is not yet so desperate. Behold! there is a medicine, potent, as a wise physician has assured me, and almost divine in its efficacy. It is composed of ingredients the most opposite to those by which thy awful father has brought this calamity upon thee and me. It is distilled of blessed herbs. Shall we not quaff it together, and thus be purified from evil?"

"Give it me!" said Beatrice, extending her hand to receive the little silver vial which Giovanni took from his bosom. She added, with a peculiar emphasis, "I will drink; but do thou await the result."

She put Baglioni's antidote to her lips; and, at the same moment, the figure of Rappaccini emerged from the portal and came slowly towards the marble fountain. As he drew near, the pale man of science seemed to gaze with a triumphant expression at the beautiful youth and maiden, as might an artist who should spend his life in achieving a picture or a group of statuary and finally be satisfied with his success. He paused; his bent form grew erect with conscious power; he spread out his hands over them in the attitude of a father imploring a blessing upon his children; but those were the same hands that had thrown poison into the stream of their lives. Giovanni trembled. Beatrice shuddered nervously, and pressed her hand upon her heart.

"My daughter," said Rappaccini, "thou art no longer lonely in the world. Pluck one of those precious gems from thy sister shrub and bid thy bridegroom wear it in his bosom. It will not harm him now. My science and the sympathy between thee and him have so wrought within his system that he now stands apart from common men, as thou dost, daughter of my pride and triumph, from ordinary women. Pass on, then, through the world, most dear to one another and dreadful to all besides!"

"My father," said Beatrice, feebly,—and still as she spoke she kept her hand upon her heart,—"wherefore didst thou inflict this miserable doom upon thy child?"

"Miserable!" exclaimed Rappaccini. "What mean you, foolish girl? Dost thou deem it misery to be endowed with marvellous gifts against which no power nor strength could avail an enemy—misery, to be able to quell the mightiest with a breath—misery, to be as terrible as thou art beautiful? Wouldst thou, then, have preferred the condition of a weak woman, exposed to all evil and capable of none?"

"I would fain have been loved, not feared," murmured Beatrice, sinking down upon the ground. "But now it matters not. I am going, father, where the evil which thou hast striven to mingle with my being will pass away like a dream-like the fragrance of these poisonous flowers, which will no longer taint my breath among the flowers of Eden. Farewell, Giovanni! Thy words of hatred are like lead[84)] within my heart; but they, too, will fall away as I ascend. Oh, was there not, from the first, more poison in thy nature than in mine?"

To Beatrice,—so radically had her earthly part been wrought upon by Rappaccini's skill,—as poison had been life, so the powerful antidote was death; and thus the poor victim of man's ingenuity and of thwarted nature, and of the fatality that attends all such efforts of perverted wisdom, perished there, at the feet of her father and Giovanni. Just at that moment Professor Pietro Baglioni looked forth from the window, and called loudly, in a tone of triumph mixed with horror, to the thunderstricken man of science, "Rappaccini! Rappaccini! and is THIS the upshot of your experiment!"

---

84) lead: 납.

Ethan Brand

Bartram the lime-burner, a rough, heavy-looking man, begrimed with charcoal, sat watching his kiln[1] at nightfall, while his little son played at building houses with the scattered fragments of marble, when, on the hill-side below them, they heard a roar of laughter, not mirthful, but slow, and even solemn, like a wind shaking the boughs of the forest.

"Father, what is that?" asked the little boy, leaving his play, and pressing betwixt his father's knees.[2]

"Oh, some drunken man, I suppose," answered the lime-burner; "some merry fellow from the bar-room in the village, who dared not laugh loud enough within doors[3] lest[4] he should blow the roof of the house off. So here he is, shaking his jolly sides at the foot of Graylock.[5]"

"But, father," said the child, more sensitive than the obtuse, middle-aged clown, "he does not laugh like a man that is glad. So the noise frightens me!"

---

1) kiln: a lime kiln. 석회가마.
2) pressing betwixt his father's knees: 소년이 겁에 질려 아버지 바지 가랑이 사이로 파고듦.
3) within doors: 집안에서.
4) lest: for fear that.
5) Graylock: 미국 동북부 매서추세츠 주에서 가장 높은 산(1,064m).

"Don't be a fool, child!" cried his father, gruffly. "You will never make a man, I do believe; there is too much of your mother in you. I have known the rustling of a leaf startle you. Hark![6] Here comes the merry fellow now. You shall see that there is no harm in him."

Bartram and his little son, while they were talking thus, sat watching the same lime-kiln that had been the scene of Ethan Brand's solitary and meditative life, before he began his search for the Unpardonable Sin. Many years, as we have seen, had now elapsed[7], since that portentous[8] night when the IDEA was first developed. The kiln, however, on the mountain-side, stood unimpaired, and was in nothing changed since he had thrown his dark thoughts into the intense glow of its furnace, and melted them, as it were, into the one thought that took possession of his life. It was a rude, round, tower-like structure about twenty feet high, heavily built of rough stones, and with a hillock of earth heaped about the larger part of its circumference[9]; so that the blocks and fragments of marble might be drawn by cart-loads,[10] and thrown in at the top. There was an opening at the bottom of the tower, like an over-mouth,[11] but large enough to admit a man in a stooping posture, and provided with a massive iron door. With the smoke and jets of flame issuing from the chinks and crevices of this door, which seemed to give admittance into the hill-side, it resembled nothing so much as the private entrance

6) Hark: to listen attentively or closely.
7) elapse: to pass or slip by.
8) portentous: 불길한, foreboding.
9) circumference: 주변, 주위.
10) cart-load: 짐마차 한 대의 짐.
11) an over-mouth: 큰 입구.

to the infernal regions, which the shepherds of the Delectable[12) Mountains were accustomed to show to pilgrims.

There are many such lime-kilns in that tract of country, for the purpose of burning the white marble which composes a large part of the substance of the hills. Some of them, built years ago, and long deserted, with weeds growing in the vacant round of the interior,[13) which is open to the sky, and grass and wild-flowers rooting themselves into the chinks of the stones, look already like relics of antiquity, and may yet be overspread with the lichens[14) of centuries to come. Others, where the limeburner still feeds his daily and night-long fire, afford points of interest to the wanderer among the hills, who seats himself on a log of wood or a fragment of marble, to hold a chat with the solitary man. It is a lonesome, and, when the character is inclined to thought, may be an intensely thoughtful occupation; as it proved in the case of Ethan Brand, who had mused to such strange purpose, in days gone by, while the fire in this very kiln was burning.

The man who now watched the fire was of a different order,[15) and troubled himself with no thoughts save[16) the very few that were requisite to his business. At frequent intervals, he flung back the clashing weight of the iron door, and, turning his face from the insufferable glare, thrust in huge logs of

12) Delectable (=delightful) Mountains: one of the rest havens for the pilgrims travelling to the Celestial City in John Bunyan's *The Pilgrim's Progress*.

13) with weeds growing in the vacant round of the interior: 가마의 텅 빈 안쪽 테두리에 잡초가 자라고 있음.

14) lichen: 이끼.

15) order: character.

16) save: with the exception of.

oak, or stirred the immense brands[17] with a long pole. Within the furnace were seen the curling and riotous flames, and the burning marble, almost molten[18] with the intensity of heat; while without,[19] the reflection of the fire quivered on the dark intricacy of the surrounding forest, and showed in the foreground a bright and ruddy little picture of the hut, the spring beside its door, the athletic and coal-begrimed figure of the lime-burner, and the half-frightened child, shrinking into the protection of his father's shadow. And when, again, the iron door was closed, then reappeared the tender light of the half-full moon, which vainly strove to trace out the indistinct shapes of the neighboring mountains; and, in the upper sky, there was a flitting congregation of clouds, still faintly tinged with the rosy sunset, though thus far down into the valley the sunshine had vanished long and long ago.

The little boy now crept still closer to his father, as footsteps were heard ascending the hill-side, and a human form thrust aside the bushes that clustered beneath the trees.

"Halloo! who is it?" cried the lime-burner, vexed at his son's timidity, yet half infected by it. "Come forward, and show yourself, like a man, or I'll fling this chunk of marble at your head!"

"You offer me a rough welcome," said a gloomy voice, as the unknown man drew nigh. "Yet I neither claim nor desire a

17) brand: 타다 남은 나무, 타고 있는 나무.
18) molten: made liquid by heat; melted.
19) without: (가마) 바깥은.

kinder one, even at my own fireside."

To obtain a distincter view, Bartram threw open the iron door of the kiln, whence immediately issued a gush of fierce light, that smote full upon the stranger's face and figure. To a careless eye there appeared nothing very remarkable in his aspect, which was that of a man in a coarse brown, country-made suit of clothes, tall and thin, with the staff and heavy shoes of a wayfarer. As he advanced, he fixed his eyes — which were very bright — intently upon the brightness of the furnace, as if he beheld, or expected to behold, some object worthy of note within it.

"Good evening, stranger," said the lime-burner; "whence come you,[20] so late in the day?"

"I come from my search," answered the wayfarer; "for, at last, it is finished."

"Drunk! — or crazy!" muttered Bartram to himself. "I shall have trouble with the fellow. The sooner I drive him away, the better."

The little boy, all in a tremble, whispered to his father, and begged him to shut the door of the kiln, so that there might not be so much light; for that there was something in the man's face which he was afraid to look at, yet could not look away from. And, indeed, even the lime-burner's dull and torpid sense began to be impressed by an indescribable something in that thin, rugged, thoughtful visage, with the grizzled hair hanging wildly about it, and those deeply sunken eyes, which gleamed like fires

20) whence come you: =where do you come from?

within the entrance of a mysterious cavern. But, as he closed the door, the stranger turned towards him, and spoke in a quiet, familiar way, that made Bartram feel as if he were a sane and sensible man, after all.

"Your[21] task draws to an end, I see," said he. "This marble has already been burning three days. A few hours more will convert the stone to lime."

"Why, who are you?" exclaimed the lime-burner. "You seem as well acquainted with my business as I am myself."

"And well I may be," said the stranger; "for I followed the same craft many a long year, and here, too, on this very spot. But you are a newcomer in these parts. Did you never hear of Ethan Brand?"

"The man that went in search of the Unpardonable Sin?" asked Bartram, with a laugh.

"The same," answered the stranger. "He has found what he sought, and therefore he comes back again."

"What! then you are Ethan Brand himself?" cried the lime-burner, in amazement. "I am a new-comer here, as you say, and they call it eighteen years since you left the foot of Graylock. But, I can tell you, the good folks still talk about Ethan Brand, in the village yonder, and what a strange errand took him away from his lime-kiln. Well, and so you have found the

21) well: well acquainted.

Unpardonable Sin?"

"Even so!" said the stranger, calmly.

"If the question is a fair one," proceeded Bartram, "where might it be?"

Ethan Brand laid his finger on his own heart.

"Here!" replied he.

And then, without mirth in his countenance, but as if moved by an involuntary recognition of the infinite absurdity of seeking throughout the world for what was the closest of all things to himself, and looking into every heart, save his own, for what was hidden in no other breast, he broke into a laugh of scorn. It was the same slow, heavy laugh, that had almost appalled the lime-burner when it heralded[22)] the wayfarer's approach.

The solitary mountain-side was made dismal by it. Laughter, when out of place,[23)] mistimed,[24)] or bursting forth from a disordered state of feeling, may be the most terrible modulation of the human voice. The laughter of one asleep, even if it be a little child, — the madman's laugh, — the wild, screaming laugh of a born idiot, — are sounds that we sometimes tremble to hear, and would always willingly forget. Poets have imagined no utterance of fiends or hobgoblins so fearfully appropriate as a

22) herald: to announce.

23) out of place: not proper; not suitable.

24) mistime: to time badly.

laugh. And even the obtuse lime-burner felt his nerves shaken, as this strange man looked inward at his own heart, and burst into laughter that rolled away into the night, and was indistinctly reverberated among the hills.

"Joe," said he to his little son, "scamper down to the tavern in the village, and tell the jolly fellows there that Ethan Brand has come back, and that he has found the Unpardonable Sin!"

The boy darted away on his errand, to which Ethan Brand made no objection, nor seemed hardly to notice it. He sat on a log of wood, looking steadfastly at the iron door of the kiln. When the child was out of sight, and his swift and light footsteps ceased to be heard treading first on the fallen leaves and then on the rocky mountain-path, the lime-burner began to regret his departure. He felt that the little fellow's presence had been a barrier between his guest and himself, and that he must now deal, heart to heart, with a man who, on his own confession, had committed the one only crime for which Heaven could afford no mercy. That crime, in its indistinct blackness, seemed to overshadow him, and made his memory riotous with a throng of evil shapes that asserted their kindred with the Master Sin, whatever it might be, which it was within the scope of man's corrupted nature to conceive and cherish. They were all of one family; they went to and fro between his breast and Ethan Brand's, and carried dark greetings from one to the other.

Then Bartram remembered the stories which had grown traditionary in reference to this strange man, who had come upon him like a shadow of the night, and was making himself at home in his old place, after so long absence, that the dead people, dead and buried for years, would have had more right to be at home, in any familiar spot, than he. Ethan Brand, it was said, had conversed with Satan himself in the lurid blaze of this very kiln. The legend had been matter of mirth heretofore, but looked grisly now. According to this tale, before Ethan Brand departed on his search, he had been accustomed to evoke a fiend from the hot furnace of the lime-kiln, night after night, in order to confer with him about the Unpardonable Sin; the man and the fiend each laboring to frame the image of some mode of guilt which could neither be atoned for nor forgiven. And, with the first gleam of light upon the mountain-top, the fiend crept in at the iron door, there to abide the intensest element of fire until again summoned forth to share in the dreadful task of extending man's possible guilt beyond the scope of Heaven's else[25)] infinite mercy.

While the lime-burner was struggling with the horror of these thoughts, Ethan Brand rose from the log, and flung open the door of the kiln. The action was in such accordance with the idea in Bartram's mind, that he almost expected to see the Evil One issue forth, red-hot, from the raging furnace.

"Hold! hold!" cried he, with a tremulous attempt to laugh; for he was ashamed of his fears, although they overmastered him. "Don't, for mercy's sake, bring out your Devil now!"

"Man!" sternly replied Ethan Brand, "what need have I of the Devil? I have left him behind me, on my track. It is with such half-way sinners as you that he busies himself. Fear not, because

---

25) else: otherwise.

I open the door. I do but act by old custom, and am going to trim your fire, like a lime-burner, as I was once."

He stirred the vast coals, thrust in more wood, and bent forward to gaze into the hollow prison-house of the fire, regardless of the fierce glow that reddened upon his face. The lime-burner sat watching him, and half suspected this strange guest of a purpose, if not to evoke a fiend, at least to plunge into the flames, and thus vanish from the sight of man. Ethan Brand, however, drew quietly back, and closed the door of the kiln.

"I have looked," said he, "into many a human heart that was seven times hotter with sinful passions than yonder furnace is with fire. But I found not there what I sought. No, not the Unpardonable Sin!"

"What is the Unpardonable Sin?" asked the lime-burner; and then he shrank farther from his companion, trembling lest his question should be answered.

"It is a sin that grew within my own breast," replied Ethan Brand, standing erect with a pride that distinguishes all enthusiasts of his stamp.[26)] "A sin that grew nowhere else! The sin of an intellect[27)] that triumphed over the sense of brotherhood with man and reverence for God, and sacrificed everything to its own mighty claims! The only sin that deserves a recompense of immortal agony! Freely, were it to do again, would I incur the

---

26) stamp: characteristic nature or quality.

27) the sin of an intellect ~ mighty claims!: the Unpardonable Sin에 대한 Hawthorne의 정의. 작가의 일지에 이와 같이 메모되어 있다.

guilt. Unshrinkingly I accept the retribution!"

"The man's head is turned," muttered the lime-burner to himself. "He may be a sinner like the rest of us, — nothing more likely, — but, I'll be sworn, he is a madman too."

Nevertheless, he felt uncomfortable at his situation, alone with Ethan Brand on the wild mountain-side, and was right glad to hear the rough murmur of tongues, and the footsteps of what seemed a pretty numerous party, stumbling over the stones and rustling through the underbrush. Soon appeared the whole lazy regiment that was wont to infest the village tavern, comprehending[28)] three or four individuals who had drunk flip[29)] beside the bar-room fire through all the winters, and smoked their pipes beneath the stoop[30)] through all the summers, since Ethan Brand's departure. Laughing boisterously, and mingling all their voices together in unceremonious talk, they now burst into the moonshine and narrow streaks of firelight that illuminated the open space before the lime-kiln. Bartram set the door ajar again, flooding the spot with light, that the whole company might get a fair view of Ethan Brand, and he of them.

There, among other old acquaintances, was a once ubiquitous man, now almost extinct, but whom we were formerly sure to encounter at the hotel of every thriving village throughout the country. It was the stage-agent. The present specimen of the genus was a wilted and smoke-dried man, wrinkled and

28) comprehending: including.

29) flip: a mixed drink made with an alcoholic beverage and often including beaten eggs.

30) stoop: a small porch, platform, or staircase leading to the entrance of a building.

red-nosed, in a smartly cut, brown, bobtailed coat, with brass buttons, who, for a length of time unknown, had kept his desk and corner in the bar-room, and was still puffing what seemed to be the same cigar that he had lighted twenty years before. He had great fame as a dry joker,[31] though, perhaps, less on account of any intrinsic humor than from a certain flavor of brandy-toddy and tobacco-smoke, which impregnated all his ideas and expressions, as well as his person. Another well-remembered, though strangely altered, face was that of Lawyer Giles, as people still called him in courtesy; an elderly ragamuffin,[32] in his soiled shirtsleeves and tow-cloth[33] trousers. This poor fellow had been an attorney, in what he called his better days, a sharp practitioner, and in great vogue[34] among the village litigants[35]; but flip,[36] and sling,[37] and toddy,[38] and cocktails, imbibed at all hours, morning, noon, and night, had caused him to slide from intellectual to various kinds and degrees of bodily labor, till at last, to adopt his own phrase, he slid into a soap-vat.[39] In other words, Giles was now a soap-boiler,[40] in a small way. He had come to be but the fragment of a human being, a part of one foot having been chopped off by an axe, and an entire hand torn away by the devilish grip of a steam-engine. Yet, though the corporeal hand was gone, a spiritual member remained; for,

---

31) a dry joker: a person with a dry sense of humor.

32) ragamuffin: a shabbily clothed, dirty child. 누더기를 걸친 추레한 사람.

33) tow-cloth: 삼베 천.

34) in great vogue: 크게 인기를 얻어.

35) litigant: (a party) engaged in a law suit. 소송당사자.

36) flip: 맥주, 브랜디에 계란, 향료, 설탕 등을 넣어 끓인 음료.

37) sling: a drink of brandy, whiskey, or gin, sweetened and, usually, lemon-flavored.

38) toddy: a drink of brandy or other liquor mixed with hot water, sugar, and spices.

39) vat: a large vessel, as a tub, cistern, or barrel.

40) soap-boiler: 비누제조인.

stretching forth the stump, Giles steadfastly averred that he felt an invisible thumb and fingers with as vivid a sensation as before the real ones were amputated. A maimed and miserable wretch he was; but one, nevertheless, whom the world could not trample on, and had no right to scorn, either in this or any previous stage of his misfortunes, since he had still kept up the courage and spirit of a man, asked nothing in charity, and with his one hand—and that the left one—fought a stern battle against want and hostile circumstances.

Among the throng, too, came another personage, who, with certain points of similarity to Lawyer Giles, had many more of difference. It was the village doctor; a man of some fifty years, whom, at an earlier period of his life, we introduced as paying a professional visit to Ethan Brand during the latter's supposed insanity. He was now a purple-visaged, rude, and brutal, yet half-gentlemanly figure, with something wild, ruined, and desperate in his talk, and in all the details of his gesture and manners. Brandy possessed this man like an evil spirit, and made him as surly and savage as a wild beast, and as miserable as a lost soul; but there was supposed to be in him such wonderful skill, such native gifts of healing, beyond any which medical science could impart, that society caught hold of him, and would not let him sink out of its reach. So, swaying to and fro upon his horse, and grumbling thick accents at the bedside, he visited all the sick-chambers for miles about among the mountain towns, and sometimes raised a dying man, as it were, by miracle, or quite as often, no doubt, sent his patient to a grave that was dug many a year too soon. The doctor had an everlasting pipe in his mouth, and, as somebody said, in allusion to his habit of swearing, it was always alight with hell-fire.

These three worthies pressed forward, and greeted Ethan Brand each after his own fashion, earnestly inviting him to partake of the contents of a certain black bottle, in which, as they averred, he would find something far better worth seeking than the Unpardonable Sin. No mind, which has wrought itself by intense and solitary meditation into a high state of enthusiasm, can endure the kind of contact with low and vulgar modes of thought and feeling to which Ethan Brand was now subjected. It made him doubt — and, strange to say, it was a painful doubt — whether he had indeed found the Unpardonable Sin, and found it within himself. The whole question on which he had exhausted life, and more than life, looked like a delusion.

"Leave me," he said bitterly, "ye brute beasts, that have made yourselves so, shrivelling up your souls with fiery liquors! I have done with you. Years and years ago, I groped into your hearts and found nothing there for my purpose. Get ye gone!"

"Why, you uncivil scoundrel," cried the fierce doctor, "is that the way you respond to the kindness of your best friends? Then let me tell you the truth. You have no more found the Unpardonable Sin than yonder boy Joe has. You are but a crazy fellow, — I told you so twenty years ago,-neither better nor worse than a crazy fellow, and the fit companion of old Humphrey, here!"

He pointed to an old man, shabbily dressed, with long white hair, thin visage, and unsteady eyes. For some years past this aged person had been wandering about among the hills, inquiring of all travellers whom he met for his daughter. The girl, it seemed, had gone off with a company of circus-performers, and occasionally tidings of her came to the village, and fine stories were told of her glittering appearance as she rode on horseback in the ring, or performed marvellous feats on the tight-rope.

The white-haired father now approached Ethan Brand, and gazed unsteadily into his face.

"They tell me you have been all over the earth," said he, wringing his hands with earnestness. "You must have seen my daughter, for she makes a grand figure in the world, and everybody goes to see her. Did she send any word to her old father, or say when she was coming back?"

Ethan Brand's eye quailed[41)] beneath the old man's. That daughter, from whom he so earnestly desired a word of greeting, was the Esther of our tale, the very girl whom, with such cold and remorseless purpose, Ethan Brand had made the subject of a psychological experiment, and wasted, absorbed, and perhaps annihilated her soul, in the process.

"Yes," he murmured, turning away from the hoary wanderer, "it is no delusion. There is an Unpardonable Sin!"

While these things were passing, a merry scene was going forward in the area of cheerful light, beside the spring and before the door of the hut. A number of the youth of the village, young men and girls, had hurried up the hill-side, impelled by curiosity to see Ethan Brand, the hero of so many a legend familiar to their childhood. Finding nothing, however, very

---

41) quail: to shrink back in fear; cower.

remarkable in his aspect, — nothing but a sunburnt wayfarer, in plain garb and dusty shoes, who sat looking into the fire as if he fancied pictures among the coals, — these young people speedily grew tired of observing him. As it happened, there was other amusement at hand. An old German Jew travelling with a diorama[42] on his back, was passing down the mountain-road towards the village just as the party turned aside from it, and, in hopes of eking[43] out the profits of the day, the showman had kept them company to the lime-kiln.

"Come, old Dutchman," cried one of the young men, "let us see your pictures, if you can swear they are worth looking at!"

"Oh yes, Captain," answered the Jew, — whether as a matter of courtesy or craft, he styled[44] everybody Captain, — "I shall show you, indeed, some very superb pictures!"

So, placing his box in a proper position, he invited the young men and girls to look through the glass orifices of the machine, and proceeded to exhibit a series of the most outrageous scratchings and daubings,[45] as specimens of the fine arts, that ever an itinerant showman had the face to impose upon his circle of spectators. The pictures were worn out, moreover, tattered, full of cracks and wrinkles, dingy with tobacco-smoke, and otherwise in a most pitiable condition. Some purported to be cities, public edifices, and ruined castles in Europe; others represented Napoleon's battles and Nelson's sea-fights; and

42) diorama: 디오라마館.(입체의 소형 모형에 의한) 實景.

43) eke: to earn with great effort or strain.

44) style: to call or name.

45) daub: a crude painting.

in the midst of these would be seen a gigantic, brown, hairy hand, — which might have been mistaken for the Hand of Destiny, though, in truth, it was only the showman's, — pointing its forefinger to various scenes of the conflict, while its owner gave historical illustrations. When, with much merriment at its abominable deficiency of merit, the exhibition was concluded, the German bade little Joe put his head into the box. Viewed through the magnifying-glasses, the boy's round, rosy visage assumed the strangest imaginable aspect of an immense Titanic child, the mouth grinning broadly, and the eyes and every other feature overflowing with fun at the joke. Suddenly, however, that merry face turned pale, and its expression changed to horror, for this easily impressed and excitable child had become sensible that the eye of Ethan Brand was fixed upon him through the glass.

"You make the little man to be afraid, Captain," said the German Jew, turning up the dark and strong outline of his visage from his stooping posture. "But look again, and, by chance, I shall cause you to see somewhat that is very fine, upon my word!"

Ethan Brand gazed into the box for an instant, and then starting back, looked fixedly at the German. What had he seen? Nothing, apparently; for a curious youth, who had peeped in almost at the same moment, beheld only a vacant space of canvas.

"I remember you now," muttered Ethan Brand to the showman.

"Ah, Captain," whispered the Jew of Nuremberg,[46] with a dark smile, "I find it to be a heavy matter in my show-box, — this Unpardonable Sin! By my faith, Captain, it has wearied my shoulders, this long day, to carry it over the mountain."

"Peace," answered Ethan Brand, sternly, "or get thee into the furnace yonder!"

The Jew's exhibition had scarcely concluded, when a great, elderly dog — who seemed to be his own master, as no person in the company laid claim to him — saw fit to render himself the object of public notice. Hitherto, he had shown himself a very quiet, well-disposed old dog, going round from one to another, and, by way of being sociable, offering his rough head to be patted by any kindly hand that would take so much trouble. But now, all of a sudden, this grave and venerable quadruped,[47] of his own mere motion, and without the slightest suggestion from anybody else, began to run round after his tail, which, to heighten the absurdity of the proceeding, was a great deal shorter than it should have been. Never was seen such headlong eagerness in pursuit of an object that could not possibly be attained; never was heard such a tremendous outbreak of growling, snarling, barking, and snapping, — as if one end of the ridiculous brute's body were at deadly and most unforgivable enmity with the other. Faster and faster, round about went the cur;[48] and faster and still faster fled the unapproachable brevity

46) the Jew of Nuremberg: 유대인에 대한 차별법이 통과된 Nuremberg 출신의 유대인. 이 법은 통칭 'Nuremberg Laws'로서 히틀러와 나치당이 1935년 뉴렘버그에서 통과시킨 법이다. 유대인의 독일 시민권과 독일계와의 혼인이나 성적관계를 금지한 법안.

47) quadruped: A four-footed animal.

48) cur: An inferior dog: mongrel.

of his tail; and louder and fiercer grew his yells of rage and animosity; until, utterly exhausted, and as far from the goal as ever, the foolish old dog ceased his performance as suddenly as he had begun it. The next moment he was as mild, quiet, sensible, and respectable in his deportment, as when he first scraped acquaintance with the company.

As may be supposed, the exhibition was greeted with universal laughter, clapping of hands, and shouts of encore, to which the canine performer responded by wagging all that there was to wag of his tail, but appeared totally unable to repeat his very successful effort to amuse the spectators.

Meanwhile, Ethan Brand had resumed his seat upon the log, and moved, as it might be, by a perception of some remote analogy between his own case and that of this self-pursuing cur, he broke into the awful laugh, which, more than any other token, expressed the condition of his inward being. From that moment, the merriment of the party was at an end; they stood aghast, dreading lest the inauspicious sound should be reverberated around the horizon, and that mountain would thunder it to mountain, and so the horror be prolonged upon their ears. Then, whispering one to another that it was late, — that the moon was almost down,-that the August night was growing chill, — they hurried homewards, leaving the lime-burner and little Joe to deal as they might with their unwelcome guest. Save for these three human beings, the open space on the hill-side was a solitude, set in a vast gloom of forest. Beyond that darksome verge, the firelight glimmered on the stately trunks and almost black foliage of pines, intermixed with the lighter verdure of sapling oaks, maples, and poplars, while here and there lay the gigantic corpses of dead trees, decaying on the leaf-strewn soil. And it seemed to little Joe — a timorous and imaginative child — that the silent forest was holding its breath until some fearful thing should happen.

Ethan Brand thrust more wood into the fire, and closed the door of the kiln; then looking over his shoulder at the lime-burner and his son, he bade, rather than advised, them to retire to rest.

"For myself, I cannot sleep," said he. "I have matters that it concerns me to meditate upon. I will watch the fire, as I used to do in the old time."

"And call the Devil out of the furnace to keep you company, I suppose," muttered Bartram, who had been making intimate acquaintance with the black bottle above mentioned. "But watch, if you like, and call as many devils as you like! For my part, I shall be all the better for a snooze.[49] Come, Joe!"

As the boy followed his father into the hut, he looked back at the wayfarer, and the tears came into his eyes, for his tender spirit had an intuition of the bleak and terrible loneliness in which this man had enveloped himself.

When they had gone, Ethan Brand sat listening to the crackling of the kindled wood, and looking at the little spirits of fire that issued through the chinks of the door. These trifles, however, once so familiar, had but the slightest hold of his

---

49) snooze: to take a light nap.

attention, while deep within his mind he was reviewing the gradual but marvellous change that had been wrought upon him by the search to which he had devoted himself. He remembered how the night dew had fallen upon him,—how the dark forest had whispered to him,—how the stars had gleamed upon him,—a simple and loving man, watching his fire in the years gone by, and ever musing as it burned. He remembered with what tenderness, with what love and sympathy for mankind and what pity for human guilt and woe, he had first begun to contemplate those ideas which afterwards became the inspiration of his life; with what reverence he had then looked into the heart of man, viewing it as a temple originally divine, and, however desecrated,[50)] still to be held sacred by a brother; with what awful fear he had deprecated the success of his pursuit, and prayed that the Unpardonable Sin might never be revealed to him. Then ensued that vast intellectual development, which, in its progress, disturbed the counterpoise between his mind and heart. The Idea that possessed his life had operated as a means of education; it had gone on cultivating his powers to the highest point of which they were susceptible; it had raised him from the level of an unlettered laborer to stand on a star-lit eminence, whither the philosophers of the earth, laden with the lore of universities, might vainly strive to clamber after him. So much for the intellect! But where was the heart? That, indeed, had withered,—had contracted,—had hardened,—had perished! It had ceased to partake of the universal throb. He had lost his hold of the magnetic chain of humanity. He was no longer a brother-man, opening the chambers or the dungeons of our common nature by the key of holy sympathy, which gave him a right

50) desecrate: to violate the sacredness of.

to share in all its secrets; he was now a cold observer, looking on mankind as the subject of his experiment, and, at length, converting man and woman to be his puppets, and pulling the wires that moved them to such degrees of crime as were demanded for his study.[51)]

Thus Ethan Brand became a fiend. He began to be so from the moment that his moral nature had ceased to keep the pace of improvement with his intellect. And now, as his highest effort and inevitable development, —as the bright and gorgeous flower, and rich, delicious fruit of his life's labor, —he had produced the Unpardonable Sin!

"What more have I to seek? what more to achieve?" said Ethan Brand to himself. "My task is done, and well done!"

Starting from the log with a certain alacrity in his gait and ascending the hillock of earth that was raised against the stone circumference of the lime-kiln, he thus reached the top of the structure. It was a space of perhaps ten feet across, from edge to edge, presenting a view of the upper surface of the immense mass of broken marble with which the kiln was heaped. All these innumerable blocks and fragments of marble were redhot and vividly on fire, sending up great spouts of blue flame, which quivered aloft and danced madly, as within a magic circle, and sank and rose again, with continual and multitudinous[52)] activity. As the lonely man bent forward over this terrible body of fire,

---

51) When they had gone으로 시작하여 거의 두 페이지에 달하는 이 전체 문단은 Ethan Brand의 meditation으로 이 단편의 핵심 부분을 이룬다. Ethan Brand의 transformation을 잘 보여주고 있다.

52) multitudinous: very numerous, having many parts.

the blasting heat smote up against his person with a breath that, it might be supposed, would have scorched and shrivelled him up in a moment.

Ethan Brand stood erect, and raised his arms on high. The blue flames played upon his face, and imparted the wild and ghastly light which alone could have suited its expression; it was that of a fiend on the verge of plunging into his gulf of intensest torment.

"O Mother Earth," cried he, "who art no more my Mother, and into whose bosom this frame shall never be resolved! O mankind, whose brotherhood I have cast off,

and trampled thy great heart beneath my feet! O stars of heaven, that shone on me of old,[53] as if to light me onward and upward! — farewell all, and forever. Come, deadly element of Fire,-henceforth my familiar friend! Embrace me, as I do thee! "

That night the sound of a fearful peal of laughter rolled heavily through the sleep of the lime-burner and his little son; dim shapes of horror and anguish haunted their dreams, and seemed still present in the rude hovel, when they opened their eyes to the daylight.

"Up, boy, up!" cried the lime-burner, staring about him. "Thank Heaven, the night is gone, at last; and rather than pass such another, I would watch my lime-kiln, wide awake, for a twelvemonth. This Ethan Brand, with his humbug[54] of an

53) of old: in the past.

54) humbug: nonsense.

Unpardonable Sin, has done me no such mighty favor, in taking my place!"

He issued from the hut, followed by little Joe, who kept fast hold of his father's hand. The early sunshine was already pouring its gold upon the mountain-tops, and though the valleys were still in shadow, they smiled cheerfully in the promise of the bright day that was hastening onward. The village, completely shut in by hills, which swelled away gently about it, looked as if it had rested peacefully in the hollow of the great hand of Providence. Every dwelling was distinctly visible; the little spires of the two churches pointed upwards, and caught a fore-glimmering of brightness from the sun-gilt skies upon their gilded weather-cocks.[55] The tavern was astir, and the figure of the old, smoke-dried stage-agent, cigar in mouth, was seen beneath the stoop. Old Graylock was glorified with a golden cloud upon his head. Scattered likewise over the breasts of the surrounding mountains, there were heaps of hoary mist, in fantastic shapes, some of them far down into the valley, others high up towards the summits, and still others, of the same family of mist or cloud, hovering in the gold radiance of the upper atmosphere. Stepping from one to another of the clouds that rested on the hills, and thence to the loftier brotherhood that sailed in air, it seemed almost as if a mortal man might thus ascend into the heavenly regions. Earth was so mingled with sky that it was a day-dream to look at it.

To supply that charm of the familiar and homely, which Nature so readily adopts into a scene like this, the stage-coach was rattling down the mountain-road, and the driver sounded his horn, while Echo caught up the notes, and intertwined them into

55) weather-cock: a weather vane (indicating wind direction), esp. one in the form of a rooster.

a rich and varied and elaborate harmony, of which the original performer could lay claim to little share. The great hills played a concert among themselves, each contributing a strain of airy sweetness.

Little Joe's face brightened at once.

"Dear father," cried he, skipping cheerily to and fro, "that strange man is gone, and the sky and the mountains all seem glad of it!"

"Yes," growled the lime-burner, with an oath, "but he has let the fire go down, and no thanks to him if five hundred bushels of lime are not spoiled. If I catch the fellow hereabouts again, I shall feel like tossing him into the furnace!"

With his long pole in his hand, he ascended to the top of the kiln. After a moment's pause, he called to his son.

"Come up here, Joe!" said he.

So little Joe ran up the hillock, and stood by his father's side. The marble was all burnt into perfect, snow-white lime. But on its surface, in the midst of the circle,—snow-white too, and thoroughly converted into lime,—lay a human skeleton, in the attitude of a person who, after long toil, lies down to long repose. Within the ribs—strange to say—was the shape of a human heart.

"Was the fellow's heart made of marble?" cried Bartram, in some perplexity at this phenomenon. "At any rate, it is burnt into what looks like special good lime; and, taking all the bones together, my kiln is half a bushel the richer for him."

So saying, the rude lime-burner lifted his pole, and, letting it fall upon the skeleton, the relics of Ethan Brand were crumbled into fragments.

Essays in Criticism

The Supernatural Encounters in the Short Fiction of Nathaniel Hawthorne: Dream the Impossible Dream*

Kimberly Renee

The 1770's ushered in a new literary genre that changed the world. Known as Romanticism, the literature produced in Europe between 1775 and 1830 was marked by strong cultural achievement and enthusiastic experimentation. In the early nineteenth century, Romanticism crossed the Atlantic and settled in America, where the genre continued to flourish. Characterized by an emphasis on the supernatural, imagination, and nature, American Romanticism stressed faith and emotion over reason and logic. The Romantic literature rebelled against the formal traditions of the seventeenth and eighteenth centuries. Perhaps one of the greatest American Romantics is Nathaniel Hawthorne. Revered for his use of allegory and symbol, Hawthorne is known for his ability to intertwine religion and nature with the supernatural. In his short fiction, Hawthorne uses the supernatural encounters of his characters to lead them to self-discovery and overall understanding.

In the literary world, many critics have referred to Hawthorne as a dreamer. He himself described himself as a dreamer "dissatisfied with dreaming." He wanted to "test his dreams against a reality he could not control, to determine their truth" (Waggoner 31). He tried to dismiss the meaningfulness of his own dreams, however he also contemplated their validity. Hawthorne battled with his belief in dreams in comparison to

* http://voices.yahoo.com/the-supernatural-encounters-short-fiction-of-165694.html

his religious beliefs. Hawthorne was born on July 4, 1804 in Salem, Massachusetts. Heavily influenced by his hometown and religious upbringing, many of Hawthorne's stories are set in Puritan England and involve his views on the Puritan church. The church was very strict and conservative in its views. In the eyes of the Puritan church, the supernatural world was seen as evil. This belief manifested itself in the Salem witch trial in which those thought to be witches were persecuted and killed. Hawthorne uses many tactics to display his views and criticisms of the church and other occurrences of his time.

One device that Hawthorne uses is the dream. Throughout his literary career, Hawthorne used dreams to give his readers insight into the hidden truths in the worlds of his characters. He gave great consideration to the importance of dreams and there interpretation. In a notebook journal Hawthorne stated:

> To write a dream, which shall resemble the real course of a dream, with all its inconsistency, its strange transformation, which are all taken as a matter of course, its eccentricities an aimlessness-with nevertheless a leading idea running through the whole. Up to this old age of the world, no such thing ever has been written. (Gollin 1)

Hawthorne believed that that ability to write a realistic dream was of paramount importance in his career. Through the use of dreams, Hawthorne sought to reveal the interior of his characters, their inner fears and desires.

In Hawthorne's work " a dream may take shape as a spectral procession, a preternatural hallucination, or simply a mystifying episode imperfectly recalled when awake" (Gollin 94). In many of his short stories, Hawthorne follows his characters into a dream state where they encounter phantoms of loved ones and friends. In the end, they return to consciousness with a startling and sometimes disturbing view of their society. Through the dream, the character is allowed to come to terms with the reality of their existence. And, the reader is invited into the dream world, and into the innermost thoughts of the character.

One way in which Hawthorne deals with these things is through the physical journey of a character. In "My Kinsman, Major Molineux" (1831), Robin embarks on a quest that introduces him to a number of peculiar occurrences in which he tries to decipher their purpose. His adventures occur in a dream like manner in which Robin goes from innocence to experience. In the story, Robin is looking for his kinsman, but on the way, he essentially finds his true self.

Robin wanders through the town as if "a spell was on him" (10). He encounters a two-faced man who encourages him to wait for his relative at the church. Robin then allows his imagination to get the best of him. He imagines that his kinsman may might be dead and "glide through yonder gate, and nod and smile to him in passing dimly by" (12). To combat his negative thought, he thinks of family to create a more positive feeling. However, soon another negative enters the mind of Robin. He slips into a dream in which his family is gathering in the house and he is mysteriously locked out, excluded from the rest of his family. Unable to deal with this prospect Robin immediately awakens. Like many dreamers, Robin is confused by his dream and is unsure of how it relates to his quest for Major Molineux.

The dream is symbolic of Robin's journey, because it reveals what Robin does not yet know, or want to know. Being cut off from his family forces Robin to grow up and be independent. He is alone and must learn to rely on himself. He has left his youth behind, and will be unable to retain it. He has entered into an adult world that he must embrace. In the end, Robin has another encounter that although it is real, it seems rather dreamlike. He comes face to face with the kinsmen that he originally sought to find. However, he realizes that he does not need Major Molineux to "rise in the world"(17). Of the stories that incorporate dream and journey, "My Kinsman, Major Molineux" is the most hopeful. In the end, the reader is left with the impression that Robin will achieve great things in life.

This sense of hopefulness is not the case in "Young Goodman Brown"(1835). In the story, Hawthorne addresses one of the seven deadly sins and the hypocrisy of the Puritan church. In "Young Goodman Brown" Hawthorne chronicles the disturbing dream of a young Puritan man in Salem. In the dream, Goodman Brown comes face to face with his fears and is forced to examine the nature of evil in man. He is disgusted by the evil he encounters, not realizing his own involvement. Goodman Brown is too consumed with spiritual pride to recognize his own flaws.

The story begins with Goodman Brown leaving his wife, Faith for an overnight errand. She begs him not to go, but he does so anyway. During his errand, he enters the forest and his mental journey begins. His first encounter is with a "fellow-traveler" with a staff in his hand(66). The traveler's staff eventually leads Goodman Brown one a journey that ultimately concludes at the Devil's ceremony, which destroys his faith in his man. During the journey, he encounters several church members consorting with the devil. Throughout the journey, he is unsure of the things he sees and hears. His mind vacillates between further pursuit of the evil and complete rejection. Near the end of his journey, Goodman believes that he hears his wife call him. At this moment, Goodman Brown loses all faith in the world and declares that there is "no good on earth" (71). The suggestion that the woman he hears is Faith causes him to lose his personal convictions. He then allows the staff to lead him again: "with the instinct that guides mortal man to evil" (71). Because of his complete loss of faith, Goodman Brown had nothing to keep him from evil.

The climax of the journey occurs when Goodman Brown witnesses a ritual of evil. When the ceremony begins, he steps forward: "He had no power to retreat one step, nor to resist, even in thought" (74). Goodman Brown at this point seems to be in a trance and he loses control of his body as he is unconsciously entering this service of converts to the devil. After the sermon, Goodman Brown comes face to face with Faith. The leader declares that "Evil is the nature of mankind" and he welcomes the converts to "communion of your race" (74). Brown then snaps out from his trance and yells "Faith! Faith! Look up to Heaven and resist the wicked one!" At this, the ceremony ends and Brown finds himself alone. He does not know whether Faith, his wife, had kept her faith, but he finds himself alone that leads him to believe that he is also alone in his faith.

The ordeal that Goodman Brown experiences completely shatters and devastates him when he awakens from his dream. As he walks the streets of Salem in the daylight, he his unable to separate his dream from reality. His dream reveals to him that the capability for evil resides in everyman. Goodman is unable to cope with this discovery. What makes the experience worst is that everyone that is important to Goodman Brown is in the dream. They are not the people that he thought them to be. The rest of his life is destroyed because of his inability to face this truth and live with it. Although Hawthorne does attempt to reveal knowledge to his characters through their dream, in the case of Goodman Brown, Hawthorne takes it a step further. Hawthorne also shows what can happen if one misinterprets this knowledge. The dream, has planted the seed of doubt in Brown's mind, which consequently cuts him off from his fellow man and leaves him alone and depressed. The truth is that Goodman Brown despises these people because he sees that same traits in himself. Like the people in his dream, he questions his own religion. However, he projects his own fears onto those around him. The dream is a manifestation of all of the insecurities he has about himself and the choices he has made in life. However, he is too proud to acknowledge his own faults. His life ends alone and miserable because he was never able to look at himself and realize that what he believed were everyone else's faults were his as well. He is completely isolated from his society. Hawthorne uses the dream to reveal Goodman Brown's inner thoughts and fear. In "The Celestial-Railroad" (1843) the narrator takes a journey through a "gate of dreams" (131). His intended destination is the Celestial City. However, his journey, which he has no control of, takes him on a different path. As the story begins, the narrator is on a train traveling by train with a gentleman named Mr. Smooth-it-away. Although he is seemingly calm, the narrator soon realizes that something is wrong. He observes that the engine looks as if it would send its passengers "to the infernal regions" (134). His foreshadowing lets the reader know that the destination of the train is not heaven.

Throughout the train ride, the narrator becomes increasingly fearful and worried about the sights and sounds of the ride. As the train enters the "treaded Valley," the narrator acknowledges is own heart palpitations. On one occasion the narrator almost comes face to face with his fear:

> I almost thought, that they were my own sins that appalled me there. These were freaks of imagination-nothing more, certainly, — mere delusions, which I ought to be heartily ashamed of-but, all through the Dark Valley, I was tormented , and pestered, and dolefully bewildered, with the same kind of waking dreams. (138)

Once the train emerges from the valley and enters into the daylight, he once again gains control and dismisses the seriousness of his experience.

Like Goodman Brown, when the narrator emerges from his dream when he can no longer face the truths of his dream. Although he was on a journey to hell, he is spared. When he awakens, he remembers the event, but is unable to acknowledge and recognize his own faults. In the end he states "Thank Heaven, it was a dream" (144). This final comment is ironic because the narrator thanks heaven, but will never reach heaven either. However, he is so deluded that he does not realize this fact. This story is perhaps one of Hawthorne's most pessimistic. Until the narrator faces the truth he has no hope of ever reaching the Celestial City, heaven.

Like most dreams, the journeys of these characters all stopped abruptly without a final conclusion. Hawthorne allows his characters to reject his own involvement in the horrors he encounters. However, the encounters break down the self assured individuals who set out on these journeys. As a result, the characters are revealed to be vulnerable and human. Each of the characters is changed by his experience, some for the better and some for the worst.

In "The Birth-mark" (1843) the dream depicted stems from the obsessions of the main character. In the story, Hawthorne combines his affinity for dreams with his curiosity of science. The first story written after Hawthorne's marriage, "The Birth-mark" focuses on the relationship between a newlywed couple (Newman 29). In the story, Aylmer, a scientist, puts aside him passion for science to marry Georgiana, a beautiful woman. Shortly after they are married, he becomes obsessed with a tiny birthmark on Georgiana left cheek. The slight imperfection consumes Aylmer and he dreams that he is cutting away the birthmark on his wife's face. However, at first he does not recall the dream. When he is able to recall the details of the dream he is somewhat ashamed. The narrator explains " Truth often finds its way to the mind close muffled in robes of sleep, and then speaks uncompromising directness in regard to which we practise an unconscious self-deception during our waking moments" (121). Hawthorne believed that even when the conscious mind tried to forget the truth, the subconscious knows only the truth. At this moment both Aylmer and Georgiana realize Aylmer's inability to live with the scar.

In addition to the use of dreams, Hawthorne also exhibits

his beliefs about science. In the story, Aylmer perceives the birthmark as a sign of imperfection. Instead of accepting that nothing in life is perfect, he sees the birthmark as a test to his power as scientist. Aylmer "reads it as a sign of the inevitable imperfection of all things in nature. And sees in it a challenge to man's ability to transcend nature" (Fetterley 165). He accepts the challenge, but soon realizes the consequences of his actions. The dream serves as a foreshadowing prophecy for the actions that follow. In his dream he surgically removes the birthmark that haunts him. The dream "hides a guilty secret" that Aylmer is unable to tell his wife or admit to himself. He knows that the removal of the scar will prove to be fatal to Georgiana (Gollin 113). Despite this revelation, he attempts to carry out his desire and remove the scar. Aylmer concocts a drug that will make the birthmark disappear. He administers the drug to Georgiana, and like his subconscious knows is true, she dies as a result of the drug. In the end, Aylmer gets his wish; Georgiana is perfect, however she is also dead. This is a common theme in Romantic literature, the death of a beautiful woman.

"The Wives of the Dead" (1832) tells the story of two recent widows. Mary and Margaret are sisters-in-law who, within days of each other, have been informed that their husbands have died. The sisters-in-law try to console each other and help the other cope with the pain of their loss. During the night, both sisters receive news that their husband is alive. Perhaps the most ironic aspect of the story stems from the fact that both sisters seem to be in a dream state when they receive the wonderful news that their husbands are alive. In the story, Hawthorne "brings us to a profound awareness of just how indistinct the boundaries between inner and out life can become, especially in times of crisis" (Friedlander).

In their attempts to protect one another, the sisters-in-law suppress their own feelings. Mary first sets her grief aside to focus on Margaret, but Margaret also exemplifies this later. When she believes that her husband is alive, Margaret's first impulse is to share her wonderful news with the one who understands her most, Mary. However, her excitement is quickly replaced with sorrow for Mary:

> Joy flashed into her heart, and lighted it up at once; and breathless, and with winged steps, she flew to the bedside of her sister. She paused, however, at the door of the chamber, while a thought of pain broke in upon her. 'Poor Mary!' said she to herself. 'Shall I waken her, to feel her sorrow sharpened by my happiness? No; I will keep it within my own bosom till the morrow.' (66)

Margaret is unable to hurt Mary. She feels guilty for seemingly having her prayers answered while her sister-in-law is still hurting. She "felt as if her own better fortune had rendered her involuntarily unfaithful" (66). She cannot bear for her happiness to show while she knows her sister is still in pain. She suppresses her own happiness to protect the feelings of Mary. Mary makes the same sacrifice for Margaret. When she believes that her beloved husband is alive, she too thinks first of sharing the news with her dear sister. However, when thoughts of her sister's unhappiness arise, she decides otherwise: "[S]he remembered that Margaret would awake to thoughts of death and woe, rendered not the less bitter by their contrast with her own felicity" (68). Just like Margaret, Mary is unable to pour salt into the wounds of her sister-in-law by expressing her overwhelming joy and happiness.

Margaret also has a similar encounter. After deciding not to tell Mary of her good news, Margaret thinks, "Happy is it, and strange, that the lighter sorrows are those from which dreams are chiefly fabricated" (66). She believes that the look of "motionless contentment" (66) on Mary's face is nothing more that the result of a wishful fantasy. Mary also displays these thoughts. As Mary watches Margaret's "rose-tinted" cheeks, "vivid smile," and "expression of joy," she thinks to herself, "My poor sister! You will waken too soon from that happy dream" (68). Mary believes that Margaret's joy exists only in the delusions of her dreams. Both women are convinced that the other is dreaming.

Through their thoughts and actions, Hawthorne reveals that although Mary and Margaret care about each other and would never intentionally hurt one another, deep inside, they subconsciously want the happiness that they think they are hiding from one another and are unable to believe that they both can have this happiness. Hawthorne's perception of the relationship between these two women seems contradictory. Although they seem selfless and caring, they have secret desires that are selfish. By showing Mary and Margaret torn between their own feelings and each other's feelings, Hawthorne exemplifies the torment women face by trying to stifle their true feelings in order to protect the ones they love. Hawthorne is saying that women are sometimes false in the appearances they portray because they do not want to hurt the other's feelings.

By the end of his career, Hawthorne's fascination with

supernatural began to manifest itself in other ways. He abandoned use of dreams as a means of revelation. This transformation probably occurred out of his own fears. Because of his self- proclaimed status as a dreamer, he never knew what he might reveal about himself. Hawthorne used his writing to sort out all of his ideas. Perhaps because he feared what he might learn about himself through the process of writing, Hawthorne changed his focus.

Works Cited

Fetterley, Judith. Women Beware Science: "The Birthmark." *Critical Essays on Hawthorne's Short Stories*. Ed. Albert J Von Frank. Boston: GK Hall and Co., 1991.

Friedlander, Benjamin. Hawthorne's "Waking Reality." *The American Transcendental Quarterly*. 13.1 (1999) 51-64.

Gollin, Rita K. *Nathaniel Hawthorne and the Truth of Dreams*. Baton Rouge: Louisiana State UP, 1979.

Hawthorne, Nathaniel. "The Birth-mark." *Nathaniel Hawthorne's Tales*. Ed. James McIntosh. New York: WW Norton and Company, 1987. 118-31.

---- "The Celestial Rail-road." *Nathaniel Hawthorne's Tales*. 131-44.

---- "My Kinsman, Major Molineux." *Nathaniel Hawthorne's Tales*. 3-17.

---- "Rappacini's Daughter." *Nathaniel Hawthorne's Tales*. 186-208.

- - - - "The Wives of the Dead." *The Oxford Book of American Literature*. Ed. Joyce Carol Oates. Oxford: Oxford UP, 1992. 62-7.

- - - - "Young Goodman Brown." *Nathaniel Hawthorne's Tales*. 65-75.

Newman, Lea Bertani Vozar. *A Reader's Guide to the Short Stories f Nathaniel Hawthorne*. Boston: GK Hall and Co., 1979.

Waggoner, Hyatt. *Hawthorne: A Critical Study*. Cambridge: Harvard UP, 1963.

Pride of Intellect Punished in the Short Fiction of Nathaniel Hawthorne*

From the first date of their publishing, Nathaniel Hawthorne's works have never been dismissed as purely entertaining, or fodder for the masses. Both his earliest writing under pen names and his accredited later works have always been respected; early admirers include Henry Wadsworth Longfellow, Herman Melville, and Edgar Allen Poe. Poe said of one of Hawthorne's short stories that "Every words tells, and there is not a word which does not tell." Each word "tells" because the stories are packed with symbols of the day and allegories for our lives- he saw in his own work what he frankly described as "an inveterate love of allegory" (Arvin xii).

While never representing himself as a moral authority or openly espousing traditionally Protestant values, Hawthorne's short fiction reads as a series of illustrations about human joy and human folly. The allegories are quite clearly understandable in his stories involving science and scientists, particularly Aylmer in "The Birthmark" and Rappaccini in "Rappaccini's Daughter." Both stories portray men of secular learning who use their knowledge not to cure or truly heal, but to alter that which they deem unworthy, and with disastrous results. In "The Birthmark" and "Rappaccini's Daughter," Hawthorne condemns mankind's prideful idolization of science as damaging to all that is good in humanity and spirituality.

---

* http://www.freeonlineresearchpapers.com/hawthorne-for-the-masses

Both fascinating to ponder and very relevant in any examination of Hawthorne's work is the environment that spawned both his genius and his values. Repetitive themes and tendencies can be better understood by exploring what Hawthorne was exposed to as a youth. He was born in 1804 in Salem, Massachusetts, into a culture still strongly influenced by its Puritan ancestry, and few aspects of his writing can be described as untouched by it. Peter Conn characterizes the relationship in his article "Finding a Voice in a New Nation" by telling us that "the Puritan ancestors who provided Hawthorne with his amplest materials also gave him his angle of vision and instructed him in his technique" (83). Maintaining a morally pure lifestyle was for centuries surrounding his lifespan of paramount importance in New England- ample material indeed, for works very much centering on sexual morality, such as The Scarlet Letter. His "angle of vision" and "technique," while subtler, are still products of a Calvinist set of ideas, where mankind is generally undeserving, and many of the stories illustrate our various failings. Certainly "The Birthmark" and "Rappaccini's Daughter" do nothing to praise human efforts, with one scientist killing off his lovely wife and the other his pretty daughter. In discussing Hawthorne's studies of human nature, Newton Arvin describes the state of mind that gave birth to such tales:

> What he found made it impossible for Hawthorne to share the great glad conviction of his age that, as Emerson had told it, 'love and good are inevitable, and in the course of things'; he came closer to feeling that guilt and terrible wrong are inevitable; that at any rate, they are terribly deeply meshed in the texture of human experience. (Intro xv.)

Humanity and their efforts seemed more generally apt to failure than success, for Nathan; considering this, and the nonexistence of any higher considerations in his upbringing other than God's sovereignty, it is unsurprising that we should read two short stories about tragedy and failure resulting from scientists attempting to alter Creation.

More specifically, Hawthorne condemned human efforts and endeavors that he saw as prideful or self-superior. "To pride himself on one's intellectual powers or attainments, to cultivate the intellect at the expense of the sympathies··· this was for Hawthorne the deadliest form that human guilt could take" (Arvin xvi). What could be more 'intellectual at the expense of human sympathy' than one person performing dangerous cosmetic procedures on another, harming that person's body and mind? This is the picture that Hawthorne paints in "The Birthmark," with the main character, Aylmer, pridefully failing his young wife in several ways. We are told that "he had devoted himself··· too unreservedly to scientific studies ever to be weaned from them by any second passion." The author that we have met cannot possibly approve of his hero loving his science more than his wife, and he goes on to set us up for a powerful outcome later: "Such a union accordingly took place, and was attended with truly remarkable consequences and a deeply impressive moral." Whatever happens will be remarkable and bring home to us a "moral," which is no less than we would expect from the New Englander. Aylmer almost immediately shows us how he feels about God's creation, telling his young wife that her birthmark "shocks me, as being the visible mark of earthly imperfection." The husband hurts his wife here, declaring a feature of her body unattractive and goes on to declare an intention of removing the shocking mark. A mark of earthly imperfection would not be appropriate for humans to try and alter, but he makes the attempt. Knowing what we do about Hawthorne's disapproval of "pride of intellect," Aylmer's arrogance must be condemned. He exhorts his wife "doubt not my power. I have already given this matter the deepest thought-thought which might almost have enlightened me to create a being"(152). His belief in his own abilities is continually set up for us, even to claims of being able to create life- surely God's province alone- with no consideration for his wife's true welfare. Barbara Eckstein comments that science has become religion for Aylmer, and so surely attempting to modify his wife through his science is akin to worship for him (Eckstein 511).

The scientist Rappaccini in "Rappaccini's Daughter" is even less kind than misguided Aylmer, railing against one who condemned the turning of his own daughter to poison, in the name of science, "Wouldst thou, then, have preferred the condition of a weak woman…?"(209). Even prior to learning of his daughter's impending death, we cannot like or sympathize with this man who used his daughter as a scientific experiment.

Humankind is not perfect- Biblically, since the sin in Eden, perfection is out of our reach, and considering the two men of science that strive to create perfection in their subjects adds another element to Hawthorne's condemnation of such practices. Leland S. Person Jr. distills the point that examining these characterizations brings up: "Hawthorne depicts character after character who destroys what is human"(Person 437). Our two examples, Aylmer and Rappaccini, bear this out dramatically. Early in the story, we learn that Dr. Rappaccini creates an incredibly beautiful garden, but is not content to cultivate for medicine the fruits and flowers that he finds; rather, he engineers new and terrible breeds, as another story character tells:

> It is his theory that all medicinal virtues are comprised within those substances which we term vegetable poisons. These he cultivates with his own hands, and is said even to have produced new varieties of poison, more horribly deleterious than Nature, without the assistance of this learned person, would ever have plagued the world withal (186).

The scientist who uses his learning to alter nature is suspect already, but Rappaccini deliberately creates harmful plants, perverting the earth's bounty. He has gone farther, however, in changing his young daughter according to his purposes: she has "been nourished with poisons from her birth upward, until… she herself has become the deadliest poison in existence" (201). Natural, unaltered flowers wither at her touch.

Butterflies fall dead from the sky when she breathes on them. At this point in the tale, Rappaccini has already destroyed his daughter, although she lives. He claims that he has improved on what God created, but his version of perfection deprives the girl of all human contact, and ultimately results in her death.

"The Birthmark" also depicts a scientist seeking the perfection that is denied to humans, inevitably failing. Hawthorne repeatedly describes Aylmer's view of his wife's birthmark as an "imperfection," and the only thing holding Georgiana back from being the ultimate physical specimen. The cure takes her young life, but that is a risk that the husband/physician declared that he was willing to take, by applying his admittedly imperfect science to a piece of his wife-science that the "large folio" wherein he records all experiments shows to fail as often as it succeeds (158). But when Georgiana says that she worships her husband, he demonstrates that he has not learned from earlier failures, telling her that if he succeeds in removing the birthmark, she can "worship me if you will. I shall deem myself hardly unworthy of it" (159). This arrogance is offensive even to a modern reader, and would have read as nearly blasphemous when it was published; nowhere is Hawthorne sympathetic to his learned characters: "mechanists like Aylmer [and] Rappaccini sinfully assume that knowledge of mechanism gives them power over life" (Person 437).

Examination of Nathaniel Hawthorne's early environs has shed light on his disdain for personal pride in human endeavors and his creation of characters that meet tragedy once they committed this sin, but the short fiction considered herein more specifically showcases the grievous punishments meted out to men of science who got beyond themselves. Interestingly, the America of the eighteenth and nineteenth centuries was not one likely to produce writers with immense respect for the fields of scientific research; only in the 1840s did the term "scientist" come into popular usage, as a descendant and variant of 'philosopher' or 'chemical experimenter.' Glen Scott Allen describes the state of American science in these decades by telling readers that "many university professors of the time moonlighted as 'consultants,' offering their services as soil analysts, patent advisers… and the like." He goes on to quote a European naturalist's characterization of the state of science in the US, that neither a man of the day "'nor any other American have a mind for purely scientific researches; they look for practical result" (Allen 6). Few favors were done for the indifferent reputation of scientists by the hawking of pseudosciences such as phrenology and mesmerism. The great Puritanical inheritance of dependence on the will of the Almighty, coupled with the perception of a narrow distinction between unregulated charlatans and 'men of science,' was enough to produce a nation with little adoration for the profession. In the eyes of his first readers, contemporaries, Hawthorne's blaspheming scientists may very much have deserved their punishments.

While science and medical treatment are not condemned wholesale as flouting God's will in the twenty-first century, traces of the attitudes of Hawthorne's ancestors can be found today. A unique perspective on two old short stories recently surfaced in American politics: George W. Bush's President's Council on Bioethics began their first meetings with a reading of "The Birthmark." The executive director of the committee, created to address moral and ethical (even Biblical) questions surrounding cloning and stem cell research, is a zealous Christian and selected the tale for his fellow committee members to examine. Discussing the story and its likely applications in the meetings, Fred Edwords elaborates:

Here we have an image of science as inadequate because it fails to consider the supernatural- and an image of scientists as prideful and self-defeating perfectionists who should be satisfied with nature. Such was a common literary view in 1843. But the advance of both time and science hasn't helped much··· biological research continues to suffer from a negative literary image (Edwords 2).

Modern Americans, in a culture far more permissive, less devout, and more centered on self esteem- a form of that deadly pride- love to consume tales wherein people who manipulate biology fail miserably; Jurassic Park and The Island of Dr. Moreau come to mind. Certainly Hawthorne found no less sympathetic an audience in his day.

Our close examination of language, setting, plot and nearly any other elements of "The Birthmark" and "Rappaccini's Daughter" yields a condemnation of worshipping science and of the arrogance of humans who do so, neglecting what is human and what is spiritual. Men who use their superior scientific knowledge to pervert, but not to heal, are painted as selfish and punished; concurrently, the notion of 'perfecting' humanity is destroyed. They got beyond themselves and suffered for it. Stepping back from these two short stories and considering other major works of Hawthorne's bears out this conclusion. The Scarlet Letter is more commonly recalled as a moral tale, where the mores of Puritan New England and human frailty are masterfully portrayed, but it also speaks of the dangers assuming "life is strictly a function of 'mechanism; and that having knowledge of the mechanism is to have power over life itself" (Trepanier 317). Chillingworth is the vehicle for this lesson in the novel; he too feels the pride of the scientist, and Hawthorne does not reward him for it.

While admittedly removed from our lives by the span of a century and a half, the author's personal views and fiction defining them on science, human failings, pride and the necessity of respect for nature (creation) are still fascinating today. Our own political system today echoes with the uniquely American struggle to define what is important and acceptable, and what is crossing the line of what is divine: congressional committees are making decisions on biological research and bioethics with a dead advisor, born two hundred years ago, and this policy is cheered on by many. Certainly Hawthorne never foresaw an outcome like this, but a reading of his work from this frame of reference is modern and relevant, whatever the personal beliefs of the reader.

Works Cited

Allen, Glen Scott. "Master Mechanics and Evil Wizards: Science and the American Imagination." *Massachusetts Review*, Winter 92/93, Vol. 33. Academic Search Elite. EBSCOhost. 1 March 2007.

Arvin, Newton. Introduction. *Hawthorne's Short Stories by Nathaniel Hawthorne*. New York: Random House, 1946.

Conn, Peter. "Finding a Voice in a New Nation." *Readings on Nathaniel Hawthorne*. Ed. Clarice Swisher. San Diego: Greenhaven Press, 1996.

Eckstein, Barbara. "Hawthorne's 'The Birthmark': Science and Romance as Belief." *Studies in Short Fiction*, Fall 1989, Vol 26. Academic Search Elite. EBSCOhost. 1 March 2007.

Edwords, Fred. "Getting Started on the Wrong Foot." *Humanist*, March/April 2002, Vol 62. Academic Search Elite. EBSCOhost. 1 March 2007.

Hawthorne, Nathaniel. "The Birthmark." *Hawthorne's Short Stories*. Ed. Newton Arvin. New York: Random House, 1946.

---- "Rappacini's Daughter." *Hawthorne's Short Stories*. Ed. Newton Arvin. New York: Random House, 1946.

Person Jr., Leland S. "Hawthorne and His Culture: Three Recent Views." *Studies in the Novel*, Winter 1992, Vol 24. Academic Search Elite. EBSCOhost. 1 March 2007.

Pfister, Joel. "Hawthorne as a Cultural Theorist." *The Cambridge Companion to Nathaniel Hawthorne*. Ed. Richard Millington. Cambridge, UK: Press Syndicate of the University of Cambridge, 2004.

Trepanier, Lee. "The Need for Renewal: Nathaniel Hawthorne's Conservatism" *Modern Age*, Fall 2003, Vol. 45. Academic Search Elite. EBSCOhost. 1 March 2007.

이영옥

미국 하와이대학교 미국학 박사
한국 영어영문학회 회장
한국 현대영미소설학회 회장 역임
현 성균관대학교 영어영문학과 명예교수

저서
『젠더와 역사: 미국소수인종문학의 이해』(태학사) 외 다수

역서
『소설과 현대』 D. Daiches 저 (탐구당) 외 다수

Hawthorne's Short Stories

WITH ESSAYS IN CRITICISM

초판 1쇄 발행 _ 2014년 6월 10일

편 주 자 • 이 영 옥
발 행 인 • 정 현 걸
발 행 • 신 아 사
인 쇄 • 예지인쇄
출판등록 • 1956년 1월 5일 (제9–52호)
주 소 • 서울시 은평구 통일로 59길 4(2F)
전 화 • 02)382–6411 · 팩스 02)382–6401
홈페이지 • www.shinasa.co.kr
E–MAIL • shinasa@daum.net

ISBN 978–89–8396–859–3(93840)

정가 13,000원